# Design Patterns and Contracts

# Design Patterns and Contracts

Jean-Marc Jézéquel

Michel Train

Christine Mingins

 **ADDISON-WESLEY**

An imprint of Addison Wesley Longman, Inc.

Reading, Massachusetts • Menlo Park, California • New York
Harlow, England • Don Mills, Ontario • Sydney • Mexico City
Madrid • Amsterdam

Gamma/Helm/Johnson/Vlissides, DESIGN PATTERNS, (88, 89, 98, 99, 108, 109, 119, 127, 128, 141, 153, 154, 164, 165, 177, 178, 187, 198, 199, 209, 210, 225, 226, 236, 237, 245, 246, 259, 260, 276, 277, 285, 286, 294, 295, 296, 306, 307, 316, 317, 327, 334, and 335). © 1995 by Addison-Wesley Publishing Company. Reprinted by permission of Addison Wesley Longman.

The publisher offers discounts on this book when ordered in quantity for special sales. For more information, please contact:

AWL Direct Sales
Addison Wesley Longman, Inc.
One Jacob Way
Reading, Massachusetts 01867
(781) 944-3700

Visit AW on the Web: www.awl.com/cseng/

*Library of Congress Cataloging-in-Publication Data*

Jézéquel, Jean-Marc, 1964-
    Design patterns and contracts / Jean-Marc Jézéquel, Michel Train, Christine Mingins.
        p. cm.
    Includes bibliographical references (p. ).
    ISBN 0-201-30959-9 (alk. paper)
    1. Computer software--Development.   2. Software patterns.   I. Train, Michel.   II. Mingins, Christine.   III. Title.
    QA76.76.D47J49   1999
    005.1--dc21                                          99-39841
                                                              CIP

ISBN 0-201-30959-9

Text printed on recycled paper
1 2 3 4 5 6 7 8 9 10—MA—0302000199

First printing, October 1999

*To Chantal, Gwenaëlle, Nolwenn, Erwan, and Armelle*

*To Catherine and Erwan*

*To our parents*

# Contents

# Preface

The idea of systematically identifying and documenting design patterns as autonomous entities was born in the late 1980s. It was brought into the mainstream by the Hillside Group, such people as Beck, Ward, Coplien, Booch, Kerth, and Johnson. However, the main event in this emerging field was the 1995 publication of the book *Design Patterns: Elements of Reusable Object-Oriented Software* (Gamma et al., 1995) by the so-called Gang of Four (GoF): Erich Gamma, Richard Helm, Ralph Johnson, and John Vlissides.

Today, design patterns are widely accepted as useful tools for guiding and documenting the design of object-oriented software systems. Design patterns play many roles in the development process. They provide a common vocabulary for design, reduce system complexity by naming and defining abstractions, constitute a base of experience for building reusable software, and act as building blocks from which more complex designs can be built.

Design patterns can be considered reusable microarchitectures that contribute to an overall system architecture. Ideally, they capture the intent behind a design by identifying the component objects, their collaborations, and the distribution of responsibilities. The purpose of this book is to show how this intention can be made *explicit*, based on the notion of *contract*. A software contract captures mutual obligations and benefits among stakeholder components—for example, between the client of a service and the suppliers, including subclasses, of that service. Contracts strengthen and deepen interface specifications. Along the lines of abstract data type theory, a common way of specifying software contracts is to use Boolean assertions called pre- and postconditions for each service offered, as well as class invariants for defining general consistency properties. Then the contract reads as follows: The client should ask a supplier for a service only in a state in which the class invariant and the precondition of the service are respected. In return, the supplier promises that the work specified in the postcondition will be done and that the class invariant will still be respected. In this way, rights and obligations of both the client and the supplier are clearly delineated, along with their responsibilities.

This idea, first implemented in the Eiffel language (Meyer, 1992a) under the name *Design by Contract*, is now available in several other programming languages, such as Java, and even in the Unified Modeling Language (UML) with the Object Constraint Language (OCL) (Warmer and Kleppe, 1999). Like the design pattern idea, the Design by Contract is not tied to any particular language, but we need to choose one for describing concrete examples. We settled on Eiffel because it provides the right paradigms to address the construction of large, high-quality object-oriented software systems and is quite easy to master. This book can thus be used as a GoF's companion for the Eiffel community; however, we believe that this book will also be most useful to people more generally interested in obtaining the greatest benefit from the design patterns ideas in a quality-based software engineering framework. We describe many examples, using the UML notation, and we also explain, in Section C.1, how Design by Contract can be used with Java through the iContract tool (Kramer, 1998).

Part I of this book establishes the framework for using design patterns. Chapter 1 introduces the notion of design patterns and their role in the software life cycle. Chapter 2 outlines the arguments for an optimal use of design patterns in a quality-oriented software engineering process, based on Design by Contract and associated technologies.

The three chapters in Part II explain how the GoF *creational*, *structural,* and *behavioral* patterns can be augmented with contracts. For each of these design patterns, we simply review its name and intent from the GoF book and then discuss specific implementation issues and provide a complete example, ready to be compiled and run, of the use of the pattern in a hypothetical application. Only the most interesting parts of the source code are presented and discussed in this book; the full source code of each example, ready to be compiled and run with a free Eiffel compiler, is available on this book's Web site (see Appendix D for the details).

Part III illustrates how one can build on design patterns to solve interesting software engineering problems. Chapter 6 explains how creational design patterns can be leveraged to simplify software configuration management without impacting on the application's overall performance. Chapter 7 discusses how to combine patterns for building graphical user interfaces.

Finally, the book contains a detailed glossary (Appendix A) of object-oriented design concepts and terminology, pointers to further information on design patterns and Design by Contract (Appendix B), and a discussion of Design by Contract in other languages (Appendix C). Appendix D tells you how to get more information about this book.

# Acknowledgments

The authors would like to thank M. Thomas, Tim Ross, Ian Gilmour, and Alain Le Guennec, who read early versions of this book and gave us a lot of feedback, as well as many pertinent suggestions. We are also grateful to Reto Kramer for allowing us to reproduce a portion of the iContract documentation.

We owe a special debt to Dominique Colnet, the main author of the GNU Eiffel compiler (also known as SmallEiffel), for the many insights he gave us on the inner working of his compiler and for his contribution to Chapter 6. Dominique also suggested an improvement to the Singleton pattern implementation.

J.-M. Jézéquel would like to thank Professor Yonezawa, from the University of Tokyo, for hosting him as a visiting scientist to Japan during most of 1996, when this book started to be discussed; as well as Bertrand Meyer and Richard Mitchell for so many fruitful discussions since then. M. Train would like to thank Rémi Houdaille for the many ideas he developed and those he helped define precisely, as well as Bruno Borghi for his deep insights into software development processes.

Finally, we would like to thank Addison-Wesley for its constant support in making this book take shape and Diane Freed, our project manager, for her good work and her ever good mood.

Jean-Marc Jézéquel      Michel Train          Christine Mingins
IRISA/CNRS          Lucent Technologies      Monash University
Rennes, France        Rennes, France       Melbourne, Australia

# PART I

# Design Patterns in a Software Engineering Context

# Chapter 1

# A Software Engineering Perspective

## 1.1 Introduction to Design Patterns

**Q.** Why isn't there a good definition of "pattern"?

**A.** Why isn't there a good definition of most engineering terms? "Pattern" seems to be on at least as good a footing as, say, "object." No one seems to mind the short slogan "a solution to a problem in a context."

However, the brevity of this slogan can cause confusion. Expanding each of these terms just a little helps:

- **Context** refers to a recurring set of situations in which the pattern applies.
- **Problem** refers to a set of forces—goals and constraints—that occur in this context.
- **Solution** refers to a canonical design form or design rule that someone can apply to resolve these forces.[1]

### 1.1.1 Key Points

Design patterns represent solutions to problems that arise when software is being developed within a particular context. Design patterns can be considered

---

1. Extract from the Patterns-Discussion FAQ, available at http://g.oswego.edu/dl/pd-FAQ /pd-FAQ.html.

**Table 1.1**
The SEI/CMM Levels

| Level | Description |
|-------|-------------|
| 1. **Initial** | The software process is characterized as ad hoc, and occasionally even as chaotic. Few processes are defined, and success depends on individual effort. |
| 2. **Repeatable** | Basic project management processes are established to track cost, schedule, and functionality. The necessary process discipline is in place to repeat earlier successes on projects with similar applications. |
| 3. **Defined** | The software process for both management and engineering activities is documented, standardized, and integrated into a standard software process for the organization. All projects use an approved, tailored version of the organization's standard software process for developing and maintaining software. |
| 4. **Managed** | Detailed measures of the software process and product quality are collected. Both the software process and products are quantitatively understood and controlled. |
| 5. **Optimized** | Continuous process improvement is enabled by quantitative feedback from the process and from piloting innovative ideas and technologies. |

reusable microarchitectures that contribute to an overall system architecture; they capture the static and dynamic structures and collaborations among key participants in software designs. Because they identify and document the essence of successful solutions to design problems, design patterns are related to the various coding idioms that exist for all programming languages. However, design patterns work at the *design* level instead of at the *implementation* level. Prosaically, design patterns are the know-how—that is, the *tricks of the trade*—that distinguish experienced designers from newcomers.

Good designers have always existed. What is new and so attractive in the idea of design patterns is the concerted effort to identify, document, and classify best practice in object-oriented design. This effort has the potential to realize a huge return on investment in the drive to improve key software quality factors, as in the Software Engineering Institute's (SEI) capability maturity model (CMM). The CMM, a process-based quality management model for assessing the level of an organization's software development (Humphrey, 1989), defines five levels of maturity, as outlined in Table 1.1.

In this context, the principal contribution of design patterns is that they explicitly capture expert knowledge and design tradeoffs and thus support the sharing of architectural knowledge among developers; the project is no longer dependent on the all-knowing oracle. The body of organizational knowledge and domain expertise—that is, its know-how—can be documented with patterns, thus paving the way for the repetition of earlier successes on projects with similar applications.

Furthermore, the architecture of a software system can be clearly documented, using design patterns as a shared vocabulary for common design structures. Design patterns, then, constitute basic building blocks of a design architecture, allowing the engineers to relate to the design at a higher level, thus reducing its apparent complexity. Instead of thinking in terms of individual classes and their behaviors, it is now possible to think in terms of collaborating classes, with their relationships and responsibilities. That is, as a software engineer, you no longer need to tell your colleagues, "This design is made of such and such classes having such and such relationships; when this event happens in this class, this method is called, which in due time triggers this other method on this other object, itself calling back the first object to get the relevant information." Instead you can simply state "Here, these classes collaborate along the lines of the Observer pattern."[2]

Your colleagues, if they are well versed in design patterns, will immediately understand the static and dynamic structures and collaborations of this part of the software architecture. Also, and as important, your colleagues will immediately be aware of the design tradeoffs that have been made among simplicity, efficiency, and nonfunctional forces, such as reusability, portability, and extensibility. In early design work, it is often enough to know that you will use a pattern at some point. The detail about how this pattern will be implemented can be filled in later.

Finally, design patterns are of clear pedagogical interest. It is often said that *the purpose of patterns is to learn from experience, preferably someone else's*. Codifying good design practice helps to distill and to disseminate experience, thereby helping others avoid frequently encountered development traps and pitfalls. Because they build on best practice in object technology, patterns also serve as exemplars of doing it properly, the object-oriented way. By looking at these examples, novice designers can move more readily toward proper use of the technology.

## 1.1.2 Understanding the Notion of Design Patterns

The origin of design patterns lies in the domain of architecture, with the seminal works of Christopher Alexander (Alexander et al., 1977):

> Each pattern describes a problem which occurs over and over again in our environment, and then describes the core of the solution to this problem in such a way that you can use this solution a million times over, without ever doing it the same way twice.

---

2. If you are not yet familiar with the Observer pattern, don't worry; it will be described in detail later.

**Table 1.2**
Learning Parallels

| Level | Stage | Becoming a Chess Master | Becoming a Software Designer |
|-------|-------|-------------------------|------------------------------|
| 1 | Learn the rules | Names of pieces, legal movements, chess board geometry and orientation, etc. | Algorithms, data structures, and programming languages |
| 2 | Learn principles | Relative value of certain pieces, strategic value of center squares, power of a threat, etc. | Modularity, object-orientation, genericity, Design by Contract, etc. |
| 3 | Learn patterns | To become a master of chess, one must study the games of other masters. These games contain patterns that must be understood, memorized, and applied repeatedly. | To truly master software design, one must study the patterns in the designs of other masters. |

It is clear that the notion underlying design patterns is related to *know-how*. It encompasses a higher-level understanding of the organization of basic components. D. C. Schmidt (http://www.cs.wustl.edu/~schmidt/cs242/learning.html) draws an interesting parallel between learning to be a chess master and learning to be a master software designer (Table 1.2).

It should be noted that when IBM Deeper Blue beat the best human chess player, Gary Kasparov, in 1997, it was due to more than simply the use of brute-force algorithms. Instead, the computer used patterns of playing borrowed from Kasparov himself; in a way, Kasparov was beaten by himself!

Software design patterns share the same essence as chess game patterns. In both contexts, the patterns can be documented, understood, memorized, and applied repeatedly to offer solutions to problems in given contexts.

## 1.1.3  An Example: The Observer Pattern

Although the range of domain-specific patterns is probably infinite, most general-purpose patterns that the average software engineer ought to know about have already been identified. One of the best-known general-purpose patterns is the Observer.

The intent of the Observer pattern is to define a one-to-many dependency among objects so that when one object changes state, all of its dependent objects, or

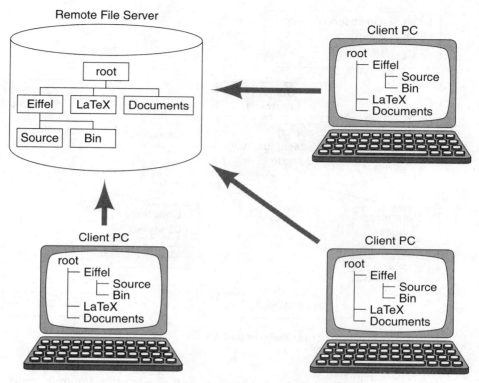

**Figure 1.1** Observer example: a network file system

receivers, are automatically notified and updated. For example, consider the network file system illustrated in Figure 1.1. Each time a change occurs in the file system, that change must be reflected on each client PC. A solution to the problem of having the PCs update their views on the system must take into account a context made of the following factors, or *forces*.

- The identity and number of receivers are not predetermined.

- New classes of receivers may be added to the system in the future.

- Polling is inappropriate—either impractical or too expensive when the number of receivers is large.

The Observer design pattern solves this problem in this context by making the remote server, the *Subject*, inform the client PCs (the *Observers*) each time an interesting change happens. Figure 1.2 uses the UML (see Section 1.2.2) class diagram notation to illustrate the relationships between *Observers* and *Subject*. Figure 1.2 describes the *static* structure of the pattern; Figure 1.3 illustrates the

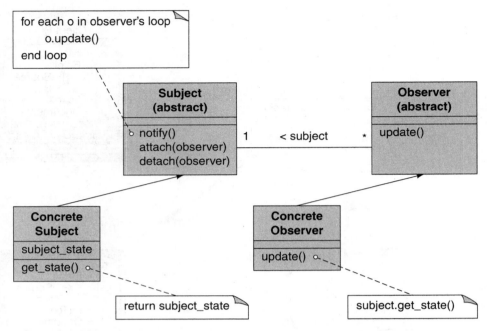

**Figure 1.2** Structure of the Observer pattern

*dynamic* collaboration between *Observers* and *Subject:* the dynamic structure of the pattern.

If you are new to this domain, you are certainly wondering why we call such a simple design trick a design pattern and what the fuss is all about. So let us consider another example: a graphics tool that lets the user manage a set of data values via a spreadsheet, a histogram, and a pie chart. All of these views of the data can be on the screen at the same time. Each time the user modifies one view, the other views must be modified accordingly.

At a certain level of abstraction, we have exactly the same design problem as for the previous example of a remote file system, with the same forces applying.

- The identity and number of the views are not predetermined.

- Novel classes of views may be added to the system in the future.

- Polling is inappropriate (too expensive).

Thus, the solution can be the same: The set of values is now the *Subject*, the views are kinds of *Observers*, and Subject and Observers interact as illustrated in Figures 1.2 and 1.3.

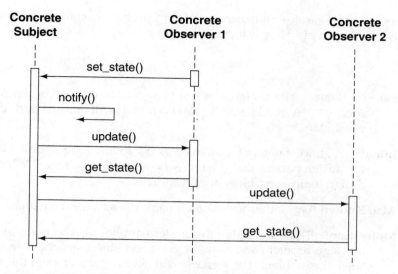

**Figure 1.3** Collaborations in the Observer pattern

What makes the Observer a design pattern is that it abstracts the static and dynamic architectures of a given solution to solve a given problem in a context. Observer is therefore applicable in many situations.

## 1.1.4 Describing Design Patterns

Because design patterns are primarily communication tools, it is very important to have a more or less standard way of describing them. Most of Alexander's pattern descriptions are of the form:

> **if**      you find yourself in *{context}*
> for example *{examples}*,
> with *{problem}*,
> entailing *{forces}*
>
> **then**   for some *{reasons}*,
> apply *{design form}* and/or *{rule}*
> to construct *{solution}*
> leading to *{new context}* and *{other patterns}*

Many stylistic variants of this format are possible. The most popular format, used in the GoF book (Gamma et al., 1995), inverts this format, starting with the design forms and/or rules and then describing problems, contexts, and examples to which they apply. Here is its basic template:

**Pattern Name:**   The pattern's name conveys the essence of the pattern succinctly. A good name is vital because it will become part of the design vocabulary.

**Intent:**   A short statement that answers the following questions: What does the design pattern do? What are its rationale and intent? What particular design issue or problem does it address?

**Also Known As:**   Other well-known names, if any, for the pattern.

**Motivation:**   The context that this pattern applies to; a scenario that illustrates a design problem and how the class and object structures in the pattern solve the problem. The scenario will help you understand the more abstract description of the pattern that follows.

**Applicability:**   Prerequisites that should be satisfied before deciding to use a pattern. In which situations can the design pattern be applied? What are examples of poor designs that the pattern can address? How can you recognize these situations?

**Structure:**   A description of the program structure that the pattern will define.

**Participants:**   A list of the participants needed to complete a pattern.

**Collaborations:**   How the participants collaborate to carry out their responsibilities.

**Consequences:**   Results, both positive and negative, of using the pattern. How does the pattern support its objectives? What are the tradeoffs and results of using the pattern? What aspect of system structure does the pattern let you vary independently?

**Implementation:**   What pitfalls, hints, or techniques should you be aware of when implementing the pattern? Are there language-specific issues?

**Sample Code and Usage:**   Code fragments that illustrate how you might implement the pattern in Eiffel, C++, Java, or Smalltalk.

**Known Uses:**   Examples of the pattern found in real systems.

**Related Patterns:**   What design patterns are closely related to this one? What are the important differences? With which other patterns should this one be used?

## 1.1.5 Notions Related to Patterns

Two notions related to that of design patterns are **architectural patterns** and **coding patterns,** or **idioms.** In Buschmann et al. (1996), these three types of patterns are defined as follows:

**Architectural Patterns:** A fundamental structural organization schema for software systems. An architectural pattern provides a set of predefined subsystems, specifies their responsibilities, and includes rules and guidelines for organizing the relationships among them.

**Design Patterns:** A scheme for refining the subsystems or components of a software system or the relationships among them. A design pattern provides a commonly recurring structure of communicating components that solves a general design problem within a particular context.

**Idioms:** A low-level pattern specific to a programming language. An idiom explains how to implement particular aspects of components or the relationships among them, using the features of the given language.

These three kinds of patterns differ in their corresponding levels of abstraction and detail. Architectural patterns are high-level strategic patterns pertaining to large-scale components and the global properties and mechanisms of a system. Design patterns are medium-scale tactical patterns that should be quite independent of any programming language. However, GoF design patterns are strongly biased toward object-oriented languages. Conversely, idioms are paradigm- and language-specific programming techniques that solve low-level implementation problems.

## 1.1.6 Design Patterns and Frameworks

Frameworks are closely related to design patterns. An object-oriented software **framework** is made up of a set of related classes that can be specialized, or instantiated, to implement an application. A framework is a reusable software architecture that provides the generic structure and behavior for a family of software applications, along with a context that specifies their collaboration and use within a given domain (Appleton, 1997).

Unlike a complete application, a framework lacks the necessary application-specific functionality. A framework can be considered a prefabricated structure, or template, of a working application, in which a number of pieces in specific places—called **plug-points,** or **hot spots**—either are not implemented or are given overridable implementations. To obtain a complete application from a framework, one has to provide the missing pieces, usually by implementing a number of call-back functions—that is, functions that are invoked by the

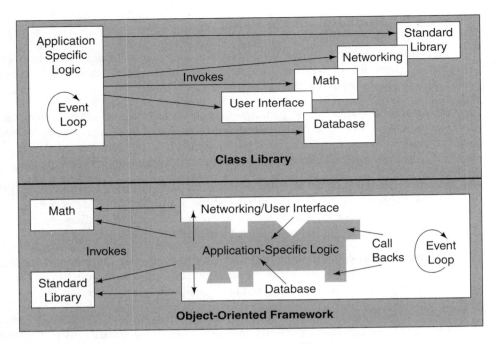

**Figure 1.4**  Difference between frameworks and class libraries

framework—to fill the plug-points. In an object-oriented context, this feature is achieved by dynamic binding: An operation can be defined in a library class but implemented in a subclass in the application-specific code. A developer can thus customize the framework to a particular application by subclassing and composing instances of framework classes (Gamma et al., 1995).

A framework is thus different from a classical class library in that the flow of control is usually bidirectional between the application and the framework (see Figure 1.4). The framework is in charge of managing the bulk of the application, and the application programmer just provides various bits and pieces. This is similar to programming some event-driven applications, when the application programmer usually has no control over the main control logic of the code.

Design patterns can be used to document the collaborations among classes in a framework. Conversely, a framework may use several design patterns, some of them general purpose, some of them domain specific. Design patterns and frameworks are thus closely related, but they do not operate at the same level of abstraction. A framework *is made of* software, whereas design patterns represent knowledge, information, and experience *about* software. In this respect, frameworks are of a physical nature, whereas patterns are of a logical nature. Frameworks are the physical realization of one or more software pattern solutions; patterns are the instructions for how to implement those solutions.

## 1.2 Design Patterns in the Software Life Cycle

### 1.2.1 A Software Engineering Process

***1.2.1.1 The Classic Life Cycle***   The size of software projects has increased by several orders of magnitude since the 1960s, making them beyond the control of a single programmer. Software development is now a cooperative process tackled from two perspectives. On the one hand, the tools used to develop software—programming languages and environments—are being continually improved to better support this scale of complexity. On the other hand, a great deal of effort is devoted to improving the *process* by which software is developed. The best results are obtained when the tools and the process fit together well.

In this context, the software development process is considered from an engineering point of view and is generally divided into several subprocesses, called **phases**. Each phase addresses different problems on the road leading from a set of requirements to a working software system. As with any other engineering domain, the increased complexity of a large system has been dealt with by modularity, or a mechanism to break down problems to a manageable size.

The first organized approaches to software development involved a sequential, unidirectional work flow between life-cycle phases, such as requirements definition, analysis, design, coding, unit testing, system integration, and system testing. The output from each phase was the basis for the next. In the United States, charts typically depict such processes as an upper-left to lower-right cascade of activities, resulting in the waterfall model (Royce, 1970); in Europe, the V model, as illustrated in Figure 1.5, is popular.

The boxes in Figure 1.5 represent the successive stages of a software development project, from the initial requirements down to the executable code—through analysis, design, and implementation—and then up to an operational system—through testing, integration and delivery. The dashed lines suggest a match between the requirements of the descending stages and the results of the ascending stages. This V model is itself the first phase in the life cycle of most large software systems, which usually foreshadow several years of both corrective and evolutive maintenance.

***1.2.1.2 The Iterative Model of the Life Cycle***   Waterfall processes are definitely an improvement over ad hoc software management techniques, providing

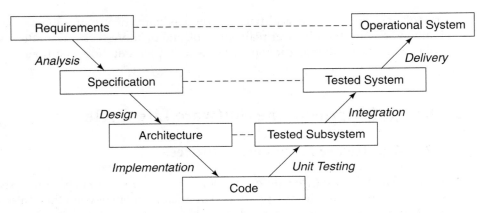

**Figure 1.5** Phases of software development in the V model

a rational, systematic, and teachable process to proceed efficiently from a well-defined functional specification to a working implementation. However, for large real systems, software specifications are usually imprecise, ambiguous, unclear, and much more subject to change than are other artifacts, because of the widely held belief in software "softness." Furthermore, during the many years when they are maintained, large applications often grow increasingly complex, up to the point that it is no longer plausible to assume that any initial design will be architecturally robust with respect to the current key requirements.

Projects using waterfall processes often fail to discover these problems until it's too late—typically, during system integration or even validation. This delay can be very costly, because architectural or design flaws often require major rework of many subsystems, including redesigning, reimplementing, and retesting. Also, since integration and testing are deferred until the last life-cycle phases, waterfall processes are known to create logistical overloads that often compromise quality.

Iterative processes, by contrast, are designed to produce a controlled sequence of implementations whose functionality increases toward that specified by the requirements but whose quality can be monitored all along the sequence. Many forms of control are possible over iterative processes, based on the choice of the decision process used to formulate the objectives and timing of the implementation produced by each iteration, such as *maximize visible progress, defer expensive tasks, accelerate end-user feedback, and synchronize with hardware availability.*

For example, the spiral model for software engineering (Boehm, 1987) encompasses the best features of both the classic life cycle and prototyping while controlling the process with a new element: risk analysis. The model defines four major activities, represented by four quadrants that are repeatedly crossed by the spiral (see Figure 1.6), as follows:

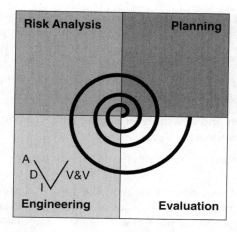

**Figure 1.6** Spiral model of software development

1.  **Planning:** Determination of objectives, alternatives, and constraints

2.  **Risk Analysis:** Analysis of alternatives and identification/resolution of risks

3.  **Engineering:** Development of the "next-level" product, using classical analysis, design, and implementation (ADI) techniques, as well as validation and verification (V&V)

4.  **Evaluation:** Assessment of the results of engineering

Beginning at the center and working outward, each iteration around the spiral results in progressively complete versions of the software. The width of the spiral can be thought of as proportional to the amount of functionality implemented in the system at a given stage. Every circuit around the spiral requires engineering that can be accomplished by using a classic life-cycle approach.

The spiral model for software engineering is the most realistic approach to the development of large-scale systems and software. This paradigm uses an "evolutionary" approach to software engineering, enabling the developer and the customer to understand and to react to risks at each evolutionary level.

*1.2.1.3 New Challenges*    The notion of object provides the basis for the development of the **software component** concept. The encapsulation and information hiding available in object-oriented languages suggest that an analogy with **hardware components** is possible. Potentially even more useful than their hardware counterparts, software components can be easily customized through inheritance: this is the **open-close** principle as stated in Meyer (1988).

Object-oriented technologies allow large-scale savings in software development by fostering the reuse of software components. This approach has a major impact on the software life cycle, which now has to integrate the following activities:

- Design of reusable software components, based on the generalization of more specific ones

- Validation and assembly of components that might come from many different sources

- Management of the components (maintenance)

*Reusing* instead of *redoing* has been the motto in software engineering for 30 years. However, to really save a lot of effort in software development, the challenge is to go beyond the mere reuse of basic components, such as those available in data structure or graphical libraries, and try to reuse design-level artifacts and full-blown frameworks. In both cases, design patterns play a major role in documenting these higher levels of reuse.

## 1.2.2  Modeling Problems and Solutions with UML

Whether or not you are relying on the spiral model of software development, a software system is something that is bound to evolve, if only because the outside world changes. Jackson (1985) showed that one of the main flaws of waterfall techniques is their neglect of this "soft" aspect of software construction. Because each module is produced to meet a precise subrequirement, no provision is made for future evolution or for dealing with potential analysis or design flaws. On the premise that *entities are more stable than functions*, Jackson's system development (JSD) method recommends that the programmer start the specification of a system with the elaboration of a "real-world" model representing the stable part of the system. This model consists of **entities** performing or receiving **actions**, the temporal pattern of which is precisely defined. Functionality specifications are added to this model at a later stage. This approach makes JSD a clear winner in terms of maintenance savings, but JSD suffers from a lack of structure and too much fuzziness.

Another popular approach, also based on modeling, consists of building entity relationship models of the problem domain (Chen, 1976). The family of methods that relies on this approach strongly emphasizes data and its organization. This approach is thus very well suited to a relational database type of application but may not fit so well with other problem domains.

Once the idea of analyzing a system through modeling has been accepted, it is no surprise that the object-oriented approach appears. Its roots lie in Simula-67, a language designed in the 1960s for simulation, which basically relies on modeling. This approach took off during the late 1980s and has led to a profusion of object-oriented analysis and design (OOA&D) methods.

Recently, a graphical modeling language, the Unified Modeling Language (UML), has been proposed as the de facto standard to describe software applications (Rumbaugh, Jacobson, and Booch, 1997). Now a standard endorsed by the OMG, UML is an evolution from Booch (1991, 1994), OMT (Rumbaugh et al., 1991), and OOSE (Object-Oriented Software Engineering) (Jacobson et al., 1992), and encompasses many of the best ideas found in previous classical and object-oriented methods. The language is quite general, allowing the modeling of a very broad class of applications while at the same time providing a bridge for communication between the user and the application system architect or designer.

Both the concepts and the graphical syntax in UML come from the community of ideas developed by various people in the object-oriented field. UML defines a number of graphical diagrams providing multiple perspectives of the system under analysis or development. The underlying model integrates these perspectives so that a self-consistent system can be analyzed and built. These diagrams are defined as follows (Rumbaugh, Jacobson, and Booch, 1997):

**Use case diagram:**    Shows the relationship among actors and use cases within a system. (A use case diagram is similar in appearance to those in OOSE.) The use case model represents external functionality of a system or a class as visible to an external interactor with the system. A use case diagram is a graph showing actors, a set of use cases enclosed by a system boundary, communication (participation) associations between the actors and the use cases, and generalizations among the use cases.

**Class diagram:**    A melding of OMT, Booch, and class diagrams of most other OO methods, class diagrams show the static structure of the model, especially the things that exist, such as classes and types, their internal structures, and their relationships to other things. (See Figure 1.2 for an example of a class diagram.) Class diagrams do not show temporal information, although they may contain reified occurrences of things that have or things that describe temporal behavior. UML class diagrams support Design by Contract through the use of stereotyped constraints expressed in the Object Constraint Language (OCL) (Warmer and Kleppe, 1999). (See Section C.2.)

**Behavior diagrams:**    Behavior diagrams show the evolution of the system—its *dynamics*—and are categorized as follows:

- **Statechart diagram:** Substantially based on the statecharts of David Harel, a statechart diagram shows the sequences of states that an object or an interaction goes through during its life in response to received stimuli, together with its responses and actions.

- **Activity diagram:** An activity model is a form of a state machine in which the states are activities representing the performance of operations. Transitions are triggered by the completion of the operations. An activity diagram represents a state machine of a procedure itself; the procedure is the implementation of an operation on the owning class.

- **Sequence diagram:** Sequence diagrams were found in a variety of OO methods under such names as interaction, message trace, and event trace. A sequence diagram shows an interaction arranged in time sequence. In particular, a sequence diagram shows the objects participating in the interaction by their **lifelines** and the messages they exchange, arranged in time sequence. (See Figure 1.3 for an example of a sequence diagram.) A sequence diagram does not show the associations among the objects. Sequence diagrams come in several slightly different formats intended for different purposes. A sequence diagram can exist in a generic form to describe all of the possible sequences and in an instance form to describe one actual sequence consistent with the generic form. In cases without loops or branches, the two forms are isomorphic.

- **Collaboration diagram:** Collaboration diagrams were adapted from various sources: the object diagram of Booch (1991), the Fusion method (object interaction graph) (Coleman et al., 1994), as well as others. A collaboration diagram shows an interaction organized around the objects in the interaction and their links to one another. Sequence diagrams and collaboration diagrams express similar information but show it in different ways. A collaboration diagram shows the relationships among the objects and is better for understanding all of the effects on a given object and for procedural design. On the other hand, a collaboration diagram does not show time as a separate dimension, so the sequence of messages and the concurrent threads must be determined by using sequence numbers.

**Implementation diagrams:**   Implementation diagrams show such aspects of implementation as source code structure and runtime implementation structure. They are derived from Booch's module and process diagrams, but they are now component centered rather than module centered and are far better interconnected. They come in two forms: *component diagrams* and *deployment diagrams*.

- **Component diagram:** A component diagram shows the dependencies among software components, including source code, binary code, and executables. A software module may be represented as a component type. Some components exist at compile time; some exist at link time; and some exist at runtime; some exist at more than one time. A compile-only component is meaningful only at compile time; the runtime component in this case would be an executable program. A component diagram has only a type form, not an instance form. Component instances are shown by using a deployment diagram, possibly a degenerate one without nodes.

- **Deployment diagram:** A deployment diagram shows the configuration of runtime processing elements and the software components, processes, and objects that live on them. Software component instances represent runtime manifestations of code units. Components that do not exist as runtime entities—because they have been compiled away—do not appear on these diagrams; they should be shown on component diagrams.

Among other interesting features, UML takes into account the notion of design patterns through collaboration diagrams, where collaborations have been accorded the status of first-class modeling entities and may form the basis of patterns. A collaboration is a context for interactions. A collaboration can indeed be used to specify the implementation of design constructs. A collaboration can also be viewed as a single entity from the outside. For example, a collaboration could be used to identify the presence of design patterns within a system design. A pattern is a parameterized collaboration; in each use of the pattern, actual classes are substituted for the parameters in the pattern definition.

A use of a pattern is shown as a dotted ellipse containing the name of the pattern. A dotted line is drawn from the collaboration symbol to each of the objects or classes—depending on whether it appears within an object diagram or a class diagram—that participate in the collaboration. Each line is labeled with the role of the participant. The roles correspond to the names of elements within the context for the collaboration; such names in the collaboration are treated as parameters that are bound to specify elements on each occurrence of the pattern within a model. Figure 1.7 illustrates this notation with the use of the Observer pattern, as described in Section 1.1.3. This notation has the advantage of making the use of a given pattern explicit and prominent in a class diagram, without entering into the details of its implementation.

## 1.2.3  From Problems to Solutions with Patterns

Design activities start with the output of the analysis activities and gradually shift the emphasis from the application domain to the computation domain. The purpose of object-oriented analysis is to model the problem domain so that it can be understood and can serve as a stable basis for preparing the design step. The design process can be seen as a transformation of the analysis model into an implementation model, using a number of design rules that could be expressed as design patterns (see Figure 1.8). Auxiliary classes may be introduced

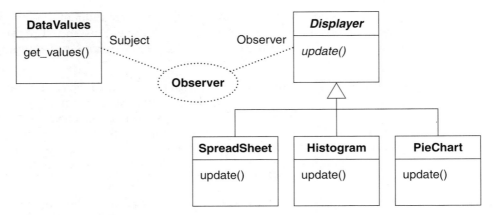

**Figure 1.7** Occurrence of the Observer pattern

at this stage to deal with complex relationships or implementation-related matters. Consistently using UML helps to avoid model ruptures and thus improves traceability. We see UML as the backbone language allowing the designer to enter progressively into the detail of the implementation by changing informal analysis and design concepts expressed with the UML into precise and detailed elements of design, still expressed in UML. The output of the object-oriented design activity is a blueprint for the implementation in an object-oriented language. The implementation should then be a mere translation from the detailed and implementation-oriented UML model.

In many organizations, the design process still follows a classical "military" model. A small number of "officers" do the "noble" task of analysis and design, plan the overall work load, and assign implementation and test tasks to the "simple soldiers." This way of working has several drawbacks.

- Implementation is not considered a "noble" task; consequently, the only aspiration of current implementers is to become designers, or even better, analysts.

- Analysts' experience can be somewhat removed from practical implementation concerns (it is well known that "diagrams do not crash"), inadvertently creating barriers to the smooth transtion among analysis, design, and implementation.

- Implementers are not empowered, and they lack the vision of the big picture (see, for example, the article about the management of the Alpha AXP program at Digital Equipment Corporation in Conklin, 1996 for the importance of this issue.)

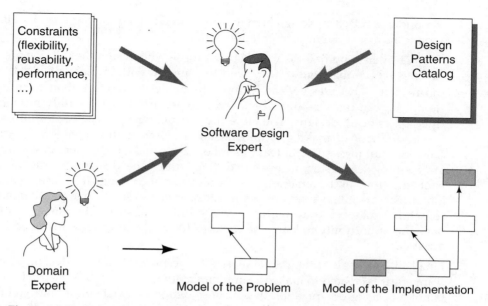

**Figure 1.8** Transforming an OO analysis by applying design patterns

But today, even the military no longer works like this, at least in the British SAS or American SEALs and probably other elite military forces as well. One of the most recent accounts of this is Andy McNab's (1993) best-seller, *Bravo Two Zero,* which relates the story of an SAS patrol behind Iraqi lines during the 1991 Gulf War. Most interesting to us is the account of the mission design. After being given a broad view on the mission objective—to cut the telecommunication line between Baghdad headquarters and Scud launchers in northern Iraq—all eight members of the SAS patrol meet to *cooperatively* design the details of their mission (what, when, where, how, and with which tools). They do not start from scratch but instead identify the problems to be solved and their contexts, and then borrow and customize solutions from the Standard Operational Procedures (SOP) handbook: for example, *get to this point behind enemy lines with enough food and amunition for the mission and without anybody else being aware* or *have a cover story ready in case of a capture*). The very same eight men then "implement" their design, being fully aware of all the implications. The bottom line of this approach is that these special forces consistently rate from five to ten times better than classical ones—and military efficiency measures, albeit somehow macabre, do exist.

Let us see what in that work procedure can readily be transposed to a software engineering project. The most striking point is the team's reliance on patterns of organization and behavior for the big picture and on SOP for the implementation details. These patterns are used as small building blocks that everyone knows and understands: The design activity can proceed at a quite high level, in terms of patterns instead of implementation details.

Another interesting point is that, because those who design the mission are also the ones who implement it, they tend to come up with implementable designs and realistic schedules.[3] Many factors—probably many more than what a single person can master—must be taken into account to successfully implement "mission-critical" designs. Therefore, by combining the expertise of all participants, the risk of making stupid mistakes or oversights is slightly reduced. This does not mean that all team members are equals. First, there is still a need for a strong leadership to pilot and "moderate" the design, asking the relevant questions and managing the process and its timing. It is also clear that junior team members may not contribute as much as senior ones, although they sometimes may come up with a few good ideas; instead, the junior members have the opportunity to learn the tricks of the trade and to feel involved in the mission.

Finally, because all of the implementers are responsible for the design, a strong team spirit is created to make the implementation possible. By construction, this is not a *blaming* organization in the sense defined in McLendon and Weinberg (1996); in case of an unexpected problem, there is no point in looking for someone to blame, as all share the responsibility. Efforts can be devoted totally to solving the problem and preventing it from appearing again instead of losing time in trying to find a scapegoat. Furthermore, when people are deeply involved in the design decision process, they take pride in being able to fulfill the expectations they have raised. And pride is probably the strongest factor in human motivation, even before money.

## 1.3  Toward Formalizing a Pattern-Based Software Process

In order to properly introduce notions of patterns into the software life cycle, we need to be able to manipulate them. The problem, however, is that patterns are not, by definition, fully formalized descriptions. They can't appear as a deliverable. In fact, they are part of the process more than of its product. What we observe is the use of patterns during the shift from one phase to the next. Patterns carry knowledge about how to organize a solution, but they are not part of the solution itself. Based on this assessment, we go back to the process definition and try to formalize how to introduce the use of patterns in a disciplined way.

---

3. This factor has also been identified by Jim Coplien (1995) as the *Architect also Implements* pattern.

## 1.3.1 The Common Phases

Each activity in the software process carries with it a transformation from one level of description to a more detailed, more implementation-aware level. To be more precise, consider the following process as an example. The phases of this process are defined by their deliverables, which are as follows:

- **System specification, or requirements analysis:** A document explaining what services users expect. It can be described in informal, natural language or more precisely through **use case** diagrams. The system specification answers the *what-for* question. Most of the time, in real systems, it is accompanied by a set of constraints. These constraints can be purely functional, but more often they are tied to implementation tradeoffs.

- **System analysis:** A document listing and describing the entities involved in the system. All of the notions that were cited or implicitly referenced by the specification document are defined here, along with their intrinsic dependencies. System analysis answers the *what* question.

- **System design:** A description of all the components, including additional implementation-oriented entities, and their collaborations. The resulting scheme aims at fulfilling the initial requirements. System design answers to the *how* question.

- **Code validation:** The use of particular idioms to translate design specifications to machine-readable code. The higher level the language, the easier the task.

The first document is obtained through either **knowledge-acquisition** techniques or an ergonomic approach called **work analysis**. We consider the resulting document as the starting point of our process.

Subsequently, each phase is a rewriting process. Its main characteristic is to proceed from ambiguous and informal to unambiguous and formal. The final code can indeed be regarded as a formal model of the system produced.

Each item that is part of the resulting document of phase $N$ is one of the following:

- A simple reformulation of an item of phase $N - 1$

- A translation of such an item designed to fit a particular implementation scheme

- An artifact item that is needed to carry out an implementation method

Using this approach, we can define traceability as the ability to *justify* each item at stage $N$ by reference to an item of a previous stage or by an implementation choice.

Stated like this, the use of patterns to obtain the resulting product remains an obscure and ad hoc manipulation merged with other actions that lead to the final transformation. This is the way it actually occurs. However, as long as we keep the process opaque, we won't be able to arrive at any conclusion and to make any improvements. The decision to apply a given pattern should be made explicit and remembered as such. Thus, we propose to document these decisions as an explicit step in the phase completion.

## 1.3.2  Two Levels of Decision

We obtain the desired effect by splitting each phase into two steps:

- Reformulation
- Collaboration identification through the use of patterns

The reformulation step maps to the naive transformation, whereby each notion of the previous level finds a corresponding counterpart at the current level or a systematic implementation. For instance, analysis classes map to design classes, relations to references or lists, and services to routines or simple features.

The next step stems from this foundation to build what will provide the real added value of the phase. The second step is to identify collaborations between items. From a naive translation, we obtain lots of concepts with lots of specific collaborations. This is where the real work begins. Going from one phase to another, as we stated before, we observe a semantics shift. Namely, we move from application semantics to operational semantics. With that idea in mind, we observe that many applicative semantics notions obey the same operational model: They are used in the same way and respond to the same protocol. Most of the time, this is the place where flexibility and evolutive concerns arise. Collaborations have to be abstract at the operational level. Then, patterns can be perceived. Abstraction from detailed application semantics is the key step toward good design and the identification of the proper patterns.

So, having abstract classes and relationships among them, we are able to deal with peculiarities in a manageable way by applying the right pattern to encapsulate them. Thus, we transform a distinction based on semantics into an operational variant, which is a standard practice in most scientific domains.

## 1.3.3  Synthesis and Transformations

This ends our second step. Most of the time, both steps are merged, and we don't pay attention to fine-process decomposition. Making it explicit allows for better control and further traceability, particularly in the decision-making process.

Taking an extreme position, we could consider the whole system as a set of nodes taking part in collaborations whose composition yields the system behavior. When collaborations are identified, we try to find the proper patterns to implement them. If none fits, we can either keep the raw implementation or propose a protopattern to solve it. In this approach, we can consider patterns as collaboration implementations.

To achieve good traceability, collaborations should be identified and described. Then, the selected pattern is referenced or, if it is new, described. Raw implementation could be considered as the *identity* pattern, since it produces no transformation of the initial model. What is important is to identify the operational semantics of all collaborations in the system. This could be done by collecting the contracts of the routines involved. The name given to the pattern helps us grasp this distributed semantics as a whole. We should try to give names to other collaborations as well, even if they do not rate the use of a particular pattern.

In practice, transformations are multiple and can be combined. This means that the result of a transformation in one phase could serve as the basis for defining a new transformation in that same phase. In the most favorable case, the transformations are supposed to conform to what is called the *layer-additive model*, meaning that patterns assemble on top of one another. It is good practice to try to stay within this model. Nevertheless, in some cases, one object may take part in two collaborations, each having side effects on the other. The best way to deal with this case is to define the composition of the two patterns as a new, composite pattern.

To conclude with the justification problem, we can say that a model item is justified either by a model item of the previous level or by a pattern introduced to build the current level. We thus have a map that goes from each notion in the requirements document down to the code. The declaration of pattern usage gives us the opportunity to justify item introductions that might otherwise have seemed to spring from nowhere.

# Chapter 2

# Object-Oriented Design with Contracts

## 2.1 Supporting Design Patterns with Contracts

Design patterns can be considered reusable microarchitectures that contribute to an overall system architecture. Ideally, design patterns capture the intent behind a design by identifying objects, their collaborations, and the distribution of responsibilities. Conversely, classes that play a role in a design pattern interact in a precise fashion; each class is expected to exhibit "proper behavior."

The notion of software contract has been defined to capture such mutual obligations and benefits among classes. Experience tells us that simply spelling out unambiguously these contracts is a worthwhile design approach (Jézéquel and Meyer, 1997), which Meyer (1992a) cornered with the **Design by Contract** approach to software construction. This approach has a sound theoretical basis in relation to partial functions and provides a methodological guideline for building robust yet modular and simple systems. In some ways, *Design by Contract* is the exact opposite of **defensive programming** (Liskov and Guttag, 1986), which recommends protecting every software module by as many checks as possible. Defensive programming makes it difficult to precisely assign responsibilities among modules and has the additional negative side effect of increasing software complexity, which eventually leads to a decrease in reliability.

Design by Contract prompts developers to specify precisely every consistency condition that could go wrong and to assign explicitly the responsibility of its enforcement to either the routine caller (the client) or the routine implementation (the contractor). Along the line of abstract data type theory, a common way of specifying software contracts is to use Boolean assertions called pre- and post-conditions for each service offered, as well as class invariants for defining general consistency properties. A contract carries mutual obligations and benefits: The client should call a contractor routine only in a state where the class invariant and the precondition of the routine are respected. In return, the contractor promises that when the routine returns, the work specified in the postcondition will be done, and the class invariant is still respected.

A failure to meet the contract terms indicates the presence of a fault, or bug. A precondition violation points out a contract broken by the client: The contractor then does not have to try to comply with its part of the contract but may signal the fault by raising an exception. A postcondition violation points out a bug in the routine implementation, which does not fulfill its promises.

Design by Contract is integrated into the type system through the notion of **subcontracting** as provided by the inheritance mechanism. That is, dynamic binding can be viewed through the perspective of a routine's subcontracting its actual implementation to a redefined version. Redefinition is, then, a semantics-preserving transformation in the sense that the redefined routine must at least fulfill the contract of the original routine and, optionally, do more, such as accepting cases that would have been rejected by the original contractor or returning a "better" result than originally promised. In other words, redefinition means that in a subclass, preconditions may only be weakened (accept more) and postconditions strengthened (do more).

## 2.1.1  Choice of a Language

Being design-level notions, both design patterns and Design by Contract can be used with any language, even non-object-oriented ones. Nonetheless, object-oriented languages are easier targets, since they are close to the design concepts used to deal with large, ever-evolving software systems. In the context of software engineering, the Eiffel language (Meyer, 1992b) is one of the most consistent and well-designed object-oriented languages on the market. Eiffel provides the right paradigms to address the construction of large, high-quality object-oriented software systems while staying quite easy to master. As Richard Wiener (1995) has noted, "Eiffel is more than a language; it is a framework for thinking about, designing and implementing object-oriented software"

Beyond classes—the modular units—Eiffel offers multiple inheritance, polymorphism, static typing and dynamic binding, genericity and a disciplined exception mechanism, and direct support for Design by Contract. For example, the rules for integrating Design by Contract with inheritance are enforced at the language level, as preconditions and postconditions are automatically inherited by redefined features. Pre- and postconditions still may be modified but only through the syntax **require else** and **ensure then,** making sure that preconditions may only be weakened (accept more) and postconditions strengthened (do more).

Eiffel is thus an ideal language for implementing an object-oriented design obtained through OOA&D methods, such as those based on UML or one of its precursors: OMT (Object Modelling Technique), BON (Business Object Notation), Fusion, and others (Jézéquel, 1996b). Eiffel has been used for a wide range of applications, from banking systems (Stephan, 1995) to scientific applications (Guidec, Jézéquel, and Pacherie, 1996) and embedded systems (Creel, 1997; Jézéquel, 1998a).

The definition of the Eiffel language (Meyer, 1992b) is in the public domain and is controlled by the Nonprofit International Consortium for Eiffel (NICE). Many Eiffel compilers and development environments are now on the market or are free (see Section B.1.1). Relying on a small standard kernel library (the **Eiffel Standard Library**, as endorsed by NICE), all of these compilers are largely compatible. All of the code examples in this book have been tested with the freely available GNU Eiffel compiler developed at LORIA (see Section B.2.1). It should be straightforward to adapt them to other environments.

Since Design by Contract can now be used with several other programming languages, such as Java, and even in the Unified Modeling Language (UML) as the Object Constraint Language (OCL) (Warmer and Kleppe, 1999), it should not be too difficult to adapt our examples to these languages. Indeed, we describe many examples using the UML notation (see Section C.2), and we explain how Design by Contract can be used with Java through the iContract tool (Kramer, 1998) in Appendix C, Section C.1.

## 2.1.2  Covariant Typing

In the implementation of many design patterns, as well as in modeling real-world problems, it is often necessary to specialize related classes jointly. Consider the following well-known example: HERBIVORES eat PLANTS. A COW is a HERBIVORE. GRASS is a PLANT.

The static structure of the pattern of relationships among these four classes is exactly the same as in Observer (187)[1] design pattern in Figure 1.2. This structure can also be found in many other design patterns: Abstract Factory (57), Factory Method (69), Bridge (93), Iterator (159), Mediator (167), and Template Method (221).

In many occurrences of this pattern structure, we face the following kind of problem: A COW eats GRASS but not other PLANTS, so the feature *eat* should have its signature redefined in the class Cow in such a way that it accepts only a GRASS argument. Eiffel is atypical in that it is one of the few languages allowing this rule,

---

1. For easy reference, each GoF pattern name is followed by the page number on which it is discussed in this book.

known as the **covariant signature redefinition**. The rest of this section enters into quite technical details. It can be skipped or skimmed over on a first reading.

Syntactically, the covariant signature redefinition constraint translates to the following rule. If the original version of a feature *f* takes an argument of type A and/or returns a type A—that is, if the feature is an attribute or a function—the redefined version may take an argument only of type B (or return a type B), such that B is a descendant of A or A itself. The inheritance varies for both in the same direction; hence, the term *covariance*. The alternative to covariance is *contravariance*, stressing the fact that the inheritance varies in the opposite direction: In the child class, the types of arguments in redefined routines must be superclasses of types in the parent's routine. The notion of no-variance—when types of arguments cannot be redefined in subclasses—is the approach taken in Java and in C++.

At first, the contravariant rule seems theoretically appealing. Recall that polymorphism means that an entity can hold objects of not only its declared type but also any descendant, or child type. Dynamic binding means that a feature call on an entity will trigger the corresponding feature call for the *actual* type of the object, which may be a descendant of the declared type of the entity. Consider the following two classes.

```
class PARENT
feature
  eat (arg: FOOD) is
    do -- some processing
    end
end -- PARENT
```

```
class CHILD
inherit
  PARENT
    redefine eat end
feature
  eat (arg: CHILD_FOOD) is
    do
      arg.mill -- some new processing,
              -- available only for CHILD_FOOD
    end
end -- CHILD
```

With contravariance—that is, when CHILD_FOOD must be a superclass or ancestor of FOOD—we can assign an object of descendant type to an entity, and all feature calls will still work, because the descendant can cope with feature arguments at least as general as those of the ancestor. In fact, the descendant object is in every way also a fully valid instance of the ancestor object: We are using inheritance to implement *true functional subtyping*.

If covariant typing is chosen without other considerations—that is, when CHILD_ FOOD must be a subclass of FOOD—however, substitutability of an object by a specialized version is lost. Assume that the routine *eat* redefined covariantly in the class CHILD performs a new operation involving the calling of a routine *mill* on its argument **arg**, which is declared of type CHILD_FOOD. Assume also that *mill* is defined in CHILD_FOOD but not in FOOD. In that case, the following code is not valid.

```
class BROKEN
feature
    p : PARENT; c : CHILD
    x : FOOD;
    wrong is
        do
            !!c.make; !!p.make; !!x.make;
            p.eat(x)     -- legal: the PARENT's version of eat is called
            p := c       -- p now holds a CHILD object
            p.eat(x)     -- the CHILD's version of eat is called, which
                         -- tries to call the nonexistent feature x.mill
        end
end -- BROKEN
```

Contravariance thus would seem to be the "right" rule. However, besides being less "natural," in the sense of real-world modeling, than the covariant one, it is indeed the source of many problems. The most surprising one appears with binary features, such as comparisons. Consider again the class PARENT and its subclass CHILD. Imagine that for these classes, we have defined a feature *equal*, which compares the current object with another object of the same type. Thus, *equal* has the functional type $(PARENT \times PARENT) \rightarrow Boolean$ in PARENT but $(CHILD \times CHILD) \rightarrow Boolean$ in CHILD. If the contravariant rule is used, the type associated with *equal* for CHILD instances is not a subtype of the one of *equal* for PARENT instances. As soon as this kind of feature is considered, and they are common, the contravariant rule prevents a subtyping relation between CHILD and PARENT. This outcome would be quite unfortunate.

Experience with Eiffel and other covariantly typed object-oriented languages, such as $O_2$ (Bancilhon, Delobel, and Kanellakis, 1992), shows that the difference between subclassing and true functional subtyping does not cause much problem in practice, because when you design a subclass that is not a true functional subtype of its superclass, you usually have a good reason to do so. If you have an OSTRICH class inheriting from a BIRD class (and changing the export clause related to *flying*), you would not write a routine to launch all birds out of a bag from a cliff: An ostrich could be among them.

This is why Eiffel does not prevent you from building inheritance structures in which true functional subtyping is not respected; unexpected special cases and exceptions always occur in the real world, even when you try to design inheritance structures that are as complete and as regular as possible. Still, Eiffel is committed to the building of better-quality software, so it must ensure that the programmer is performing only type-safe manipulations. The **system-level validity** rule allows Eiffel systems to be fully type-safe, still modeling the problem domains in a natural way, where subclassing does not always conform to true functional subtyping.

Basically, the system-level validity rule says that when a CHILD class inherits from a PARENT class but is not a true functional subtype of PARENT because a certain feature *f* has a restricted export set or has been covariantly redefined, a CHILD object *c* can be assigned to a PARENT entity *p* (either directly p := c or through parameter passing) only *if there is no risk that* f *is called on such a* p. This rule forbids such polymorphic assignment when the routine *f* might be called on a *p* entity anywhere in the same system—that is, the set of classes making a given program. Thus, a class such as BROKEN in Section 2.1.2 would be rejected by the compiler. See Meyer (1992b) for a more formal description of the system-level validity rule.

## 2.1.3  Controlled Multiple Inheritance

In languages such as C++, multiple inheritance is poorly integrated and may have a performance penalty; therefore, design guidelines for an implementation in C++ tell you to develop shallow inheritance graphs and to avoid, as much as possible, multiple inheritance and, above all, repeated inheritance. This is not necessary in Eiffel, due to two main factors. First, even if the inheritance graph leading to a class X is complex, there is no performance penalty. Finding a feature subject to dynamic binding can be done in constant time, whatever the inheritance graph. This is possible because of the inheritance semantics in Eiffel, by which each class X inheriting from a set of other classes has an equivalent form, called its **flat** form, which can be expressed without *any* inheritance. (Most Eiffel environments provide tools to show this form.) This is the client's view on X, or what the user of class X needs to know about it: the complete description of its interface. Where that interface originates is of absolutely no significance to the client. You might want to know all of its ancestor classes to understand its polymorphic behavior, but how it is constructed from those classes is irrelevant.

The other main factor allowing multiple inheritance to be better controlled in Eiffel is that inheritance of a class may be customized on a by-feature basis. For each individual feature inherited from a parent class, you may either (1) inherit the feature as it is in the parent class—same name; specification, including signature, preconditions and postconditions; body; and export status, or default behavior—or (2) change any number of these components with a feature-adaptation clause. This will be particularly helpful for the Adapter (87) design pattern, where this issue will be discussed in more detail.

## 2.2  Supporting OO Design

Because it takes object-oriented ideas seriously, Eiffel fosters a pure object-oriented design approach, without compromise. The idea is that the burden should be placed on the compiler, not on the software engineer. This was a problem in the early 1990s, when compilers were not mature enough for high-performance projects. But since then, compilation technology, based on type inference (Zendra, Colnet, and Collin, 1997), has progressed so much that performance is no longer a problem for most applications.

In this section, we review the main principles underlying a truly object-oriented design. These principles will be very helpful to us in understanding the context of the Eiffel implementation of the GoF design patterns. For more information on these principles, see Coleman et al. (1994), Meyer (1997), and Wirfs-Brock, Wilkerson, and Wiener (1990).

### 2.2.1  Encapsulation and Information Hiding

Several common prinicples can be applied.

- **One abstraction per class:** The class is the unit of modularity in Eiffel. The class is also the implementation of an abstract data type (ADT), which means that classes should be cohesive units representing complete abstractions.

  Disassociated pieces of functionality should not be encapsulated in the same class. Designing unrelated functionality in the same class makes it more difficult to understand and to maintain and undermines the "real-world modeling" benefit of the object-oriented approach for that class.

- **One class per abstraction:** In object-oriented software systems, the overall functionality is distributed across the objects, but any given abstraction, including functions, should be tied to only one class. Spreading an abstraction across a collection of objects makes change control difficult. A change in one part of an abstraction may require changes to the other, but the link may be lost in the object-oriented structure.

Each individual class should serve a particular purpose. Collaboration diagrams, such as those provided by the UML, should be reviewed to check that the same functionality is not implemented by unrelated classes and that each class is coherent, with strongly associated functionality.

- **Information hiding:** Beyond allowing us to present a controlled interface to the outside world, the encapsulation mechanism enables the underlying implementation of a class to be hidden. This mechanism should be used to keep the representation hidden and to reduce the interface dependence on the representation. Easy replacement of representations to implement the same interface is then permitted, which is useful in design, especially in promoting reuse.

- **Minimality of class interfaces:** Each feature should serve a well-understood and accepted purpose and thus be characterized by a well-defined contract: precondition, postcondition, and class invariant. Features should be orthogonal; that is, functionality should not overlap across features. To keep the class interfaces as simple as possible, features that do not need to be exported should explicitly be kept private.

Beyond these common principles, there are several schools of thought about the problem of the size of class interfaces.

- The **minimalist school** considers that the composition of functions should be left to the client, not to the server. A class provides the primitive building blocks, or atomic features, and users of the class group the primitives into useful compositions. For example, a *pop* feature of a STACK class should remove the top of the stack, and a *top* feature should select the top of the stack. Combining these two separate functions into one feature would restrict the usefulness and flexibility of the stack interface.

- The **pragmatic school** considers that pure minimalism is too extremist and admits that nonprimitive features that are still *pragmatically* useful to a class should be included for ease of use or efficiency. The class may then provide a combination of primitive features, but this is valid only when the primitives are also part of the provided interface. If it wouldn't have clashed with the "pure function" requirement (see Section 2.3.6), the feature *pop*—combining both operations of removing the top of the stack and returning it—would, for example, qualify for inclusion in the STACK interface under this pragmatic-minimalist rule.

- The **shopping list school** considers that all *potentially* useful features should be included in the class interface, provided that they respect the basic rules of minimality. The idea is that *one more feature will hurt no one—and may help someone tremendously* (Meyer, 1994).

Although the pragmatic point of view is probably the most efficient for building standalone applications, B. Meyer makes some good points about defending the shopping list approach when the design concerns reusable libraries (Meyer, 1994).

## 2.2.2  Modularity and Coupling

The following principles apply.

- **Macro organization:** The class is a necessary but insufficient vehicle for decomposition. For large systems, one of the worst organizations would consist of a flat collection of classes through which developers would have to navigate to find what they needed. A better design principle is to ensure that the universe of classes is partitioned into loosely coupled subsystems, or *clusters*. Closely coupled objects can be grouped in relevant clusters. The objects have client/server relationships, so the clusters can be structured according to usual principles, such as partitioning and layering.

- **Minimize object interactions:** The patterns of interactions for objects should be kept as simple as possible. Paraphrasing Antoine de Saint-Exupéry, we could say that *a good design is not the one to which you cannot add anything but the one from which you cannot remove anything.*

  UML collaboration diagrams are helpful for visualizing object interactions. These diagrams should have a minimal number of objects and a minimal number of references. Minimizing the number of objects limits the dispersion of an operation implementation across the object structure. Minimizing the number of references makes designs more efficient. The fewer the references, the shorter the access paths needed to implement an algorithm.

  Cycles in the collaboration diagrams denote mutual feature calls between objects. Mutual feature calls require copies of object references across object collections, known as **aliasing**. If this is the key to an algorithm, the cycle length should be reduced to localize potential aliasing, and responsibilities for modifying a multiply aliased object should be clearly spelled out.

- **Minimal interface dependencies:** Mutual interface dependencies should be reduced as much as possible across object boundaries. A guide to help achieve this is given by the *Law of Demeter* (Lieberherr and Holland, 1989), which states that for each object $o$ and each of its features $f$, the objects that can be referenced are the object itself, $o$; object-valued attributes of $o$; and arguments of $f$. An object observing this law may call the features only of the objects that are immediately referenced.

## 2.3   Idioms for Implementing Design Patterns

An idiom is a low-level pattern specific to a programming language (see Section 1.1.5). An idiom explains how to solve a particular problem in the context of a given language. In this section, we describe some of the most useful examples of Eiffel idioms, which will be used extensively in the next chapters.

### 2.3.1   Accessing the Original Version of a Redefined Feature

Sometimes, a routine has to be redefined only to add a few lines of code at the beginning, at the end, or both. This characteristic is particularly true of creation routines. Whereas in Smalltalk, you can use the *Super* object and in C++ the PARENT::*foo()* notation, in Eiffel all of the information dealing with the relations between a class and its ancestors is located within the *inheritance* clauses. This approach enforces a loose coupling between the inheritance hierarchy and the feature codes. Without the need to check all of the class features for calls on ancestor classes, it is much easier to modify an inheritance hierarchy.

The Eiffel approach—isolating the code from any inheritance information—has, however, a small drawback: Once a routine is redefined, the original version is lost. The only solution is to get two features from the original routine: one to be redefined and the other to keep the original version.

If you are responsible for the design of the parent class, you may anticipate such a need. You may provide multiple versions of the same routine body, with some versions frozen, or not redefinable.

```
class PARENT
feature foo, frozen parent_foo is
    do
        ...
    end
end -- class PARENT
-----------------------------------
class CHILD
inherit
    PARENT
        redefine foo
```

```
     end
feature foo is
   do
      parent_foo
      ...
   end
end -- class CHILD
```

Otherwise, you have to use repeated inheritance to get two versions of *foo* and to redefine one of them.

```
class PARENT
feature foo is
   do
      ...
   end
end -- class PARENT
----------------------------------
class CHILD
inherit
   PARENT
      rename foo as parent_foo
         export {NONE} all -- to ensure that none of the new features
            -- created by renaming are exported to the clients of CHILD
      end
   PARENT
      redefine foo
      select foo  -- in case of dynamic binding
      end
feature
   foo is
      do
         parent_foo
         ...
      end
end -- class CHILD
```

Recently, a new construct to deal more elegantly with this issue has been added to the Eiffel language. This construct uses a new keyword, *precursor*, providing a limited mechanism that allows the body of a redefined routine, such as *foo*, and *only* such a body, to refer to the original one, as follows.

```
class CHILD
inherit
  PARENT
    redefine foo end
feature
  foo is
    do
      ...
        precursor -- calls PARENT's foo. Invalid outside the body of foo
      ...
    end
end -- class CHILD
```

Because this third solution is not yet implemented in all Eiffel compilers, we do not use it in this book. Most often, we rely on providing multiple versions of the same routine body.

## 2.3.2  Implementing Inheritance and Delegation

The organization of object-oriented classes into class hierarchies is an aid to reuse. Classes can be tailored and specialized to produce new classes. However, reuse by inheritance is not always the best option. Classes can be extended through inheritance *or* delegation, also called composition. Deciding when to build new classes by inheritance and when to use delegation is an aspect of object-oriented design.

Inheritance should be used when the complete interface of the old class applies to the new class: *is-a* relationship. Delegation (*has-a* relationship), however, can be considered when a high proportion of code needs to be rewritten or when some of the features of the old class are irrelevant—that is, when the new class is not a true functional subtype of the old class. Places where true subtyping is violated should be documented as such. Building by composition allows the designer more control in the new class interface. The designer can decide which aspects of the old class are relevant and can be reused and which parts can be discarded.

This guideline also applies when all you need is a module-importation mechanism. Consider, for example, the class MATH as it appears in several Eiffel vendors' libraries. This class is merely a module encapsulating a number of mathematical constants, such as $\pi$, and functions, such as *sin* and *cos*. If you need these functions in another class, you could make it inherit from MATH. Inheritance then would be used as a module-importation mechanism, not as a subtyping facility. Although this is a valid use of the Eiffel inheritance mechanism, it "feels wrong" in a certain way, because this inheritance relationship does not relate to the problem domain but to implementation decisions.

In this kind of module-importation problem, it might be better to be a client of MATH rather than its heir. Still, we would like to avoid the overhead of an extra indirection and of an extra attribute. The solution, then, is to use a hidden expanded MATH object, such as *libm*, obtained through the following declaration:

```
feature {NONE}
    libm : expanded MATH
```

The class MATH declares only constants and functions, so its instances have no attributes and hence do not take space in memory. Furthermore, *libm* is an expanded object, so it is not subject to polymorphism, and all of its features may be statically bound and even in-lined by the compiler. You then can expect exactly the same space and time behavior for both solutions. In large software systems, you gain the additional benefits of the qualified call (*libm.atan*), telling you from which module the imported feature came, and of avoiding potential name clashes.

## 2.3.3 Class Variables

Sometimes, you want to share a variable among all instances of a class; this is the notion of class variable found in Smalltalk or C++. Class variables do not exist in Eiffel, but they can be obtained through *once* functions, which provide greater functionality in a more disciplined way.

*Once* functions are special routines. They have the same syntax, except for the keyword **once** used instead of **do**, to introduce the compound statement. The first time the function is called, it works exactly like a regular function. Subsequent calls, however, have no effect; they return the same value as the one returned by the first call. A *once* function can therefore be used to implement a shared attribute of reference type (initialized on its first use).

A *once* function can be included in a mix-in class. The shared attribute returned by that *once* function is then available to all instances of classes that inherit from the mix-in class. (See the Singleton Pattern for an example of the use of a *once* function.)

## 2.3.4 Finalization

Eiffel objects are garbage-collected, so there is no need for the software developer to worry about whether, how, and when to "destruct," or "free," them in the software text. But the need may arise to ensure that certain operations will automatically take place whenever the garbage collector reclaims an object. This is called **finalization** (Hayes, 1992), and is especially useful when an object manages an external resource, such as a file or a network connection. For example, it may be important to close a file when the object dealing with it is reclaimed. Finalization can generalize the garbage collector so that other resources are managed in much the same way as heap memory and with similar program structure. This generalization makes it possible to write more general and reusable code rather than having to treat certain kinds of objects very differently from normal objects.

An Eiffel class that requires finalization facilities can inherit from the standard library class MEMORY and then may redefine the procedure *dispose*—which by default does nothing—to implement the finalization actions. However, because finalization occurs asynchronously—that is, whenever the collector notices that the object is unreachable and does something about it—the finalization code should be written with care. It should concentrate on cleaning external resources and should not do remote calls on other objects, because those also may be dead and may already have been reclaimed.

## 2.3.5  Low Complexity of Routines

Each routine should be kept so short and simple that its mere name—aided by a comment at its header—is enough to understand its purpose and so that the reading of its contract is enough to know how to use it. Complicated or imbricated control structures, such as loops and switches, or both, should be avoided as much as possible. Dynamic binding should be relied on instead. In McCabe's (1976) terms, where the **cyclomatic complexity** of a software component is defined as the number of independent paths through it, a routine's cyclomatic complexity should be as small as possible. Unless you are dealing with special cases, such as parsing user input, it should stay in the range [1..3] (2 corresponds to an **if then else**). This minimal complexity will simplify routine debugging and testing dramatically. The performance penalty of having large numbers of very short routines should not be feared. Eiffel type-checking rules require so much from the compiler that it is easy for it to statically bind and even *in-line* short routines each time it is useful (Zendra, Colnet, and Collin, 1997).

## 2.3.6  Command-Query Distinction

Eiffel fosters a style of design that clearly separates commands from queries. A command is a procedure that may modify the state of an object. A query, by contrast, should return information about an object without modifying its state. A query can be an attribute or a **pure function.** A pure function is without side effects, such as $2 \times f(x) = f(x) + f(x)$. If a function is so complex that it is not clear whether it is pure, this property can be specified explicitly with a postcondition as follows:

---

**ensure**
pure_function: deep_equal(**Current**,old(deep_clone(**Current**)))

---

In addition to the theoretical advantages of this command-query distinction, pure functions enable their use in assertions and will facilitate the testing of classes.

### 2.3.7  Dealing with Optional Behaviors

In an object-oriented system, dynamic binding should be used when we want to provide the user with a set of options tuning the behavior of the system. When this is not possible or not practical, behavior tuning can be provided within a routine through explicit tests on one or more entities that hold the values of the options. Whereas in traditional software, these options are usually transmitted through routine arguments—for example, FORTRAN mathematical subroutines frequently have half a dozen option parameters in addition to their operands— the encapsulation available in object-oriented languages allows a simpler approach to be chosen by means of separately **settable options**. The entities holding the option values no longer need to belong to the argument list of the routine but can be attributes of the class. True operands, then, can be the only arguments of routines, whereas the tuning is factored out and dealt with at the object level or even at the class level if *once* functions are used to provide class attributes. Depending on the scope of an option—class, object, or routine—a setting routine (or two if the option is Boolean) may be included in the class interface.

## 2.4  Documenting the Use of Design Patterns

### 2.4.1  Importance of Documentation

Documenting the use of patterns is very important, especially for maintenance, program understanding, and communication. Within the maintenance phase of a software system life cycle, poor documentation costs even more than poor code. Analysis and design-level documentation should be available to let the future maintenance team understand the rationale behind the code. Most notably, all design decisions should be documented, along with their rationales. If the context changes in the future, the maintenance team should be able to reverse a design decision with full knowledge of all of its ramifications.

Conversely, documenting design-level decisions with design patterns or even with protopatterns seems to be a good idea. But applying a pattern somewhere in a program has an impact not only on the class structure but also on the elements of a class, such as the set of its methods or attributes. For example, the fact that a class plays the *subject* role in an Observer pattern occurrence implies that it has certain methods, such as *notify* or *changed,* and needs certain data structures, such as a collection of observers. Also, some of the code of the methods is there only because of the role the class plays in the pattern. In methods that update some of the subject's state, a call like *notify* occurs because it is a subject in the pattern occurrence. And this can be further complicated by inheritance, when the subject role is spread out over an inheritance tree.

The problem is that such detailed design-related documentation that is not part of the code is usually so badly wrong or out of date that it does not help. The documentation has to be part of the code, integrated in the version-management system, and then manipulated sensibly by browsing and extraction tools. Without the help of external tools, at least two approaches are possible: (1) use (multiple) inheritance to model that a class play a given role in a pattern; (2) rely on the structured documentation facility provided by the Eiffel *indexing* clause. We discuss advantages and drawbacks of both solutions in the following sections.

## 2.4.2  Modeling Pattern Roles with Inheritance

Here, the idea is based on fine-grain multiple inheritance of abstract pattern roles. For each role that a class can play in a pattern, an abstract class is defined to reify this role. Contracts may be specified at this level to denote the responsibilities of each class in the model. Since assertions are inherited, the concrete subclasses will be constrained to respect their ancestor contracts.

Even if no useful code is inherited, it helps document the software and provide traceability. Because of the transitivity of the inheritance relationship, a subclass always has to implement the design pattern roles its ancestors had, and standard tools—such as *short*, the Eiffel class interface extractor—are able to recover this design pattern–level information from the class text.

This approach, however, has a number of limitations. First, not all patterns have an interesting meaning at the class level: Sometimes, the code inside a method relates to the fact that it is, in some way, part of a pattern instance. (For example, in the Observer pattern discussed previously, each method modifying the subject state should include a call to *notify*.) Another problem is method parameters: Usual design patterns "transcend" implementation details, such as method signatures; how many parameters does a routine accept, and what are their types?

A possible solution to this last problem would be to declare the feature with the following signature:

```
method (arg : ANY) is
    -- ...
```

In this case, the argument can be (covariantly) redefined in subclasses to be of any type. If no argument is needed, it can be redefined to NONE, thus constraining the client to call x.method(Void), or else a compile-time error is generated. If more than one argument is needed, the method can be redefined to take an ARRAY[ANY] or an array of a more specific class. The client would then call

```
x.method(<<42,"The Answer is">>)
```

The problem, then, is that we lose the ability to statically type-check the call.

## 2.4.3  Documenting the Use of Patterns with the Indexing Clause

The Eiffel *indexing* clause provides a powerful mechanism for cataloging classes under many criteria. This clause consists of a set of pairs (index, value) following the keyword **indexing**.

Although indices are free identifiers, it is useful to define a small set of indices used consistently across all classes of a given project or, still better, at the company level. The following indices are widely used in the Eiffel world:

- **Description:** associated with a short description of the class, coming, for example, from the data dictionary elaborated during the object-modeling phase and enriched in the design phase

- **revision:** associated with a version management–specific manifest string— for example, "$Id$" for RCS (Revision Control System).

Such an index clause could be used to document the fact that a class plays a role in a pattern. The index clause element could be named *patterns*, and its values would be a list of the pattern roles it implements. A class whose instances hold both the roles of "product" in the Abstract Factory pattern and "subject" in the Observer pattern would be documented as follows.

```
Indexing
    description: "Specification of an Abstract Interface for creating %
    % parts of a Product object"
    note: "This class just serves for demonstrating the indexing clauses"
    patterns: "Abstract_Factory.product", "Observer.subject"
    status: "$State: Exp $"
    date: "$Date: 1999/05/18 08:01:22 $"
```

```
    revision: "$Revision: 1.4 $"
    author: "Jean-Marc Jezequel"
class INDEXE
creation make
feature
    make is do print("Hello world%N") end
end -- INDEXE
```

The main drawback of this approach is that indexing clauses are not inherited, so they should be repeated in subclasses. Also, they do not carry semantics information for ensuring that pattern roles are properly implemented.

## 2.4.4  Conclusion

The two solutions—based on inheritance and indexing—are not mutually exclusive. Therefore, our approach will be to always use the indexing clauses to document the pattern roles played by a class and, each time it is both useful—because interesting contracts hold between patterns participants—and not too cumbersome, to also use inheritance to reify the participation in a pattern.

But clearly, the traditional notion of paper-based documentation is not sufficient for all this. What is needed is an electronic hyperdocument that provides different but interrelated and mutually consistent views of the software being developed. One view is the design level, presented with the UML. Another view is the code itself, and yet another view is made of the pattern occurrences in the program.

Meijers (1996) describes a prototype tool based on these ideas. The program is represented in a kind of database that stores design elements, such as classes, inheritance relations, methods, code, attribute definitions, and pattern occurrences. In doing so, the database provides these different but integrated views on the program. When looking at the design, one can see—by color markers—which elements play a role in which pattern occurrences. Alternatively, a pattern occurrence can be picked up, its abstract structure viewed, and the elements in the design that play a role in the pattern highlighted.

# PART II

# GoF Design Patterns with Contracts

# Chapter 3

# Creational Patterns

The purpose of creational design patterns is to decouple knowledge of the precise type of an object from the process of creating it, that is, allocating memory and initializing its fields. Creational patterns allow for flexibility in deciding what objects are created and how and when they are created. For example, creational design patterns can be used to simplify the task of software configuration management, described in Chapter 6.

## 3.1 The Maze Example

To discuss the adaptation to Eiffel of the Gang of Four (GoF) creational design patterns, we will take the same application example: building a maze for a computer game. As illustrated in Figure 3.1, a MAZE is an indexed set of ROOMs. A ROOM knows its neighbors; possible neighbors are another ROOM, a WALL, or a DOOR to another ROOM. These possible neighbors are generalized as a MAP_SITE, which is simply a place that can be described and that one can try to *enter*.

```
deferred class MAP_SITE
feature {ANY} -- Public Commands
    describe is deferred end -- Print a terse description of this MAP_SITE
    enter is deferred end -- Try to enter into this MAP_SITE
end -- MAP_SITE
```

ROOM is the concrete subclass of MAP_SITE defining the key relationships among components in the maze. ROOM maintains references to other MAP_SITEs and stores a room number.

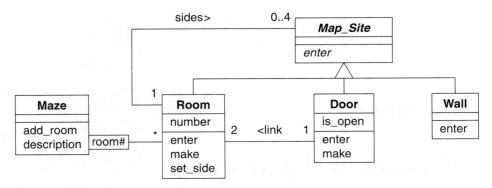

**Figure 3.1** Static model of the maze game in UML

```
class ROOM
inherit
    MAP_SITE
creation make
feature -- Creation
    make (room_number: INTEGER) is
        -- Creation and initialization
        do
            number := room_number
        end -- make
feature {ANY} -- Public Queries
    north_side, east_side, south_side, west_side : MAP_SITE
    number : INTEGER
feature {ANY} -- Public Commands
    enter is do print("You enter "); describe; print(".%N") end
    describe is do print("Room #"); io.put_integer(number) end
    set_north_side (map_site: MAP_SITE) is
        do
            north_side := map_site
        ensure north_side = map_site
        end -- set_north_side
    set_east_side (map_site: MAP_SITE) is
        do
            east_side := map_site
        ensure east_side = map_site
        end -- set_east_side
    set_south_side (map_site: MAP_SITE) is
        do
            south_side := map_site
```

```
        ensure south_side = map_site
        end -- set_south_side
    set_west_side (map_site: MAP_SITE) is
        do
            west_side := map_site
        ensure west_side = map_site
        end -- set_west_side
end -- ROOM
```

The following classes represent the wall or door that occurs on each side of a room.

```
class WALL
inherit
    MAP_SITE
feature {ANY} -- Public Commands
    describe is do print("a wall") end
    enter is do print("You hit the wall%N") end
end -- WALL
```

```
class DOOR
inherit
    MAP_SITE
creation make
feature -- Creation
    make (r1, r2 : ROOM) is
        -- Creation and initialization
        do
            room1 := r1
            room2 := r2
        ensure door_set: room1 = r1 and room2 = r2
        end -- make
feature {ANY} -- Public Queries
    room1, room2 : ROOM -- The ROOMs this DOOR is connecting
    other_side_from (room: ROOM) : ROOM is
        require adjacent_room: room = room1 or room = room2
        do
            if room = room1 then
                Result := room2
            else
                Result := room1
```

```
        end -- if
      end -- other_side_from
  is_open : BOOLEAN
feature {ANY} -- Public Commands
  describe is
    do
      if is_open then print("an open door") else print("a closed door") end -- if
    end -- describe
  enter is
    do
      if not is_open then print("You hit the door%N") end
    end -- enter
end -- DOOR
```

The MAZE itself is an indexed set of ROOMS, stored in an array. (The maze could have been a list or any other collection.) The maze is also able to describe itself.

```
class MAZE
creation make_empty
feature -- Creation
  make_empty is
    -- Creation and initialization
    do
      !!store.make(1,0)
    end -- make_empty
feature {ANY} -- Public Queries
  describe is
    -- Print a terse description of each ROOM of the MAZE
    local i : INTEGER
    do
      print("Maze made of:%N")
      from i := store.lower until i > store.upper
      loop
        if room(i) /= Void then
          room(i).describe; print(" with ")
          room(i).north_side.describe;  print(" (N), ")
          room(i).east_side.describe;   print(" (E), ")
          room(i).south_side.describe;  print(" (S), ")
          room(i).west_side.describe;   print(" (W).%N")
        end -- if
        i := i + 1
      end -- loop
    end -- description
```

```
room (i: INTEGER) : ROOM is
        -- The ith ROOM if it exists in the MAZE, or else Void
    do
        if store.valid_index(i) then Result := store.item(i) end
    end -- room
feature {ANY} -- Public Commands
    add_room (new_room : ROOM) is
        -- add a new ROOM in the MAZE
        require new_room_not_void: new_room /= Void
    do
        -- store it at position new_room.number,
        -- forcing a resize of 'store' if needed
        store.force(new_room,new_room.number)
        ensure stored: room(new_room.number) = new_room
    end -- add_room
feature {NONE} -- Private
    store : ARRAY[ROOM]
invariant
    store_not_void: store /= Void
end -- MAZE
```

## 3.2  Creating Objects in Eiffel

Before discussing the creational design patterns, let's review how objects get created in Eiffel. Objects are created as instances of classes. Let $e$ be an entity with the declared type SOMECLASS

- If SOMECLASS is an expanded type, such as INTEGER, $e$ directly holds the value of the object and is initialized according to the default initialization rules listed in Table 3.1. Thus, no creation is needed. Note that creation of an expanded object is not prohibited; it just resets the object to its default initial value.

- If SOMECLASS is a reference type—for example, ROOM—a creation instruction is needed to dynamically allocate a new object attached to $e$.

In the simplest form, if a class has no creation clause—for example, WALL—a new instance of the class is allocated, initialized—that is, its fields are given their default values—and attached to $e$ by the means of a *creation* instruction made up of two exclamation marks (!!) preceding the entity name.

**Table 3.1**
Default Initialization Rules for Entities

| Entity Type | Initial Value |
| --- | --- |
| BOOLEAN | **false** |
| CHARACTER | '%U' (NUL) |
| INTEGER | 0 |
| REAL | 0.0 |
| DOUBLE | 0.0 |
| Reference to class A | **Void** |
| Expanded class A | All attributes of A initialized to their default values |

```
local
    w : WALL -- w will be a reference to an instance of a WALL
            --   (or one of its subclasses)
do
    !!w        -- An object of type WALL is created, initialized and attached to w
end
```

If the class has one or more creation features—for example, DOOR—one of them must be called when the object is created. The creation routine for the class DOOR is the routine *make*, which takes as its argument the two ROOMS to which it will link. To create a DOOR object and attach it to an entity, the user would write as follows.

```
local
    d : DOOR
do
    !!d.make(a_room,another_room)
        -- An object of type DOOR is created,
        -- initialized, attached to d, and then the
        -- creation procedure 'make' is called on d
end
```

The effect of this instruction is the same as in the WALL example; in addition, the *make* routine is immediately called on the new object, thus allowing it to establish the class invariant.

The third form of the creation instruction allows you to create an object instance of a subclass of a class instead of a direct instance of it.

```
local
   m : MAP_SITE  -- m will be a reference to an instance
                 --   of a MAP_SITE (or one of its subclasses)
do
   !DOOR!m.make(a_room,another_room)
      -- An object of type DOOR (subclass of MAP_SITE)
      -- is created, initialized, attached to e, and then
      -- the creation procedure 'make' is called on m
end
```

The last way to get a new object is to clone an existing one. The function *clone* is available to all classes to create a new object with the same type that is a field-by-field copy of the original object. *Clone*, like *print*, is a feature defined in the class GENERAL, which is an implicit common ancestor to all classes.

```
f := clone(e)              -- now we have equal(e,f)
g := deep_clone(e)         -- now we have deep_equal(e,g)
```

If *e* is **Void**, *f* is also set to **Void**. A variant of *clone*, called *deep_clone*, also exists. This duplicates the entire structure referenced by the original object, that is, deep clones all its fields. Cloning will be discussed again in relation to the Prototype (73) pattern.

Using these creation instructions, we can now create a small example of a maze game. Remember, if you do not want to retype all of this code, the full source code of every example is available from this book's Web site (see Appendix D).

```
class BASEGAME
creation make
feature -- Creation
   make is
      -- Program entry point
      do
         my_maze := create_maze
         my_maze.describe
      end -- make
feature
   create_maze : MAZE is
      -- Create a new maze with 2 rooms connected through a door: [r1 | r2]
      local
         r1, r2 : ROOM
         door : DOOR
```

```
        wall : WALL
    do
        !!Result.make_empty
        !!r1.make(1); !!r2.make(2); !!door.make(r1,r2)
        Result.add_room(r1); Result.add_room(r2)
        -- Now set up r1
        !!wall; r1.set_north_side(wall)
        r1.set_east_side(door)
        !!wall; r1.set_south_side(wall)
        !!wall; r1.set_west_side(wall)
        -- Now set up r2
        !!wall; r2.set_north_side(wall)
        !!wall; r2.set_east_side(wall)
        !!wall; r2.set_south_side(wall)
        r2.set_west_side(door)
    end -- create_maze
feature {NONE} -- Private
    my_maze : MAZE
end -- BASEGAME
```

If we compile and execute this class as the root of an Eiffel system, we get the following output:

```
Maze made of:
Room #1 with a wall (N), a closed door (E), a wall (S), a wall (W).
Room #2 with a wall (N), a wall (E), a wall (S), a closed door (W).
```

## 3.3 Using Creational Design Patterns

The problem with creating a maze this way is that code defining the topology of the maze—that is, its logical layout—is tightly mingled with code defining precisely which constituent we use to build the maze. It is impossible to reuse this construction process to build variants of the maze game—for instance, where some rooms could be ENCHANTED_ROOMS. The idea shared in all creational design patterns is to uncouple these two aspects of the construction of a complex object so that they can be varied independently. The following five patterns are listed in the GoF book:[1]

---

1. The names of the patterns presented in this chapter are followed by the acronym GoF and the page number on which they appear in the original GoF book (Gamma et al., 1995).

**Abstract Factory (GoF page 87)**  Provide an interface for creating families of related or dependent objects without specifying their concrete classes.

**Builder (GoF page 97)**  Separate the construction of a complex object from its representation so that the same construction process can create various representations.

**Factory Method (GoF page 107)**  Define an interface for creating an object, but let subclasses decide which class to instantiate. Factory Method lets a class defer instantiation to subclasses.

**Prototype (GoF page 117)**  Specify the kinds of objects to create, using a prototypical instance, and create new objects by cloning this prototype.

**Singleton (GoF page 127)**  Ensure that a class has only one instance, and provide a global point of access to it.

If you are not yet very familiar with these creational patterns, we recommend that you start by reading Factory Method (69) before carrying on in alphabetical order, that is, Abstract Factory (57),[2] Builder (63), Prototype (73), and Singleton (79).

---

2. Another example of the use of Abstract Factory (57) is presented in Chapter 6.

# Abstract Factory (GoF 87)     (Creational)

## Intent

Provide an interface for creating families of related or dependent objects without specifying their concrete classes.

## Also Known As

Kit

## Structure

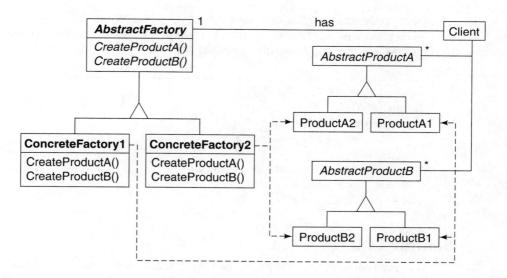

## Collaboration

- Normally, a single instance of a CONCRETEFACTORY class is created at runtime. This concrete factory creates product objects having a particular implementation. To create different product objects, clients should use a different concrete factory.

- ABSTRACTFACTORY defers creation of product objects to its CONCRETEFACTORY subclass.

## Eiffel Implementation

In some applications—and even more so when setting up frameworks—the designer may want to make sure that the design remains extensible. For example, if we want to be able to smoothly replace one product family with another one, we might wish to constrain the creation of Concrete Products by means of FACTORY classes only. In Eiffel, we can enforce this at the language level by restricting the exportation of the creation routine to the ABSTRACT FACTORY class.

```
class CONCRETE_PRODUCT
creation {ABSTRACT_FACTORY} -- Restricted use
   make
feature

   ...
```

Now, only classes inheriting from ABSTRACT_FACTORY are allowed to create such products. ABSTRACT_FACTORY can simply be defined as an interface for operations that create abstract product objects.

```
deferred class ABSTRACT_FACTORY
feature {ANY} -- Public
   new_product : ANY is
         -- Create a new product instance
      deferred
      ensure new_created: Result /= Void
      end -- new_product
end -- ABSTRACT_FACTORY
```

## Sample Code

We give some code examples based on the maze case study described earlier. To build the maze using the Abstract Factory pattern, we would use a maze factory such as the following.

```
class MAZE_FACTORY
inherit
   ABSTRACT_FACTORY
         rename new_product as new_maze redefine new_maze end;
feature {ANY} -- Public
   new_maze : MAZE is
      do
```

```
          !!Result.make_empty
      end -- new_maze
   new_wall : WALL is
      do
         !!Result
      ensure created: Result /= Void
      end -- new_wall
   new_room (number : INTEGER) : ROOM is
      do
         !!Result.make(number)
      ensure created: Result /= Void
      end -- new_room
   new_door (r1, r2 : ROOM) : DOOR is
      do
         !!Result.make(r1,r2)
      ensure created: Result /= Void
      end -- new_door
end -- MAZE_FACTORY
```

Now, imagine that we have to extend the maze game to deal with enchanted rooms (a ROOM that may contain a SPELL) and magically lockable doors (DOOR that might need a SPELL to be cast for unlocking it).

```
class ENCHANTED_ROOM
inherit
   ROOM
      rename make as make_without_spell redefine describe end;
creation make
feature -- Creation
   make (room_number: INTEGER; spell: SPELL) is
      -- Creation and initialization
      do
         make_without_spell(room_number)
         resident_spell := spell
      end -- make
feature {ANY} -- Public Queries
   resident_spell : SPELL -- protecting the ENCHANTED_ROOM
feature {ANY} -- Public Commands
   describe is do print("Enchanted room #"); io.put_integer(number) end
end -- ENCHANTED_ROOM
```

```
class LOCKED_DOOR
inherit DOOR
   redefine describe end
creation make
feature {ANY} -- Public Queries
   spell_needed : SPELL
feature {ANY} -- Public Commands
   describe is do print("a magical door") end -- describe
end -- LOCKED_DOOR
```

For this example, we do not care what a SPELL is. So let us just define it as something with a name.

```
class SPELL
feature {ANY}
   name : STRING
   set_name (new : STRING) is do name := new end
end -- SPELL
```

We would just have to specialize the maze factory to deal with enchanted rooms and other magically locked doors.

```
class ENCHANTED_MAZE_FACTORY
inherit
   MAZE_FACTORY
         redefine new_room, new_door end; -- (co-variant redefinition)
feature {ANY} -- Public
   new_room (number : INTEGER) : ENCHANTED_ROOM is
      -- Creates an ENCHANTED_ROOM
      do
         cast_a_spell
         !!Result.make(number,last_spell_cast)
      end -- new_room
   new_door (r1, r2 : ROOM) : LOCKED_DOOR is do !!Result.make(r1,r2) end
feature {NONE} -- Private
   last_spell_cast : SPELL
   cast_a_spell is do !!last_spell_cast end
end -- ENCHANTED_MAZE_FACTORY
```

Note the covariant redefinition of the result for the methods *new_room* and *new_door*. Instead of returning a ROOM and a DOOR, the methods have been specialized to return ENCHANTED_ROOM and LOCKED_DOOR.

These maze factories would be used in a maze game as follows.

---

```
class GAME_WITH_ABSTRACT_FACTORY
creation make
feature -- Creation
  make is
    -- Program entry point
    local maze_factory : MAZE_FACTORY
    do
      !!maze_factory
      my_maze := create_maze (maze_factory) -- A normal MAZE
      my_maze.describe
      !ENCHANTED_MAZE_FACTORY!maze_factory
      my_maze := create_maze (maze_factory) -- A MAZE with enchanted ROOMs
      my_maze.describe
    end -- make
feature
  create_maze (factory : MAZE_FACTORY) : MAZE is
    -- Create a new maze
    local
      r1, r2: ROOM
      door : DOOR
    do
      Result := factory.new_maze
      r1 := factory.new_room(1); r2 := factory.new_room(2)
      door := factory.new_door(r1,r2)
      Result.add_room(r1); Result.add_room(r2)
      -- Now set up r1
      r1.set_north_side(factory.new_wall)
      r1.set_east_side(door)
      r1.set_south_side(factory.new_wall)
      r1.set_west_side(factory.new_wall)
      -- Now set up r2
      r2.set_north_side(factory.new_wall)
      r2.set_east_side(factory.new_wall)
      r2.set_south_side(factory.new_wall)
      r2.set_west_side(door)
    end -- create_maze
```

```
feature {NONE} -- Private
  my_maze : MAZE
end -- GAME_WITH_ABSTRACT_FACTORY
```

If we compile and execute this class as the root of an Eiffel system, we get
the following output:

```
Maze made of:
Room #1 with a wall (N), a closed door (E), a wall (S), a wall (W).
Room #2 with a wall (N), a wall (E), a wall (S), a closed door (W).
Maze made of:
Enchanted room #1 with a wall (N), a magical door (E), a wall (S),
    a wall (W).
Enchanted room #2 with a wall (N), a wall (E), a wall (S), a magical
    door (W).
```

## Related Patterns

Abstract Factory classes are often implemented with Factory Method (69),
but they can also be implemented by using Prototype (73). A concrete factory is often a Singleton (79).

# Builder (GoF 97)      (Creational)

## Intent

Separate the construction of a complex object from its representation so that the same construction process can create various representations.

## Structure

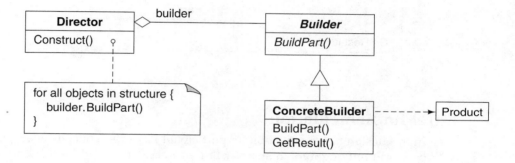

## Collaboration

- The client creates the Director object and configures it with the desired Builder object.

- Director notifies the builder whenever a part of the product should be built.

- Builder handles requests from the director and adds parts to the product.

- The client retrieves the product from the builder.

The following interaction diagram illustrates how Builder and Director co-operate with a client.

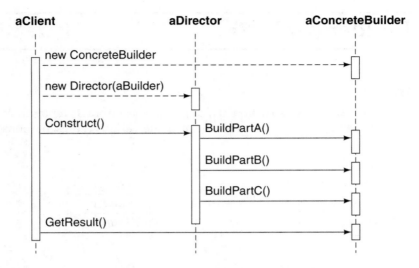

## Eiffel Implementation

In this design pattern, the builder participant has a role concrete enough to be worth reifying into an abstract BUILDER class. It would have been nice if the product resulting from the build process could have been a generic parameter of the class BUILDER [T]. But since it is not possible to instantiate entities of generic type in Eiffel, we have to rely on inheritance to redefine the product according to the desired type.

```
deferred class BUILDER
feature {ANY} -- Public Queries
   product : ANY is
         -- Returns the result of the build process
      deferred
      end -- product
feature {ANY} -- Public Commands
   build is
         -- Start to build the product
      deferred
      ensure product_not_void: product /= Void
      end -- build
end -- BUILDER
```

Eiffel puts a strong emphasis on being able to reuse a class without having to look at its source code. But the mere signature of a method—that is, its name and the type of its parameters and result—is not enough information to describe what it does. The specification of a method must include its *contract*, that is, its preconditions and postconditions. But once a method, such as *build* in the preceding BUILDER, promises something—that the product will not be *Void* after it finishes—it has to keep this promise. So we cannot give it a default empty body, as was originally proposed in the GoF book for C++; the method must stay deferred. This situation will occur again several times throughout this book.

## Sample Code

According to this principle, our MAZE_BUILDER will be an abstract class, with deferred methods for building each component of the maze.

```
deferred class MAZE_BUILDER
inherit
    BUILDER
        rename product as maze, build as build_maze redefine maze end;
feature {ANY} -- Public Queries
    maze : MAZE is deferred end -- the MAZE being built
feature {ANY} -- Public Commands
    build_maze is
        -- Initialize the 'maze'
        deferred
        end -- build_maze
    build_room (number : INTEGER) is
        -- Create a ROOM
        require room_not_yet_built: maze.room(number) = Void
        deferred
        ensure room_built: maze.room(number) /= Void
        end -- build_room
    build_door (n1, n2 : INTEGER) is
        -- Build a DOOR between rooms numbered n1 and n2
        deferred
        end -- build_door
end -- MAZE_BUILDER
```

Then, a standard builder could be implemented as follows.

```
class STANDARD_MAZE_BUILDER
inherit MAZE_BUILDER
feature {ANY} -- Public Queries
```

```
    maze : MAZE -- the MAZE being built
feature {ANY} -- Public Commands
  build_maze is
      -- Initialize the 'maze'
      do !!maze.make_empty end -- build_maze
  build_room (number : INTEGER) is
      -- Create a ROOM and build the WALLs around it
    local
      room : ROOM
      wall : WALL
    do
      !!room.make(number)
      maze.add_room(room)
      !!wall; room.set_north_side(wall)
      !!wall; room.set_east_side(wall)
      !!wall; room.set_south_side(wall)
      !!wall; room.set_west_side(wall)
    end -- build_room
  build_door (n1, n2 : INTEGER) is
      -- Build a DOOR between rooms numbered n1 and n2
      -- and replace their adjoining wall
    local
      door : DOOR
      r1, r2 : ROOM
    do
      r1 := maze.room(n1); r2 := maze.room(n2)
      !!door.make(r1,r2)
      r1.set_east_side(door)
      r2.set_west_side(door)
    end -- build_door
end -- STANDARD_MAZE_BUILDER
```

It could then be used in an application as follows.

```
class GAME_WITH_BUILDER
creation make
feature -- Creation
  make is
      -- Program entry point
    local maze_builder : MAZE_BUILDER
    do
      !STANDARD_MAZE_BUILDER!maze_builder
      my_maze := create_maze (maze_builder)
```

```
            my_maze.describe
        end -- make
feature
    create_maze (builder : MAZE_BUILDER) : MAZE is
        -- Create a new maze
        do
            builder.build_maze
            builder.build_room(1)
            builder.build_room(2)
            builder.build_door(1,2)
            Result := builder.maze
        end -- create_maze
    feature {NONE} -- Private
    my_maze : MAZE
end -- GAME_WITH_BUILDER
```

## Related Patterns

Abstract Factory (57) is similar to Builder but returns the product immediately, not as a separate final step. Composite (99) is what the Builder often builds, for example, in the minicompiler example used to illustrate Facade (109), we use a Builder to construct the Abstract Syntax Tree.

# Factory Method (GoF 107)     (Creational)

## Intent

Define an interface for creating an object, but let subclasses decide which class to instantiate. Factory Method lets a class defer instantiation to subclasses.

## Also Known As

Virtual Constructor

## Structure

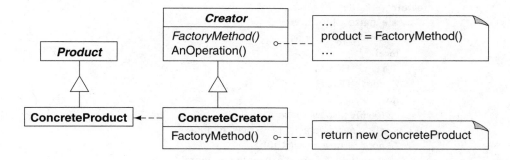

## Collaboration

- Creator relies on its subclasses to define the factory method so that it returns an instance of the appropriate ConcreteProduct.

## Eiffel Implementation

By definition, Factory Methods are functions with a side effect: They create a new instance each time they are called. It is therefore important to document them as such. Here, a naming convention may help to make clear what is going on. For example, we can decide to name every Factory Method by prepending the string *new_* to the name of the class of the object it creates. Thus, a Factory Method for the creation of ROOMS would be named *new_ room*.

## Sample Code

Factory Methods can be used in the maze example to separate the object creations from the maze layout settings. The idea is that each time we want to create a maze component, we call a Factory Method, such as *new_room*, instead of creating it directly.

```
class GAME_WITH_FACTORY_METHOD
creation make
feature -- Creation
  make is
    -- Program entry point
    do
      my_maze := create_maze
      my_maze.describe
    end -- make
feature -- Factory Methods
  create_maze : MAZE is
    -- Create a new maze
    local
      r1, r2: ROOM
      door : DOOR
    do
      Result := new_maze
      r1 := new_room(1); r2 := new_room(2)
      door := new_door(r1,r2)
      Result.add_room(r1); Result.add_room(r2)
      -- Now set up r1
      r1.set_north_side(new_wall)
      r1.set_east_side(door)
      r1.set_south_side(new_wall)
      r1.set_west_side(new_wall)
      -- Now set up r2
      r2.set_north_side(new_wall)
      r2.set_east_side(new_wall)
      r2.set_south_side(new_wall)
      r2.set_west_side(door)
    end -- create_maze
  new_maze : MAZE is
    do
      !!Result.make_empty
    ensure created: Result /= Void
    end -- new_maze
```

```
    new_wall : WALL is
      do
        !!Result
      ensure created: Result /= Void
      end -- new_wall
    new_room (number : INTEGER) : ROOM is
      do
        !!Result.make(number)
      ensure created: Result /= Void
      end -- new_room
    new_door (r1, r2 : ROOM) : DOOR is
      do
        !!Result.make(r1,r2)
      ensure created: Result /= Void
      end -- new_door
feature {NONE} -- Private
  my_maze : MAZE
end -- GAME_WITH_FACTORY_METHOD
```

These Factory Methods, being virtual by default, can be redefined in sub-classes. Thus, to get a variant of the game containing ENCHANTED_ROOMS and LOCKED_DOORS instead of plain ROOMS and DOORS, we simply redefine the method *new_room*.

```
class ENCHANTED_GAME
inherit
  GAME_WITH_FACTORY_METHOD
      redefine new_room, new_door end; -- (co-variant redefinition)
creation make
    -- the 'make' definition is inherited from GAME_WITH_FACTORY_METHOD
feature {ANY} -- Public
  new_room (number : INTEGER) : ENCHANTED_ROOM is
    -- Creates an ENCHANTED_ROOM
    do
      cast_a_spell
      !!Result.make(number,last_spell_cast)
    end -- new_room
  new_door (r1, r2 : ROOM) : LOCKED_DOOR is do !!Result.make(r1,r2) end
feature {NONE} -- Private
  last_spell_cast : SPELL
  cast_a_spell is do !!last_spell_cast end
end -- ENCHANTED_GAME
```

Alternatively, we could have given factory methods a parameter to let it know which variant of ROOM and DOOR we wanted. Either way, if we compile and execute this last class as the root of an Eiffel system, we get the following output:

```
Maze made of:
Enchanted room #1 with a wall (N), a magical door (E), a wall (S),
    a wall (W).
Enchanted room #2 with a wall (N), a wall (E), a wall (S), a magical
    door (W).
```

## Related Patterns

Abstract Factory (57) is often implemented with Factory Methods. Factory Methods are typically called within Template Method (221). A more advanced use of Factory Methods will be presented in Chapter 6, in connection with software configuration management.

# Prototype (GoF 117) (Creational)

## Intent

Specify the kinds of objects to create, using a prototypical instance, and create new objects by cloning this prototype.

## Structure

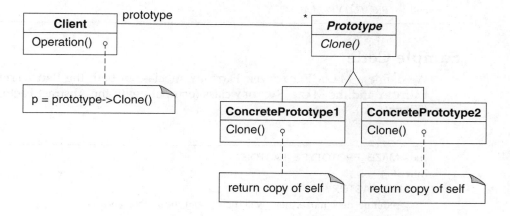

## Collaboration

- A client asks a prototype to clone itself.

## Eiffel Implementation

In many languages, the most difficult part of this pattern is implementing the clone operation correctly. However, the implementation of this pattern is quite straightforward in Eiffel, since both operations *clone* and *deep_clone* are defined in the Eiffel Standard Library to belong to the class GENERAL, ancestor of all other classes. So, the only difficult choice is which version of cloning to use. The function *clone* creates a new object that is a field-by-field copy of the original object and has the same type, whereas the function *deep_clone* duplicates the entire structure referenced by the original object, that is, recursively deep clones all of its fields.

Since it appears that there is no best solution, we provide a toggle in the class PROTOTYPE_FACTORY to let the client choose at runtime.

```
class PROTOTYPE_FACTORY
feature {ANY} -- Public Queries
  is_deep_cloning : BOOLEAN
        -- Whether deep cloning is enabled. Shallow cloning is the default.
feature {ANY} -- Public Commands
  select_deep_clone is
        -- Enable deep cloning of the prototypes
        do is_deep_cloning := True ensure is_deep_cloning end
  select_shallow_cloning is
        -- Enable shallow cloning of the prototypes
        do is_deep_cloning := False ensure not is_deep_cloning end
end -- PROTOTYPE_FACTORY
```

## Sample Code

We define a MAZE_PROTOTYPE_FACTORY subclass of both the PROTOTYPE_FACTORY and the MAZE_FACTORY class (compare with the Abstract Factory (57) pattern).

```
class MAZE_PROTOTYPE_FACTORY
inherit
  MAZE_FACTORY
    redefine new_maze, new_wall, new_room, new_door end;
  PROTOTYPE_FACTORY
creation  make
feature -- Creation
  make (maze : MAZE; wall : WALL; room : ROOM; door : DOOR) is
        -- Initialize the factory with prototypes of the objects
        -- it will create.
      require
        maze_not_void: maze /= Void;  wall_not_void: wall /= Void
        room_not_void: room /= Void;  door_not_void: door /= Void
      do
        prototype_maze := maze
        prototype_wall := wall
        prototype_room := room
        prototype_door := door
      end -- make
feature {ANY} -- Public
  new_maze : MAZE is
      do
        if is_deep_cloning then
```

```
                Result := deep_clone(prototype_maze)
            else
                Result := clone(prototype_maze)
            end -- if
            Result.make_empty -- Re-initialize new_maze
        end -- new_maze
    new_wall : WALL is
        do
            if is_deep_cloning then
                Result := deep_clone(prototype_wall)
            else
                Result := clone(prototype_wall)
            end -- if
        end -- new_wall
    new_room (number : INTEGER) : ROOM is
        do
            if is_deep_cloning then
                Result := deep_clone(prototype_room)
            else
                Result := clone(prototype_room)
            end -- if
            Result.make(number) -- Re-initialize new_room
        end -- new_room
    new_door (r1, r2 : ROOM) : DOOR is
        do
            if is_deep_cloning then
                Result := deep_clone(prototype_door)
            else
                Result := clone(prototype_door)
            end -- if
            Result.make(r1,r2) -- Re-initialize new_maze
        end -- new_door
feature {NONE} -- Private (prototype objects)
    prototype_maze : MAZE
    prototype_wall : WALL
    prototype_room : ROOM
    prototype_door : DOOR
invariant
    prototype_maze_not_void: prototype_maze /= Void
    prototype_wall_not_void: prototype_wall /= Void
    prototype_room_not_void: prototype_room /= Void
    prototype_door_not_void: prototype_door /= Void
end -- MAZE_PROTOTYPE_FACTORY
```

Notice how we use the creation procedures to **reinitialize** the newly cloned object: Indeed, Eiffel creation procedures can be used like normal procedures. We can then use the MAZE_PROTOTYPE_FACTORY to create various kinds of mazes.

```
class GAME_WITH_PROTOTYPE
inherit GAME_WITH_ABSTRACT_FACTORY
        redefine make end;
creation make
feature -- Creation
    make is
            -- Program entry point
        local
            maze_prototype_factory : MAZE_PROTOTYPE_FACTORY
            maze : MAZE; wall : WALL; room : ROOM; door : DOOR
        do
            -- First make a standard MAZE by passing instances of
            -- MAZE, WALL, ROOM and DOOR
            !!maze.make_empty; !!wall; !!room.make(0); !!door.make(Void,Void)
            !!maze_prototype_factory.make(maze,wall,room,door)
            my_maze := create_maze (maze_prototype_factory)
            my_maze.describe
            -- Now make an enchanted MAZE by passing instances of
            -- ENCHANTED_ROOM and LOCKED_DOOR
            !ENCHANTED_ROOM!room.make(0,Void)
            !LOCKED_DOOR!door.make(Void,Void)
            !!maze_prototype_factory.make(maze,wall,room,door)
            my_maze := create_maze (maze_prototype_factory)
            my_maze.describe
        end -- make
end -- GAME_WITH_PROTOTYPE
```

If we compile and execute this class as the root of an Eiffel system, we get the following output:

```
Maze made of:
Room #1 with a wall (N), a closed door (E), a wall (S), a wall (W).
Room #2 with a wall (N), a wall (E), a wall (S), a closed door (W).
Maze made of:
Enchanted room #1 with a wall (N), a magical door (E), a wall (S),
    a wall (W).
Enchanted room #2 with a wall (N), a wall (E), a wall (S), a magical
    door (W).
```

## Related Patterns

A Prototype factory can be implemented along the lines of Abstract Factory (57). Designs that make heavy use of Composite (99) and Decorator (105) patterns can often benefit from Prototype as well.

# Singleton (GoF 127) (Creational)

## Intent

Ensure that a class has only one instance, and provide a global point of access to it.

## Structure

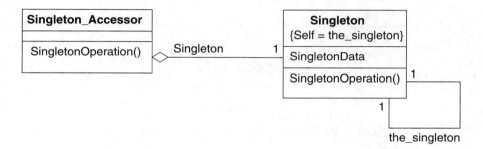

## Collaboration

- Clients access a Singleton instance solely through Singleton's Instance operation.

## Eiffel Implementation

In Eiffel, the only way to control the number of instances of a class is to use a *once* function. *Once* routines are special routines. They have the same syntax as regular routines except that the keyword **once** is used instead of **do** to introduce the compound statement. The first time the routine is called, it works exactly like a regular routine. Subsequent calls, however, have no effect; the body of the routine is not executed. If the *once* routine is a function, the value it returns is the same as the value returned by the first call. This mechanism enables

- The initialization of a data structure without an explicit initialization statement.

- The sharing of values that are computed at runtime. This is related to the notion of class variable found in Smalltalk or C++, whereby variables are shared among all instances of a class.

Thus, a *once* function can be used to always return a reference to the same instance to all callers. We base our Eiffel implementation of the Singleton design pattern on this property. Accordingly, we split the pattern into two classes:

- SINGLETON: A class that should have a unique instance
- SINGLETON_ACCESSOR: A class that provides an access point to the Singleton

To specify that a class may have only one instance, we can make it inherit from the following SINGLETON class.

```
class SINGLETON
feature {NONE} -- Private
   frozen the_singleton : SINGLETON is
         -- The unique instance of this class
      once
         Result := Current
      end -- singleton
invariant
   only_one_instance:  Current = the_singleton
end -- SINGLETON
```

Indeed, if we try to create two instances of such a SINGLETON, we get a violation of the class invariant.

To provide a global point of access to a Singleton, we propose to use a SINGLETON_ACCESSOR with a feature called *singleton*, which should be redefined in concrete subclasses to be a *once* function, creating the singleton object, either directly or by using any of the other creational patterns.

```
deferred class SINGLETON_ACCESSOR
feature {NONE} -- Private
   singleton : SINGLETON is
         -- Access to a unique instance.
         -- Should be redefined as a once function in concrete subclasses
      deferred
      end -- singleton
   is_real_singleton : BOOLEAN is
         -- Do multiple calls to 'singleton' return the same result?
      do
```

```
        Result := singleton = singleton
     end -- is_real_singleton
invariant
   singleton_is_real_singleton: is_real_singleton
end -- SINGLETON_ACCESSOR
```

The SINGLETON_ACCESSOR is simply a way to make available a *shared* instance of SINGLETON to all subclasses and/or clients. To access the singleton object, client classes may either subclass SINGLETON_ACCESSOR or use an instance of it. In the latter case, SINGLETON_ACCESSOR should have no state; it just encapsulates one or more *once* functions and other functions free of side effects. So, even if many instances of the SINGLETON_ACCESSOR are created, they are, for all purposes, absolutely identical, just as this number 3 is identical to this other 3.

This implementation has one small drawback. Since in Eiffel, SINGLETON and SINGLETON_ACCESSOR may not be the same class, the SINGLETON_ACCESSOR has to either repeat all of the SINGLETON public interface or violate the Law of Demeter by exposing the singleton itself. In the following code example, the former solution is taken.

## Sample Code

In the maze example, if we want to use the same MAZE_FACTORY everywhere (compare with Abstract Factory (57)), we have to make the class MAZE_FACTORY inherit from SINGLETON and then define a class MAZE_FACTORY_ACCESSOR to provide a global point of access to it. MAZE_FACTORY_ACCESSOR redefines the *singleton* inherited from SINGLETON_ACCESSOR into a *once* function to create the MAZE_FACTORY singleton. As the icing on the cake, this *once* function could use the value of an environment variable (say, MAZESTYLE) to select the type of the maze factory to be created.

```
class MAZE_FACTORY_ACCESSOR
inherit
   SINGLETON_ACCESSOR
      redefine singleton end;
feature {ANY} -- Public
   new_maze : MAZE is
      do
         Result := singleton.new_maze
      ensure created: Result /= Void
```

```
        end -- new_maze
    new_wall : WALL is
        do
            Result := singleton.new_wall
        ensure created: Result /= Void
        end -- new_wall
    new_room (number : INTEGER) : ROOM is
        do
            Result := singleton.new_room(number)
        ensure created: Result /= Void
        end -- new_room
    new_door (r1, r2 : ROOM) : DOOR is
        do
            Result := singleton.new_door(r1, r2)
        ensure created: Result /= Void
        end -- new_door
feature {NONE} -- private
    singleton : MAZE_FACTORY is
            -- Return a unique instance of a MAZE_FACTORY
        local
            maze_style : STRING
        once
            maze_style := get_environment_variable("MAZESTYLE")
            if maze_style = Void then
                !!Result
            elseif maze_style.is_equal("enchanted") then
                !ENCHANTED_MAZE_FACTORY!Result
            else -- Default to MAZE_FACTORY
                !!Result
            end -- if
        end -- singleton
end -- MAZE_FACTORY_ACCESSOR
```

We can then use this MAZE_FACTORY_ACCESSOR as follows.

```
class GAME_WITH_SINGLETON_FACTORY
creation make
feature -- Creation
    make is
            -- Program entry point
        local maze_factory : MAZE_FACTORY_ACCESSOR
```

```
        do
            !!maze_factory
            my_maze := create_maze (maze_factory)
            my_maze.describe
        end  -- make
feature
    create_maze (factory : MAZE_FACTORY_ACCESSOR) : MAZE is
        -- Create a new maze
        local
            r1, r2: ROOM
            door : DOOR
        do
            Result := factory.new_maze
            r1 := factory.new_room(1); r2 := factory.new_room(2)
            door := factory.new_door(r1,r2)
            Result.add_room(r1); Result.add_room(r2)
            -- Now set up r1
            r1.set_north_side(factory.new_wall)
            r1.set_east_side(door)
            r1.set_south_side(factory.new_wall)
            r1.set_west_side(factory.new_wall)
            -- Now set up r2
            r2.set_north_side(factory.new_wall)
            r2.set_east_side(factory.new_wall)
            r2.set_south_side(factory.new_wall)
            r2.set_west_side(door)
        end  -- create_maze
feature {NONE}  -- Private
    my_maze : MAZE
end  -- GAME_WITH_SINGLETON_FACTORY
```

If we compile and execute this class as the root of an Eiffel system, we get the following output:

```
Maze made of:
Room #1 with a wall (N), a closed door (E), a wall (S), a wall (W).
Room #2 with a wall (N), a wall (E), a wall (S), a closed door (W).
```

Now if we set the environment variable MAZESTYLE to be "enchanted," for example, on a UNIX system running the *csh* command interpreter, with the command *setenv MAZESTYLE enchanted*, and we rerun this program, we get the following output:

```
Maze made of:
Enchanted room #1 with a wall (N), a magical door (E), a wall (S),
    a wall (W).
Enchanted room #2 with a wall (N), a wall (E), a wall (S), a magical
    door (W).
```

## Related Patterns

Many patterns can be implemented using the Singleton pattern. See Abstract Factory (57), Builder (63), and Prototype (73).

# Chapter 4

# Structural Patterns

Structural patterns pertain to how classes and objects are composed to form larger structures. In this chapter, we show how the GoF structural patterns can be implemented with Eiffel. As in Chapter 3, we review the name and the intent of the pattern before discussing Eiffel-specific implementation issues and providing a complete example of the use of the pattern in a complete and self-contained, albeit toy, application. The examples we use are broadly based on those in the GoF book: We just add the few necessary classes to fill in the blanks and to obtain something we can definitively watch running.

**Adapter (GoF page 139)** Convert the interface of a class into another interface clients expect. Adapter lets classes with otherwise incompatible interfaces work together.

**Bridge (GoF page 151)** Decouple an abstraction from its implementation so that the two can vary independently.

**Composite (GoF page 163)** Arrange objects into tree structures to represent part/whole hierarchies. Composite lets clients treat individual objects and compositions of objects uniformly.

**Decorator (GoF page 175)** Attach additional responsibilities to an object dynamically. Decorator provides a flexible alternative to subclassing for extending functionality.

**Facade (GoF page 185)** Provide a unified interface to a set of interfaces in a subsystem. Facade defines a higher-level interface that makes the subsystem easier to use.

**Flyweight (GoF page 195)**  Use sharing to support large numbers of fine-grained objects efficiently.

**Proxy (GoF page 207)**  Provide a surrogate, or placeholder, for another object to control access to it.

# Adapter (GoF 139)                    (Structural)

## Intent

Convert the interface of a class into another interface clients expect. Adapter lets classes with otherwise incompatible interfaces work together.

## Also Known As

Wrapper

## Structure

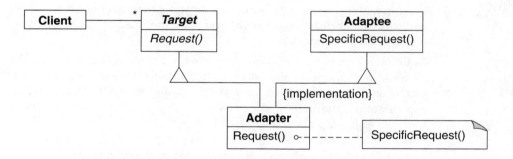

An object adapter relies on object composition:

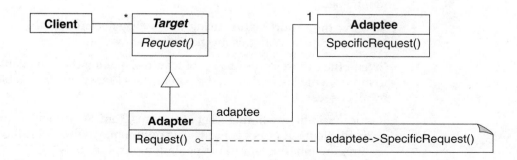

## Collaboration

- Clients call operations on an Adapter instance. In turn, the adapter calls Adaptee operations that carry out the request.

## Eiffel Implementation

This pattern comes in two flavors: the *Object Adapter* and the *Class Adapter*. The former allows dynamic changes and basically uses delegation, whereas the latter is purely static and uses multiple inheritance.

Eiffel offers a rich set of adaptation mechanisms to help in the implementation of the Class Adapter pattern, because the reuse of Eiffel classes through inheritance may be customized on a by-feature basis. A useful analogy for this mechanism is the problem of plugging an electrical razor cord into a foreign wall outlet. The solution usually is to use a plug adapter to convert the size and the form of the connectors—and, sometimes, the voltage or the frequency or both—of your cord to fit the foreign wall outlet. What is done with this adapter is functionally equivalent to changing the foreign wall outlet interface. As a client, you may then use the adapter interface instead of the original one.

In Eiffel, for each individual feature inherited from a parent class, you may either inherit the feature as it is in the parent class—same name; specification, including signature, preconditions, and postconditions; body; and export status, the default behavior—or change any of these components with the following mechanisms:

- **Renaming,** or giving a new name to an inherited feature.

- **Redefining,** or changing, the feature's specification or body or both. If you want to redefine a feature, you must declare it in the **redefine** subclause of the inheritance clause. This change is, however, constrained; it must respect the semantics of the original feature. The signature must be covariantly compatible with the original, the precondition can only be weakened, and the precondition must be strengthened.

- **Changing the export status,** using the *export* subclause of the inheritance clause. With this mechanism, you may either

  - Extend the export status of a set of features, making them available to more client classes than in the parent class ("ANY" means visible by all classes).

  - Reduce visibility by hiding a set of features from some clients—or even all clients, if NONE is used. This option may be useful if the features are inherited for implementation purposes only.

- **Undefine** a feature (*undefine* clause), useful mainly for choosing one of a set of competing implementations for a feature name in some cases of multiple inheritance.

- **Select** a feature (*select* clause) as the target for dynamic binding when there are ambiguities in some cases of repeated inheritance.

## Sample Code

Consider the case of a class SHAPE, defining the interface of a graphical object with an editable shape.

```
deferred class SHAPE
feature {ANY} -- Queries
    bottom_left, top_right : POINT2D is deferred end
    new_manipulator : MANIPULATOR is deferred end -- Factory Method
end -- SHAPE
```

The problem is to *adapt* a preexisting class TEXT_VIEW in such a way that it can be used as a SHAPE.

```
class TEXT_VIEW
creation
    make
feature -- Creation
    make (x,y,w,h : INTEGER) is
        -- Creation and initialization
        do
            !!origin.make(x,y)
            width := w; height := h
        ensure
            origin_set: origin.x = x and origin.y = y
            dim_set: width = w and height = h
        end -- make
feature {ANY} -- Queries
    origin : POINT2D
    width, height : REAL
    is_empty : BOOLEAN
invariant origin_not_void: origin /= Void
end -- TEXT_VIEW
```

SHAPE assumes a bounding box defined by its opposing corners. In contrast, TEXT_VIEW is defined by its origin, height, and width.

## Class Adapter

The following class TEXT_SHAPE is an *adapter* between these various interfaces. It uses multiple inheritance to inherit both the desired interface and the existing implementation.

---

```
class TEXT_SHAPE
inherit
  SHAPE
  TEXT_VIEW
      rename origin as bottom_left -- to allow a merge with SHAPE's
      export {NONE} width, height -- private inheritance: these features are hidden
      redefine make end
      -- is_empty is inherited without modification
creation make
feature -- Creation
  make (x,y,w,h : INTEGER) is
    -- Creation and initialization
    do
      !!bottom_left.make(x,y)
      width := w; height := h
      is_empty := True
    end -- make
feature {ANY} -- Queries
  top_right : POINT2D is
      -- Returns the top right point of the shape
      -- The Result could be cached if this method is to be called often
    do
      !!Result.make(bottom_left.x+width, bottom_left.y+height)
    end -- top_right
  new_manipulator : MANIPULATOR is
      -- Factory Method
    do
      !!Result.make(Current)
    end -- new_manipulator
end -- TEXT_SHAPE
```

---

## Object Adapter

On the other hand, Object Adapter uses object composition to combine classes with various interfaces: It implements the desired interface by delegating the actual work to a private instance of a TEXT_VIEW. Only minor adaptations are necessary.

```
class TEXT_SHAPE2
inherit
  SHAPE
creation make
feature -- Creation
  make (x,y,w,h : INTEGER) is
      -- Creation and initialization
      do
        !!text.make(x,y,w,h)
      end -- make
feature {ANY} -- Queries
  bottom_left : POINT2D is
      do
        Result := clone(text.origin)
      end -- bottom_left
  top_right : POINT2D is
      do
        !!Result.make(text.origin.x+text.width, text.origin.y+text.height)
      end -- top_right
  is_empty : BOOLEAN is
      -- Delagate the call to 'text' version
      do
        Result := text.is_empty
      end -- is_empty
  new_manipulator : MANIPULATOR is
      -- Factory Method
      do
        !!Result.make(Current)
      end -- new_manipulator
feature {NONE} -- Private
  text : TEXT_VIEW
invariant
  text_not_void: text /= Void
end -- TEXT_SHAPE2
```

## Using Adapters

The following example shows how both versions of these adapters can be used.

```
class MAIN
creation
  make
feature -- Creation
  make is
    -- Creation and initialization
    local t : SHAPE
    do
      !TEXT_SHAPE!t.make(1,2,3,4)
      show_shape(t)
      !TEXT_SHAPE2!t.make(1,2,3,4)
      show_shape(t)
    end -- make
  show_shape (t : SHAPE) is
    -- show the bounding box of t
    do
      print("Bottom left = ("); print(t.bottom_left.out); print(")%N")
      print("Top right = ("); print(t.top_right.out); print(")%N")
    end -- show_shape
end -- MAIN
```

If we compile and execute this class as the root of an Eiffel system, we get the following output:

```
Bottom left = (1.000000,2.000000)
Top right = (4.000000,6.000000)
Bottom left = (1.000000,2.000000)
Top right = (4.000000,6.000000)
```

## Related Patterns

Bridge (93) has a structure similar to Object Adapter but has a different intent. Bridge is meant to separate an interface from its implementation so that each can be varied easily and independently. Adapter is meant to change the interface of an *existing* object. Decorator (105) enhances another object without changing its interface. Proxy (131) defines a representative, or surrogate, for another object and does not change its interface.

# Bridge (GoF 151)                    (Structural)

## Intent

Decouple an abstraction from its implementation so that the two can vary independently.

## Also Known As

Handle/Body

## Structure

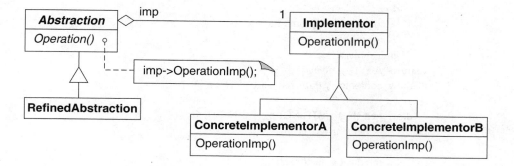

## Collaboration

- Abstraction fowards client requests to its Implementor object.

## Eiffel Implementation

The **Bridge** pattern implementation is based on the use of a polymorphic **handle** on one of the various possible implementations of an abstraction. Since Eiffel features automatic garbage collection, this handle might be in turn freely shared among a number of abstractions, without raising complex issues of memory management.

## Sample Code

Consider the implementation of a portable Window abstraction in a user interface toolkit. This abstraction should enable us to write applications that work on both X Windows and OS/2 Presentation Manager, for example.

The Bridge pattern is used to uncouple the abstraction from a given implementation.

We describe this Window/WindowImp implementation example mainly as in the GoF book. The only difference is that here, the Implementor is passed as a parameter to the Window creation routine.

```
deferred class WINDOW
feature -- Creation
   make (a_contents : VIEW; window_imp : WINDOW_IMP) is
      -- Creation and initialization
      -- Simple case where the implementation is passed as a parameter
      require
         a_contents_not_void: a_contents /= Void
         window_imp_not_void: window_imp /= Void
      do
         contents := a_contents
         imp := window_imp
      end -- make
feature {ANY} -- Commands
   draw_contents is deferred end -- Draw the contents
   -- ...
   draw_text (text : STRING; p : POINT2D) is
         -- Draw a text at 'p'
      do
         imp.device_text(text,p.x,p.y)
      end -- draw_text
feature {NONE} -- Private
   imp : WINDOW_IMP -- interface to the underlying windowing system
   contents : VIEW -- the window's contents
invariant
   imp_not_void: imp /= Void
end -- WINDOW
```

Thus, at creation time, a WINDOW receives a reference to a WINDOW_IMP, which declares the interface to the underlying windowing system.

```
deferred class WINDOW_IMP
feature {ANY} -- Queries & Commands
   -- a lot of routines..., plus
   device_text(text: STRING; x,y: REAL) is deferred end
   device_bitmap(bitmap: STRING; x,y: REAL) is deferred end
end -- WINDOW_IMP
```

Among the multiple possible variants of a WINDOW, we can define, for instance, an APPLICATION_WINDOW that is able to draw the VIEW instance it holds.

```
class APPLICATION_WINDOW
inherit
   WINDOW
creation make -- Creation routine (inherited)
feature {ANY} -- Commands
   draw_contents is
         -- Draw the contents
      do
         contents.draw_on(Current)
      end  -- draw_contents
end -- APPLICATION_WINDOW
```

A VIEW is a representation of the thing we want to display. For the sake of simplicity, we define a simple VIEW of the string "A message".

```
class VIEW
feature {ANY} -- Commands
   draw_on (w : WINDOW) is
         -- simulates that the view contents is being drawn on w
      require w_not_void: w /= Void
      local place : POINT2D
      do
         !!place.make(2,5)
         w.draw_text("A message",place)
      end -- draw_on
end -- VIEW
```

Another example of a WINDOW subclass would be the ICON_WINDOW, which would draw only a bitmap.

```
class ICON_WINDOW
inherit
   WINDOW
creation make -- Creation routine inherited
feature {ANY} -- Commands
   draw_contents is
         -- Draw the contents
      do
```

```
        imp.device_bitmap(bitmap_name,0.0,0.0)
    end   -- draw_contents
feature {NONE} -- Private
  bitmap_name : STRING is "Flashy Bitmap"
end -- ICON_WINDOW
```

Let's now look at two possible Implementors for the class WINDOW, that is, subclasses of WINDOW_IMP. First, we look at a class XWINDOW_IMP to simulate an X Window–specific implementation; then we consider a PMWINDOW_IMP to simulate a Presentation Manager–specific version.

```
class XWINDOW_IMP
inherit WINDOW_IMP
feature {ANY} -- Queries & Commands
  -- a lot of routines..., plus
  device_text(text: STRING; x,y: REAL) is
    do
        print("Printing: "); print(text)
        print(" on an X-window at ("); io.put_real(x)
        io.put_character(','); io.put_real(y); print(").%N")
    end -- device_text
  device_bitmap(bitmap: STRING; x,y: REAL) is
    do
        print("Putting a bitmap "); print(bitmap)
        print(" on an X-window at ("); io.put_real(x)
        io.put_character(','); io.put_real(y); print(").%N")
    end -- device_bitmap
end -- XWINDOW_IMP
```

In this example, the Presentation Manager version is basically the same as the previous one.

```
class PMWINDOW_IMP
inherit WINDOW_IMP
feature {ANY} -- Queries & Commands
  -- a lot of routines..., plus
  device_text(text: STRING; x,y: REAL) is
    do
        print("Printing: "); print(text)
        print(" on a PM-window at ("); io.put_real(x)
        io.put_character(','); io.put_real(y); print(").%N")
    end -- device_text
```

```
device_bitmap(bitmap: STRING; x,y: REAL) is
    do
        print("Putting a bitmap "); print(bitmap)
        print(" on a PM-window at ("); io.put_real(x)
        io.put_character(','); io.put_real(y); print(").%N")
    end -- device_bitmap
end -- PMWINDOW_IMP
```

We construct a simple driver class to show the effect of choosing the relevant window implementation at runtime. For each of the two variants, we create an application window and an icon window and make them draw their contents.

```
class MAIN
creation make
feature -- Creation
    make is
            -- Creation and initialization
        local
            imp : WINDOW_IMP
        do
            print("X-windows example -> ")
            !XWINDOW_IMP!imp; window_example(imp)
            print("PM windows example -> ")
            !PMWINDOW_IMP!imp; window_example(imp)
        end -- make
feature {ANY} -- Commands
    window_example (imp : WINDOW_IMP) is
            -- Creates 2 windows and make them draw their contents
        local
            aw : APPLICATION_WINDOW
            iw : ICON_WINDOW
            v : VIEW
        do
            !!v
            !!aw.make(v,imp) -- make an application Window
            !!iw.make(v,imp) -- make an icon window
            aw.draw_contents; iw.draw_contents -- draw both contents
        end -- window_example
end -- MAIN
```

By building and running a system with this class as the root class, we get the following output:

```
X-windows example -> Printing: A message on an X-window at
     (2.000000,5.000000).
Putting a bitmap Flashy Bitmap on an X-window at (0.000000,0.000000).
PM windows example -> Printing: A message on a PM-window at
     (2.000000,5.000000).
Putting a bitmap Flashy Bitmap on a PM-window at (0.000000,0.000000).
```

## Related Patterns

An Abstract Factory (57) can create and configure a particular bridge. The Adapter (87) pattern, geared toward making unrelated classes work together, is usually applied to systems after they have been designed. Bridge, on the other hand, is used up front in a design to let abstractions and implementations vary independently.

# Composite (GoF 163)                    (Structural)

## Intent

Compose objects into tree structures to represent part/whole hierarchies. Composite lets clients treat individual objects and compositions of objects uniformly.

## Structure

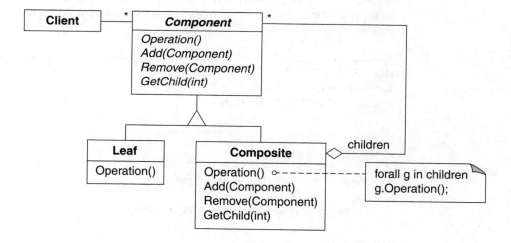

A typical Composite object structure might look like this:

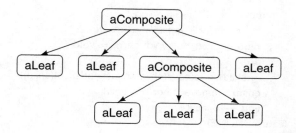

## Collaboration

- Clients use the COMPONENT class interface to interact with objects in the composite structure. If the recipient is a Leaf, the request is handled directly. If the recipient is a Composite, it usually forwards requests to its child components, possibly performing additional operations before and/or after forwarding.

## Eiffel Implementation

The following issues might be considered when implementing the Composite pattern.

- A Composite has basically a tree structure. It is therefore natural to represent it as such: as a generic class with a *parent* and a set of *children*.

---

```
class COMPOSITE [T]
feature {ANY} -- Queries
   parent : COMPOSITE [T] is do end
         -- optional parent, default to Void. If an explicit reference
         -- to the parent is needed, redefine as an attribute.
   has (child : T) : BOOLEAN is
         -- does 'child' belong to the composite?
      require child_not_void: child /= Void
      do
         Result := children.fast_has(child) -- identity comparison
      end -- has
feature {ANY} -- Commands
   add (new_child : T) is
         -- add 'new_child' to the composite
      require new_child_not_void: new_child /= Void
      do
         children.add_last(new_child)
      ensure added: has(new_child)
      end -- add
   remove (child : T) is
         -- remove T from the composite
      require child_not_void: child /= Void
      do
         children.remove(children.fast_index_of(child))
      ensure removed: not has(child)
      end -- remove
feature {NONE} -- Private
```

```
    children : COLLECTION [T]
            -- holding the parts.
invariant
    children_not_void: children /= Void
end -- COMPOSITE
```

Whether a Composite maintains a reference to its parent is left open at this stage. Concrete subclasses may choose to either maintain it by defining the feature *parent* as an attribute or ignore it—and not pay any penalty—by defining it as a *Void* constant.

- Many designs specify an ordering on the children of Composite. In that case, the feature *children* can be redefined as an ordered collection. Thus, with the preceding definition of COMPOSITE, the choice of the data structure (such as a list, array, or hash table) for storing the composite children may be decided on a per object basis. In our following code examples, we implement this by providing a number of variants for class creation features.

- For costly operations, it might be useful to *cache* the result of children traversal. You may implement this transparently in Eiffel; there is no difference, from the client's point of view, between a parameterless function and an attribute.

## Sample Code

In Eiffel, there is no reason why the leaf components should be bothered by the declaration of child management features. For instance, a class EQUIPMENT modeling computer parts, such as drives, bus, chassis, and cabinets, can simply be defined as follows.

```
deferred class EQUIPMENT
feature {ANY} -- Queries
    name : STRING
            -- Name of this equipment
    power : REAL is deferred end
            -- Electric power consumption
    net_price, discount_price : REAL is deferred end
            -- cost of this equipment
feature {ANY} -- Commands
    make (its_name : STRING) is
        -- Initialization
      require
        its_name_not_void: its_name /= Void
```

```
    do
        name := its_name
    end -- make
invariant
    name_not_void: name /= Void
    positive_power: power >= 0.0
    positive_price: discount_price >= 0.0
    real_discount: net_price >= discount_price
end -- EQUIPMENT
```

Subclasses of EQUIPMENT might include leaf classes that represent disk drives, integrated circuits, and so on.

```
class FLOPPY_DISK
inherit EQUIPMENT
creation make -- inherited from EQUIPMENT
feature {ANY} -- Queries
    power : REAL is 10.0
    net_price : REAL is 20.0
    discount_price : REAL is
        -- No discount on such a single item
    do
        Result := net_price
    end -- discount_price
end -- FLOPPY_DISK
```

The clean semantics of multiple inheritance in Eiffel makes it easy to define a composite piece of equipment as a COMPOSITE_EQUIPMENT.

```
class COMPOSITE_EQUIPMENT
inherit
    COMPOSITE [EQUIPMENT] -- Handle parent and children management features
    EQUIPMENT
        redefine make end;
feature -- Creation
    make (its_name : STRING) is
        -- Creation and initialization of the children as an ARRAY
    do
        name := its_name
        !ARRAY[EQUIPMENT]!children.make(1,0)
    end -- make
    make_with_list  (its_name : STRING) is
```

```
         -- Creation and initialization of the children as a LINKED_LIST
     do
         name := its_name
         !LINK_LIST[EQUIPMENT]!children.make
     end -- make_with_list
feature {ANY} -- Queries
   net_price : REAL is
         -- Sum the net prices of the subequipments
     local
         i : INTEGER
     do
         from i := children.lower until i > children.upper
         loop
             Result := Result + children.item(i).net_price
             i := i + 1
         end -- loop
     end -- net_price
   discount_price : REAL is
     do
         Result := net_price * 0.9
     end -- discount_price
   power : REAL is 0.0 -- Should be a computation
invariant
   filiation: parent /= Void implies parent.has(Current)
end -- COMPOSITE_EQUIPMENT
```

A CHASSIS is a kind of COMPOSITE_EQUIPMENT.

```
class CHASSIS
inherit COMPOSITE_EQUIPMENT
creation make, make_with_list -- inherited creation methods
feature {ANY} -- Public queries
   length, width : REAL -- in centimeters
end -- CHASSIS
```

Other equipments, such as CABINET or BUS, may be defined in similar ways. This gives us everything we need to assemble equipment into a primitive PC.

```
class MAIN
creation make
feature -- Creation
```

```
make is
    -- Creation and assembly of a primitive PC whose price is displayed
    local
        cabinet : CABINET -- Will hold a CHASSIS
        chassis : CHASSIS -- Will contain a BUS and a FLOPPY_DISK
        bus : BUS -- Will hold a CARD
        e : EQUIPMENT -- Temporary for storing basic equipment
    do
        !!cabinet.make("PC Cabinet")
        !!chassis.make("PC Chassis")
        cabinet.add(chassis)
        !!bus.make("MCA Bus")
        !CARD!e.make("16Mbs Token Ring"); bus.add(e)
        chassis.add(bus)
        !FLOPPY_DISK!e.make("3.5 Floppy"); chassis.add(e)
        io.put_string("The net price is ")
        io.put_real(cabinet.net_price); io.put_new_line
    end -- make
end -- MAIN
```

If we compile and execute this class as the root of an Eiffel system, we get
the following output:

```
The net price is 90.000000
```

## Related Patterns

Often, the component-parent link is used for a Chain of Responsibility
(141). Decorator (105) is often used with Composite. Flyweight (121) lets
you share components, but they can no longer refer to their parents. Iterator
(159) should be used to traverse Composites. Visitor (227) localizes operations and behaviors that would otherwise be distributed across Composites
and LEAF classes.

# Decorator (GoF 175) (Structural)

## Intent

Attach additional responsibilities to an object dynamically. Decorator provides a flexible alternative to subclassing for extending functionality.

## Also Known As

Wrapper

## Structure

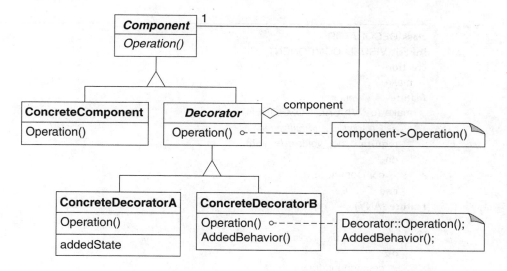

## Collaboration

- Decorator forwards requests to its component object. Decorator may optionally perform additional operations before and after forwarding the request.

## Eiffel Implementation

Once again, the implementation of this pattern is based on the use of delegation instead of inheritance to forward requests from a newly defined object to a reused one.

## Sample Code

Let VISUAL_COMPONENT be the abstract class defining visual objects that can be drawn and resized.

```
deferred class VISUAL_COMPONENT
feature {ANY} -- Commands
   draw is deferred end -- draw on the screen
   resize is deferred end -- resize the component
end -- VISUAL_COMPONENT
```

A DECORATOR, then is, a VISUAL_COMPONENT containing a VISUAL_COMPONENT. Its default behavior is simply to forward requests to its component:.

```
class DECORATOR
inherit VISUAL_COMPONENT
creation
   make
feature -- Creation
   make (c : VISUAL_COMPONENT) is
      -- Creation and initialization
      require c_not_void: c /= Void
      do
         component := c
      end -- make
feature {ANY} -- Commands
   draw is
      -- draw on the screen
      do
         component.draw
      end -- draw
   resize is
      -- resize the component
      do
         component.resize
      end -- resize
feature {NONE} -- Private
   component : VISUAL_COMPONENT
invariant
   component_not_void: component /= Void
end -- DECORATOR
```

The class BORDER_DECORATOR is an example of a VISUAL_COMPONENT decorated with a border

---

```
class BORDER_DECORATOR
inherit
  DECORATOR
    rename make as decorator_make
    redefine draw end;
creation
  make
feature -- Creation
  make (c : VISUAL_COMPONENT; border_width : INTEGER) is
    -- Creation and initialization
    require positive_width : border_width >= 0
    do
      decorator_make(c)
      width := border_width
    end -- make
feature {ANY} -- Commands
  draw is
    -- draw on the screen
    do
      component.draw
      draw_border
    end -- draw
feature {NONE} -- Private
  width : INTEGER
    -- width of the border around the component
  draw_border is
    -- draw a border
    do
      io.put_string("Drawing a border of width ")
      io.put_integer(width); io.put_new_line
    end -- draw_border
invariant
  positive_width : width >= 0
end -- BORDER_DECORATOR
```

---

Assuming that the class WINDOW features a procedure *set_contents* to graphically display its parameter within the window, here is how decorated objects might be used. (The class SCROLL_DECORATOR is not described here, since it has the same structure as BORDER_DECORATOR.)

```
class MAIN
creation make
feature -- Creation
    make is
            -- Creation and initialization
        local
            t : TEXT_VIEW
            s : SCROLL_DECORATOR
            b : BORDER_DECORATOR
        do
            !!t.make("Here is a text")
            set_contents(t) -- Display text without decoration
            !!s.make(t)
            !!b.make(s,1)
            set_contents(b) -- Redisplay text with decorations
        end -- make
feature {ANY} -- Commands
    set_contents (c : VISUAL_COMPONENT) is
            -- Draw c in this window
        do
            c.draw -- Simulates the drawing
        end -- set_contents
end -- MAIN
```

The resulting output is:

```
Here is a text
Here is a text
Drawing a scroll bar
Drawing a border of width 1
```

## Related Patterns

Unlike an Adapter (87), Decorator changes only an object's responsibilities, not its interface. An Adapter will give an object a completely new interface.

A Decorator can be viewed as a degenerate Composite (99) with only one component. However, a Decorator adds additional responsibilities; it isn't intended for object aggregation.

A Decorator lets you change the skin of an object. A Strategy (215), by contrast, lets you change the guts.

# Facade (GoF 185)                    (Structural)

## Intent

Provide a unified interface to a set of interfaces in a subsystem. Facade defines a higher-level interface that makes the subsystem easier to use.

## Structure

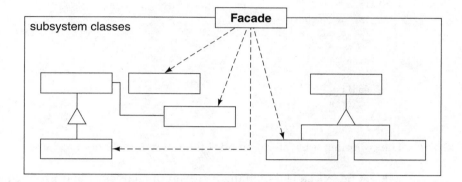

## Collaboration

- Clients communicate with the subsystem by sending requests to Facade, which forwards them to the appropriate subsystem objects(s). Although the subsystem objects perform the actual work, the facade may have to do work of its own to translate its interface to subsystem interfaces.

- Clients that use the facade don't have to access its subsystem objects directly.

## Eiffel Implementation

A good way to dissociate a Facade from the full subsystem is to implement the two in different *clusters*. A cluster is not an Eiffel language-level notion. Any mechanism that allows you to group several related classes might be used. In most UNIX, Windows, or DOS systems, a cluster is usually a directory containing a set of files, themselves containing class descriptions.

For a subsystem called, for example, *compilation_system*, we might thus provide two clusters: one for the classes making the *Facade*, such as *compilation_system_facade*; and another for all of the other classes of the subsystem, such as *compilation_system_core*. This way, a client of the subsystem would know directly which classes might be of interest.

## Sample Code

Consider the following compilation subsystem for handling sample programs:

```
read n
while n > 1 do
   is_odd_number := n % 2
   if is_odd_number then
      n := ( 3 * n ) + 1
   else
      n := n / 2
   endif
   print n
end
```

The compiler subsystem includes the following elements:

- A SCANNER class, taking a stream of characters and producing a stream of TOKENs, one token at a time.

- A PARSER class, using a NODE_BUILDER to construct an Abstract Syntax Tree from the SCANNER's tokens. The PARSER interacts with the NODE_BUILDER according to the Builder (63) pattern. The PARSER could have constructed the tree directly, but this way the tree construction is decoupled from the parsing of an input stream, thus allowing for other ways of handling the tree, such as using a graphical editor.

- A PROGRAM_NODE, representing an abstract node in the Abstract Syntax Tree, and all of its concrete subclasses: BIN_EXPRESSION, ASSIGNMENT, CONDITIONAL, WHILE, and so on. Here is, for instance, the class CONDITIONAL.

---

```
class CONDITIONAL
inherit STATEMENT
creation make
feature -- Creation
   make (cond: EXPRESSION; true_part, false_part: BLOCK) is
```

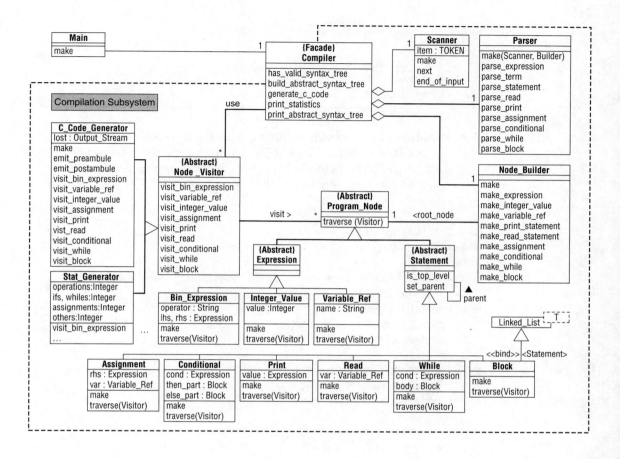

-- *Creation and initialization*
**require**
    cond_not_void: cond /= **Void**
    true_part_not_void: true_part /= **Void**
    false_part_not_void: false_part /= **Void**
**do**
    condition := cond
    then_part := true_part; then_part.set_parent(**Current**)
    else_part := false_part; else_part.set_parent(**Current**)
**end** -- *make*
**feature** {ANY} -- *Queries*
  condition : EXPRESSION
  then_part, else_part : BLOCK
**feature** {ANY} -- *Commands*
  traverse (visitor : NODE_VISITOR) **is**

```
                -- let visitor visit the current node
        do
            visitor.visit_conditional (Current)
        end -- traverse
end -- CONDITIONAL
```

- A NODE_VISITOR defining the interface for traversing the Abstract
  Syntax Tree. This is a Visitor (227) encapsulating the traversal code.
  Concrete subclasses might be code generators, optimizers, or simply
  classes collecting statistics on the source program.

```
class STAT_GENERATOR
inherit NODE_VISITOR
feature {ANY} -- Queries
    operations, ifs, whiles, assignments, others : INTEGER -- Accumulates
                -- occurrences of such program nodes as traversing is going
feature {ANY} -- Commands
    visit_binary_expression (node : BINARY_EXPRESSION) is
            -- Visit a BINARY_EXPRESSION
        do
            operations := operations + 1
            node.left.traverse(Current)
            node.right.traverse(Current)
        end -- visit_binary_expression
    visit_variable_ref (node : VARIABLE_REF) is do end
    visit_integer_value (node : INTEGER_VALUE) is do end
    visit_assignment (node : ASSIGNMENT) is
            -- Visit an ASSIGNMENT
        do
            assignments := assignments + 1
            node.right_hand_side.traverse(Current)
        end -- visit_assignment
    visit_print (node : PRINT) is
            -- Visit a PRINT
        do
            others := others + 1
            node.expression.traverse(Current)
        end -- visit_print
    visit_read (node : READ) is
            -- Visit a READ
        do
            others := others + 1
```

```
        end -- visit_read
    visit_conditional (node : CONDITIONAL) is
            -- Visit a CONDITIONAL
        do
            ifs := ifs + 1
            node.condition.traverse(Current)
            node.then_part.traverse(Current)
            node.else_part.traverse(Current)
        end -- visit_conditional
    visit_while (node : WHILE) is
            -- Visit a WHILE
        do
            whiles := whiles + 1
            node.condition.traverse(Current)
            node.loop_body.traverse(Current)
        end -- visit_while
    visit_block (node : BLOCK) is
            -- Visit a BLOCK
        local i : INTEGER
        do
            from i := 1 until i > node.count
            loop
                node.item(i).traverse(Current)
                i := i + 1
            end -- loop
            if node.is_top_level then
                io.put_string("Number of 'if' statements: ")
                io.put_integer(ifs); io.put_new_line
                io.put_string("Number of 'while' statements: ")
                io.put_integer(whiles); io.put_new_line
                io.put_string("Number of ':=' statements: ")
                io.put_integer(assignments); io.put_new_line
                io.put_string("Number of other (read, print) statements: ")
                io.put_integer(others); io.put_new_line
                io.put_string("Number of binary operations: ")
                io.put_integer(operations); io.put_new_line
            end -- if
        end -- visit_block
end -- STAT_GENERATOR
```

Something more useful would be a simple C code generator, that is, a NODE_VISITOR generating a C program. (You would just need to call the C compiler as a back end to get an executable program.)

```
class C_CODE_GENERATOR
inherit NODE_VISITOR
creation make
feature -- Creation
   make (s: OUTPUT_STREAM) is
      -- Creation and initialization
      do
         iostream := s
      end -- make
feature {ANY} -- Queries
   iostream : OUTPUT_STREAM
feature {ANY} -- Commands
   visit_binary_expression (node : BINARY_EXPRESSION) is
      -- Emit C code for this node
      do
         iostream.put_character('(')
         node.left.traverse(Current)
         iostream.put_character(')')
         iostream.put_string(node.operator)
         iostream.put_character('(')
         node.right.traverse(Current)
         iostream.put_character(')')
      end -- visit_binary_expression
   visit_variable_ref (node : VARIABLE_REF) is
      -- Emit C code for this node
      do
         iostream.put_character('V') -- to avoid name clashes with C
         iostream.put_string(node.name)
      end -- visit_variable_ref
   visit_integer_value (node : INTEGER_VALUE) is
      -- Emit C code for this node
      do
         iostream.put_integer(node.value)
      end -- visit_integer_value
   visit_assignment (node : ASSIGNMENT) is
      -- Emit C code for this node
      do
         indentation
         node.variable.traverse(Current)
         iostream.put_character('=')
         node.right_hand_side.traverse(Current)
         iostream.put_character(';'); iostream.put_new_line
      end -- visit_assignment
```

```
visit_print (node : PRINT) is
        -- Emit C code for this node. PRINT is implemented with a printf()
    do
        indentation; iostream.put_string("printf(%"%%d!n%",")
        node.expression.traverse(Current)
        iostream.put_character(')')
        iostream.put_character(';'); iostream.put_new_line
    end -- visit_print
visit_read (node : READ) is
        -- Emit C code for this node. READ is implemented with a scanf()
    do
        indentation; iostream.put_string("scanf(%"%%d%",&")
        node.variable.traverse(Current)
        iostream.put_character(')')
        iostream.put_character(';'); iostream.put_new_line
    end -- visit_read
visit_conditional (node : CONDITIONAL) is
        -- Emit C code for this node
    do
        indentation; iostream.put_string("if (")
        node.condition.traverse(Current)
        iostream.put_character(')')
        node.then_part.traverse(Current)
        indentation; iostream.put_string("else")
        node.else_part.traverse(Current)
    end -- visit_conditional
visit_while (node : WHILE) is
        -- Emit C code for this node
    do
        indentation; iostream.put_string("while (")
        node.condition.traverse(Current)
        indentation; iostream.put_character(')')
        node.loop_body.traverse(Current)
    end -- visit_while
visit_block (node : BLOCK) is
        -- Emit C code for this node
    local i : INTEGER
    do
        if node.is_top_level then
            emit_preambule (node)
        end -- if
        iostream.put_character('{'); iostream.put_new_line
        indent
        from i := 1 until i > node.count
```

```
      loop
         node.item(i).traverse(Current)
         i := i + 1
      end -- loop
      dedent
      indentation; iostream.put_character('}'); iostream.put_new_line
      if node.is_top_level then
         emit_postambule (node)
      end -- if
   end -- visit_block
emit_preambule (node : BLOCK) is
      -- Emit code that precedes the main body
   local i : INTEGER
   do
      iostream.put_string("#include <stdio.h>%Nint ")
      -- list the variables used in the program
      from i:=1 until i > node.var_table.count
      loop
         visit_variable_ref(node.var_table.item(i))
         iostream.put_string(", ")
         i := i + 1
      end -- loop
      iostream.put_string("_exit_code = 0;%N") -- Add one extra variable
      iostream.put_string("void main ()") -- all the code is generated as
                                          -- a single procedure
   end -- emit_preambule
emit_postambule (node : BLOCK) is
      -- Emit code that follows the main body
   do
   end -- emit_postambule
feature {NONE} -- Private
   depth : INTEGER
   indent is
         -- increment depth
      do
         depth := depth + 1
      end -- indent
   dedent is
         -- decrement depth
      require depth > 0
      do
         depth := depth - 1
      end -- dedent
   indentation is
```

```
            -- Print a number of blank characters according to depth
        local i: INTEGER
        do
            from i := depth * 2 until i = 0
            loop
                iostream.put_character(' ')
                i:=i-1
            end -- loop
        end -- indentation
invariant
    depth_positive: depth >= 0
end -- C_CODE_GENERATOR
```

We define a class COMPILER as a *facade* hiding the bulk of this compilation subsystem under a much simpler interface.

```
class COMPILER
feature {ANY} -- Queries
    has_valid_abstract_syntax_tree : BOOLEAN is
            -- Whether the input stream has been correctly parsed
        do
            Result := ast /= Void
        end -- has_valid_abstract_syntax_tree
feature {ANY} -- Commands
    build_abstract_syntax_tree (in_stream: INPUT_STREAM) is
        -- Build an Abstract Syntax Tree by reading on 'in_stream'
        require in_stream_not_void: in_stream /= Void
        do
            !!scanner.make(in_stream)
            !!builder.make
            !!parser.make(scanner,builder)
        end -- build_abstract_syntax_tree
    generate_c_code (out_stream: OUTPUT_STREAM) is
            -- Generate C code on 'out' for the Abstract Syntax Tree
        require
            out_stream_not_void: out_stream /= Void
            valid_abstract_syntax_tree: has_valid_abstract_syntax_tree
        local code_gen : C_CODE_GENERATOR
        do
            !!code_gen.make(out_stream)
            ast.traverse(code_gen)
        end -- generate_c_code
    print_statistics is
```

```
            -- Print statistics on the number of each kind of constructs
            -- in the Abstract Syntax Tree
        local stat_gen : STAT_GENERATOR
        do
            if ast /= Void then
                !!stat_gen; ast.traverse(stat_gen)
            end -- if
        end -- print_statistics
    print_abstract_syntax_tree is
            -- Print a representation of the Abstract Syntax Tree on STDOUT
        local printer : AST_PRINTER
        do
            if ast /= Void then
                !!printer; ast.traverse(printer)
            end -- if
        end -- print_abstract_syntax_tree
feature {NONE}
    scanner : SCANNER
    parser : PARSER
    builder : NODE_BUILDER
    ast : PROGRAM_NODE is
            -- Root of the Abstract Syntax Tree
        do
            if builder /= Void then Result := builder.root_node end
        end -- ast
end -- COMPILER
```

This COMPILER facade could be used, for example, in a front-end compilation system integrating a C code generator and the printing of some statistics about the program. In the following example, the user can choose between the two options with a command line switch -*stat*.

```
class MAIN
creation make
feature -- Creation
    make is
            -- Read a program in the toy language on STDIN
            -- If "-stat" is given as the first argument, produces statistics on STDOUT
            -- else generates corresponding C code
        local
            compiler : COMPILER -- The FACADE to the compilation subsystem
        do
            !!compiler; compiler.build_abstract_syntax_tree(std_input)
            if argument_count >= 1 and then argument(1).is_equal(" -stat") then
```

```
          compiler.print_statistics
      else -- Generate C code
          compiler.generate_c_code(std_output)
      end -- if
    end -- make
end -- MAIN
```

If we compile this class as the root of an Eiffel system, executing it on the preceding sample program with the command line switch *-stat* produces the following output:

```
Number of 'if' statements: 1
Number of 'while' statements: 1
Number of ':=' statements: 3
Number of other (read, print) statements: 2
Number of binary operations: 5
```

If we omit the command line switch, we trigger the C code generation, which produces the following output:

```
#include <stdio.h>
int Vn, Vis_odd_number, _exit_code = 0;
void main (){
  scanf("%d",&Vn);
  while ((Vn)>(1)  ){
    Vis_odd_number=(Vn)%(2);
    if (Vis_odd_number){
      Vn=((3)*(Vn))+(1);
    }
    else{
      Vn=(Vn)/(2);
    }
    printf("%d\n",Vn);
  }
}
```

## Related Patterns

Abstract Factory (57) can be used with Facade to provide an interface for creating subsystem objects in a subsystem-independent way. Abstract Factory can also be used as an alternative to Facade to hide platform-specific classes. Mediator (167) is similar to Facade in that it abstracts functionality of existing classes.

Usually only one Facade object is required. Thus, a Facade object is often a Singleton (79).

# Flyweight (GoF 195)                    (Structural)

## Intent

Use sharing to support large numbers of fine-grained objects efficiently.

## Structure

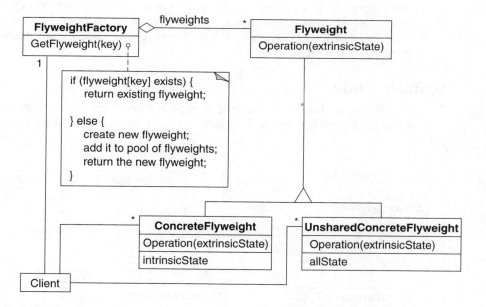

The following object diagram shows how flyweights are shared:

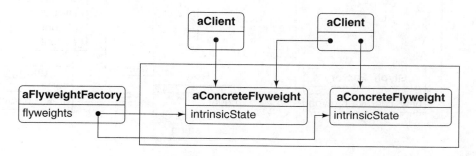

## Collaboration

- State that a flyweight needs to function must be characterized as either intrinsic or extrinsic. Intrinsic state is stored in the ConcreteFlyweight object; extrinsic state is stored or computed by Client objects. Clients pass this state to the flyweight when they invoke its operations.

- Clients should not instantiate ConcreteFlyweights directly. Clients must obtain ConcreteFlyweight objects exclusively from the FlyweightFactory object to ensure that they are shared properly.

## Eiffel Implementation

The essence of this pattern implementation is to enable various objects to share data storage. Once again, Eiffel's automatic garbage collection reduces the burden of managing these shared spaces; they are automatically freed when no longer in use.

## Sample Code

In a document formatter example, a *glyph* is a basic graphical entity able to draw itself onto a window. Logically, a glyph has many attributes, such as

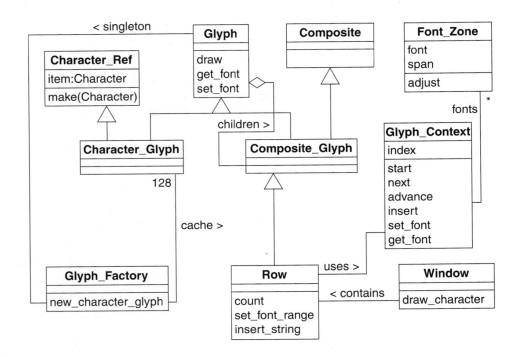

its font, color, style, and so on. In the following example, we focus on its font attribute, but the same approach can be used for any other attribute.

```
deferred class GLYPH
feature {ANY} -- Queries
   get_font (gc : GLYPH_CONTEXT) : FONT is deferred end
feature {ANY} -- Commands
   draw (w: WINDOW; gc : GLYPH_CONTEXT) is deferred end
   set_font (new_font : FONT; gc : GLYPH_CONTEXT) is deferred end
feature {NONE}
   glyph_factory : GLYPH_FACTORY is
          -- An abstract factory singleton to produce glyphs
       once
          !!Result.make
       end -- glyph_factory
end -- GLYPH
```

A CHARACTER_GLYPH is both a GLYPH and a reference to a CHARACTER.

```
class CHARACTER_GLYPH
inherit
   CHARACTER_REF
   GLYPH
creation make -- inherited from CHARACTER_REF
feature {ANY} -- Queries
   get_font (gc : GLYPH_CONTEXT) : FONT is
       do
          Result := gc.get_font
       end -- get_font
feature {ANY} -- Commands
   draw (w: WINDOW; gc : GLYPH_CONTEXT) is
          -- draw itself into w
       do
          w.draw_character(item,get_font (gc))
       end -- draw
   set_font (new_font : FONT; gc : GLYPH_CONTEXT) is
          -- Change the font of the current character
       do
          gc.set_font (new_font,1)
       end -- set_font
end -- CHARACTER_GLYPH
```

A GLYPH_CONTEXT is used to store the glyph's extrinsic state—here, its font. In this example, a GLYPH_CONTEXT stores, as a list of zones, the font information about a sequence of glyphs. A zone records a font, along with its extent. The GLYPH_CONTEXT must be kept informed of various events happening on the primary sequence of glyphs, such as its traversal (features *start* and *next*) or the insertion of new glyphs (feature *insert*). The GLYPH_CONTEXT also keeps track of font changes.

```
class GLYPH_CONTEXT
creation make
feature -- Creation
   make (font : FONT) is
      -- Creation and initialization
      require font_not_void: font /= Void
      local
         zone : FONT_ZONE
      do
         !!fonts.make
         fonts.add_last(new_zone(font,0)) -- Initialize with 0 width font
         zone_number := fonts.lower
      end -- make
feature {ANY} -- Queries
   get_font : FONT is
      -- Current font
      do
         Result := fonts.item(zone_number).font
      end -- get_font
feature {ANY} -- Commands to modify the context
   insert (quantity : INTEGER) is
      -- insert a 'quantity' of glyphs at the current place in the structure
      require positive_quantity: quantity > 0
      do
         fonts.item(zone_number).adjust(quantity)
      end -- insert
   set_font(f: FONT; span : INTEGER) is
      -- change the font for 'span' glyphs from current position.
      -- Naive implementation that cuts the current zone into 3 parts.
      -- Should try to fuse adjacent font_zones instead
      require positive_span: span > 0
      local
         right_span : INTEGER -- space left at the right of this new zone
         old_font : FONT
      do
```

```
        right_span := fonts.item(zone_number).span - (index-1+span)
        old_font := fonts.item(zone_number).font
        if index = 1 then -- replace from the beginning of the zone
            fonts.item(zone_number).make(f,span)
        else -- shorten the current zone, and insert the new one
            fonts.item(zone_number).make(old_font,index-1)
            zone_number := zone_number + 1
            fonts.add(new_zone(f,span),zone_number)
        end -- if
        if right_span > 0 then -- insert a new zone at the right, with old font
            fonts.add(new_zone(old_font,right_span),zone_number+1)
        end -- if
        index := 1 -- first glyph in the new zone
    end -- set_font
count : INTEGER is
        -- Total span of the context in number of glyphs
    local i : INTEGER
    do
        from i := fonts.lower until i > fonts.upper
        loop Result := Result + fonts.item(i).span; i:= i+1 end -- loop
    end -- count
feature {ANY} -- Commands for traversing
    start is
            -- start a traversal
        do
            zone_number := 1
            index := 1
        end -- start
    next is
            -- Advance to the next glyph
        do
            advance(1)
        end -- next
    advance (step : INTEGER) is
        -- Advance 'step' times to the next glyph
        require step_positive: step >= 0
        do
            from index := index + step
            until zone_number = fonts.upper
                or else index <= fonts.item(zone_number).span
            loop
                index := index - fonts.item(zone_number).span
                zone_number := zone_number + 1
            end -- loop
```

```
       end -- advance
feature {NONE} -- Private
    fonts : LINK2_LIST[FONT_ZONE] -- describes the list of fonts in use
    zone_number : INTEGER -- number of the current font_zone in fonts
    index : INTEGER -- Position in zone during traversals
    new_zone (f: FONT; span: INTEGER): FONT_ZONE is
        -- Factory method
      do !!Result.make(f,span) end -- new_zone
invariant
    fonts_not_empty: fonts /= Void and then fonts.count > 0
    valid_zone_number: fonts.valid_index(zone_number)
    index_positive: index >= 0
    index_in_zone: index <= fonts.item(zone_number).span + 1
end -- GLYPH_CONTEXT
```

A Row is a composite GLYPH holding CHARACTER_GLYPHS.

```
class ROW
inherit COMPOSITE_GLYPH redefine children end;
creation make
feature -- Creation
    make (font : FONT) is
        -- Creation and initialization
        require font_not_void: font /= Void
        do
            !!context.make(font)
            !!children.make(1,0)
        end -- make
feature {ANY} -- Queries
    get_font (gc : GLYPH_CONTEXT) : FONT is
        do
            Result := gc.get_font
        end -- get_font
    count : INTEGER is
        -- The number of character_glyphes in the row
        do
            Result := children.count
        end -- count
feature {ANY} -- Commands
    draw (w: WINDOW; gc : GLYPH_CONTEXT) is
        -- draw itself into w
        do
            from start; context.start until is_done
```

```
        loop
            item.draw(w,context)
            next; context.next
        end -- loop
    end -- draw
set_font (new_font : FONT; gc : GLYPH_CONTEXT) is
    -- Set the font to 'new_font' for the all row
  do
    context.start
    context.set_font(new_font,count)
  end -- set_font
set_font_range (new_font : FONT; first, last : INTEGER) is
            -- Set the font to 'new_font' for a subrange of the row
  require valid_range: first >= 1 and last <= count
  do
    context.start; context.advance(first-1)
    context.set_font(new_font,last-first+1)
  end -- set_font_range
insert_string (s : STRING; offset : INTEGER) is
  -- Insert STRING 's' starting from 'offset' in the row
  require
    s_not_empty: s /= Void and then s.count > 0
    offset_positive: offset >= 0
  local i : INTEGER
  do
    context.start; context.advance(offset-1)
    context.insert(s.count)
    from i := 1 until i > s.count
    loop
      children.add(glyph_factory.new_character_glyph(s.item(i)),offset+i-1)
      i := i + 1
    end -- loop
  ensure count = old(count) + s.count
  end  -- insert_string
feature {NONE} -- Private
  context : GLYPH_CONTEXT
  children : ARRAY[CHARACTER_GLYPH]
invariant
  coherent_context: context.count = children.count
end -- ROW
```

Note that the Row uses a GLYPH_FACTORY to make new CHARACTER_ GLYPHS, thus making it possible to share the glyph objects. If a client asks for a new CHARACTER_GLYPH, the GLYPH_FACTORY looks it up in its private table and, if one has already been allocated, returns a reference on it. Since the GLYPH_FACTORY is implemented as a Singleton (79), at most 128 CHARACTER_GLYPHs are allocated for the whole application.

```
class GLYPH_FACTORY
creation make
feature -- Creation
   make is
         -- Creation and initialization
      do
         !!char_table.make(0,127)
      end -- make
feature {ANY} -- Queries
   new_character_glyph (c: CHARACTER) : CHARACTER_GLYPH is
         -- Factory Method to create a CHARACTER_GLYPH from a CHARACTER
      do
         if char_table.item(c.code) = Void then
            !!Result.make(c)
            char_table.put(Result,c.code)
         else
            Result := char_table.item(c.code)
         end -- if
      end -- new_character_glyph
feature {NONE} -- Private
   char_table : ARRAY[CHARACTER_GLYPH]
invariant
   char_table /= Void
      end -- GLYPH_FACTORY
```

The user may insert text in a Row and change the font in a range of the Row, as in the following example, where the font changes are simulated with case changes.

```
class WINDOW
creation make
feature -- Creation
   make is
         -- Entry point to the example
      local
      r : ROW
         default_font, uppercase, lowercase : FONT -- font examples
```

```
        do
            !!default_font.make("")
            !!uppercase.make("Uppercase") -- a font named "Uppercase"
            !!lowercase.make("Lowercase") -- a font named "Lowercase"
            !!r.make(default_font)
            r.insert_string("A MuLTi-CaSeD StRiNg ExAmPlE%N",1)
            r.draw(Current,Void)
            r.set_font_range(uppercase,15,20) -- StRiNg becomes 'uppercase'
            r.draw(Current,Void)
            r.set_font_range(lowercase,2,13) -- MuLTi-CaSeD becomes 'lowercase'
            r.draw(Current,Void)
            r.insert_string("NoTHeR",2) -- Insert in a 'lowercase' context
            r.draw(Current,Void)
        end -- make
feature {ANY}
    draw_character (c : CHARACTER; font : FONT) is
            -- Draw 'c' using font 'f'
        require font_not_void: font /= Void
        do
            print(font.representation(c))
        end -- draw_character
end -- WINDOW
```

If we compile and execute this class as the root of an Eiffel system, we get the following output:

```
A MuLTi-CaSeD StRiNg ExAmPlE
A MuLTi-CaSeD STRING ExAmPlE
A multi-cased STRING ExAmPlE
Another multi-cased STRING ExAmPlE
```

## Related Patterns

The Flyweight pattern is often combined with the Composite (99) pattern to implement a logically hierarchical structure in terms of a directed-acyclic graph with shared leaf nodes. Flyweights should generally be used to implement State (197) and Strategy (215) objects.

# Proxy (GoF 207)     (Structural)

## Intent

Provide a surrogate, or placeholder, for another object to control access to it.

## Also Known As

Surrogate

## Structure

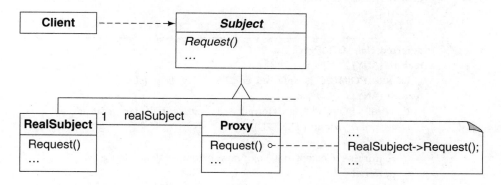

Here's a possible object diagram of a proxy structure at runtime:

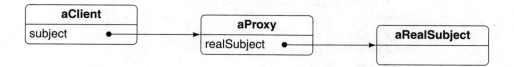

## Collaboration

- Proxy forwards requests to RealSubject when appropriate, depending on the kind of proxy.

## Eiffel Implementation

Eiffel has an interesting feature that can help implementing proxies: the uniformity of reference. Indeed, from a client point of view, there is no syntactical difference between calling a function *foo* on an object *x* and accessing the attribute *foo*: In both cases, the client calls *x.foo*. Thus, it is possible to specify an interface where the feature *foo* is deferred. Then we can implement it as an attribute in the real object and as a function in the corresponding proxy. We use this technique with the feature *extent* in the following code examples.

## Sample Code

Let us consider the case of a document editor that can embed graphical objects into a document. A somehow simplified interface for handling such graphical objects follows.

```
deferred class GRAPHIC
feature {ANY} -- Queries
    extent : POINT2D is deferred end -- size of the graphic
feature {ANY} -- Commands
    draw (at : POINT2D) is deferred end -- draw itself starting at 'at'
    resize (new_extent: POINT2D) is
            -- resize the graphic
        require new_extent_not_void: new_extent /= Void
        deferred
        ensure extent.is_equal(new_extent)
        end -- resize
    load (source: STD_FILE_READ) is
            -- load from an input stream
        require
            source_not_void: source /= Void
            not_end_of_input: not source.end_of_input
        deferred
        end   -- load
    save (destination: STD_FILE_WRITE) is
            -- save to an output stream
        require destination_not_void: destination /= Void
        deferred
        end -- save
end -- GRAPHIC
```

The class IMAGE implements the GRAPHIC interface as follows:

```
class IMAGE
inherit GRAPHIC
creation make
feature -- Creation
   make (filename : STRING) is
         -- Creation and initialization
      require filename_not_void: filename /= Void
      local f : STD_FILE_READ
      do
         !!extent.make(0,0)
         !!f.connect_to(filename)
         load(f) -- load image from the file
      end -- make
feature {ANY} -- Queries
   extent : POINT2D -- implemented as an attribute
feature {ANY} -- Commands
   draw (at : POINT2D) is
         -- simulates drawing the image
      do
         io.put_string(contents); io.put_string(" drawn at ")
         io.put_string(at.out); io.put_new_line
      end -- draw
   resize (new_extent: POINT2D) is
         -- resize the image
      do
         extent := new_extent
      end -- resize
   load  (source: STD_FILE_READ) is
         -- load from an input stream
      do
         print("Loading an image. Please wait...%N")
         extent.read(source)
         source.read_line; contents := clone(source.last_string)
      end -- load
   save (destination: STD_FILE_WRITE) is
         -- save to an output stream
      do
         print("Saving an Image...")
         destination.put_string(extent.out); destination.put_character(' ')
         destination.put_string(contents); destination.put_new_line
      end   -- save
feature {NONE} -- Private
   contents : STRING
end -- IMAGE
```

Some graphical objects, such as large raster images, can be expensive to load from disk, whereas opening a document should be as fast as possible. So we use an IMAGE_PROXY, which acts as a stand-in for the real image, creating the actual image and loading it from disk only when the document needs it—to draw itself, for example.

```
class IMAGE_PROXY
inherit GRAPHIC
creation make
feature -- Creation
   make (filename : STRING) is
      -- Creation and initialization
      require filename_not_void: filename /= Void
      local f : STD_FILE_READ
      do
         image_filename := clone(filename)
         !!cached_extent.make(0,0)
      end -- make
feature {ANY} -- Queries
   extent : POINT2D is
      -- returns the cached extent if possible, or else load the image
      do
         if cached_extent.is_zero then
            cached_extent := get_image.extent
         end -- if
         Result := cached_extent
      end -- extent
feature {ANY} -- Commands
   draw (at : POINT2D) is
      -- simulates drawing the image
      do
         get_image.draw(at)
      end -- draw
   resize (new_extent: POINT2D) is
      -- resize the image
      do
         get_image.resize(new_extent)
         cached_extent := new_extent
      end -- resize
   load  (source: STD_FILE_READ) is
      -- load from an input stream
      do
         cached_extent.read(source)
```

```
            source.read_line; image_filename := clone(source.last_string)
        end -- load
    save (destination: STD_FILE_WRITE) is
        -- save to an output stream
        do
            print("Saving an Image_Proxy...")
            destination.put_string(cached_extent.out)
            destination.put_character(' ')
            destination.put_string(image_filename); destination.put_new_line
        end   -- save
feature {NONE} -- Private
    get_image : IMAGE is
        -- returns the cached image if possible, or else load it
        do
            if actual_image = Void then
                !!actual_image.make(image_filename)
                cached_extent := actual_image.extent
            end -- if
            Result := actual_image
        end -- get_image
    image_filename : STRING -- the filename storing the actual image
    cached_extent : POINT2D -- a cache for the extent of the actual image
    actual_image : IMAGE -- loaded only when actually needed
invariant
    coherent_cache: actual_image /= Void
                    implies cached_extent.is_equal(actual_image.extent)
end -- IMAGE_PROXY
```

A TEXT_DOCUMENT could then be defined as a COLLECTION of GRAPHICS, each member of which can *draw* itself and *save* its contents to a file.

```
class TEXT_DOCUMENT
inherit LINKED_LIST[GRAPHIC]
creation make
feature {ANY} -- Commands
    save (filename: STRING) is
        -- save the current document to a file named 'filename'
        require filename_not_void: filename /= Void
        local
            f : STD_FILE_WRITE
            i : INTEGER
        do
            !!f.connect_to(filename)
```

```
        from i := 1 until i > count
        loop
           item(i).save(f)
           i := i + 1
        end -- loop
        f.disconnect
        print("Document saved.%N")
     end -- save
   draw is
        -- draw the document in a diagonal (silly but simple).
     local
        top_left : POINT2D
        i : INTEGER
     do
        !!top_left.make(0,0)
        from i := 1 until i > count
        loop
           item(i).draw(top_left)
           top_left.add(item(i).extent)
           i := i + 1
        end -- loop
     end -- draw
end -- TEXT_DOCUMENT
```

Such a TEXT_DOCUMENT could be manipulated as follows:

```
class MAIN
creation make
feature -- Creation
   make is
        -- Creation and initialization
     local
        p, new_size : POINT2D
        document : TEXT_DOCUMENT
        g1, g2 : GRAPHIC
     do
        !!document.make
        !IMAGE!g1.make("Image1") -- Image1 is a small image: we include it directly
        !IMAGE_PROXY!g2.make("Image2") -- Image2 is large, we use an image proxy
        document.add_last(g1) -- we insert both g1 and g2
        document.add_last(g2) --    into the document

        document.save("A_document") -- Image2 is not yet accessed
```

```
        document.draw -- Here we need the actual image
        !!new_size.make(5,10); g1.resize(new_size) -- resize g1
        !!new_size.make(50,100); g2.resize(new_size) -- resize g2
        -- notice that the resize operation on g2 does not change
        -- the image itself, but just its proxy
        document.save("A_document") -- Overwrite previous save
        document.draw -- Redraw with new size
    end -- make
end -- MAIN
```

If we compile and execute this class as the root of an Eiffel system, we get the following output:

```
Loading an image. Please wait...
Saving an Image...Saving an Image_Proxy...Document saved.
 Simulation of a real image drawn at 0.000000,0.000000
Loading an image. Please wait...
 Simulation of another real image drawn at 10.000000,20.000000
Saving an Image...Saving an Image_Proxy...Document saved.
 Simulation of a real image drawn at 0.000000,0.000000
 Simulation of another real image drawn at 5.000000,10.000000
```

## Related Patterns

An Adapter (87) provides a different interface to the object it adapts. In contrast, a Proxy provides the same interface as its subject.

Although a Decorator (105) can have a similar implementation to a Proxy, it has a different purpose. A Decorator adds one or more responsibilities to an object, whereas a Proxy controls access to an object.

# Chapter 5

# Behavioral Patterns

Behavioral patterns relate to algorithms and the assignment of responsibilities among objects. This chapter shows how the GoF behavioral patterns can be implemented with Eiffel. As in the previous chapters, we review the name and the intent of the pattern before discussing Eiffel-specific implementation issues and providing a complete example of the use of the pattern in a complete and self-contained, albeit hypothetical, application. Most of the examples we used are broadly based on the corresponding examples in the GoF book; we just add the few necessary classes to fill the blanks and to obtain something we can definitively watch running.

**Chain of Responsibility (GoF page 223)** Avoid coupling the sender of a request to its receiver, by giving more than one object a chance to handle the request. Chain the receiving objects and pass the request along the chain until one object handles it.

**Command (GoF page 233)** Encapsulate a request as an object, in order to parameterize clients with different requests, queue or log requests, and support undoable operations.

**Interpreter (GoF page 243)** Given a language, define a representation for its grammar, along with an interpreter that uses the representation to interpret sentences in the language.

**Iterator (GoF page 257)** Provide a way to access the elements of an aggregate object sequentially, without exposing its underlying representation.

**Mediator (GoF page 273)** Define an object that encapsulates how a set of objects interact. Mediator promotes loose coupling by keeping objects from referring to one another explicitly and lets you vary their interaction independently.

**Memento (GoF page 283)** Without violating encapsulation, capture and externalize an object's internal state so that the object can be restored to this state later.

**Observer (GoF page 293)** Define a one-to-many dependency among objects so that when one object changes state, all of its dependents are notified and updated automatically.

**State (GoF page 305)** Allow an object to alter its behavior when its internal state changes. The object will appear to change its class.

**Strategy (GoF page 315)** Define a family of algorithms, encapsulate each one, and make them interchangeable. Strategy lets the algorithm vary independently from clients that use it.

**Template Method (GoF page 325)** Define the skeleton of an algorithm in an operation, deferring some steps to subclasses. Template Method lets subclasses redefine certain steps of an algorithm without changing the algorithm's structure.

**Visitor (GoF page 331)** Define a general interface to apply various computations to a set of classes without modifying them each time.

# Chain of Responsibility (Behavioral) (GoF 223)

## Intent

Avoid coupling the sender of a request to its receiver by giving more than one object a chance to handle the request. Chain the receiving objects and pass the request along the chain until one object handles it.

## Structure

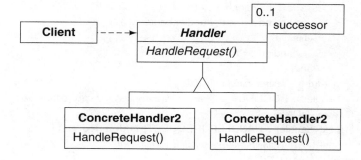

A typical object structure might look like this:

## Collaboration

- When a client issues a request, the request propagates along the chain until a ConcreteHandler object takes responsibility for handling it.

## Eiffel Implementation

The basic implementation scheme of this pattern is to send the request to a known handler and to assume that the request will be forwarded along a chain of handlers until the relevant one is reached. This idea can be reified in Eiffel by combining genericity and inheritance. The request to be handled can be a generic parameter to a class HANDLER implementing this basic scheme: Concrete subclasses would then just decide whether to use the default behavior of propagating the request to the next handler in the chain or to redefine the request handling.

```
deferred class HANDLER [REQUEST] -- REQUEST is a generic type parameter
feature {ANY}
  default_handle, handle (r : REQUEST) is
      -- Forwards the request 'r' to the next handler in the chain
    do
      if next_handler /= Void then
        next_handler.handle(r)
        handled := next_handler.handled
      else
        handied := False
      end -- if
    end -- default_handle, handle
  handled : BOOLEAN -- Whether last request has successfully been handled
feature {NONE}
  next_handler : HANDLER [REQUEST] is deferred end
      -- Implement the responsibility chain link
end -- HANDLER
```

The generic notion of HANDLER can be specialized in subclasses. Indeed, the link implementing the responsibility chain (*next_handler*) most often also exists at the analysis level as a kind of problem domain relationship X. The designer must then *merge* the problem domain relationship with the feature *next_handler*, basically saying: *I use this X relationship to implement my responsibility chain.* This can be achieved by renaming and redefining the feature *next_handler*, as in the WIDGET class in the following sample code.

## Sample Code

To illustrate this point, we now use Chain of Responsibility to handle events in a graphical context. The client is an EVENT_MANAGER responsible for the proper processing of the incoming events. From the event description, it computes the target WIDGET and asks it to handle this event. To keep the description short, we suppose that the widget selection is done elsewhere and that the resulting widget is provided to the manager as the focus widget. The EVENT_MANAGER is defined as follows.

```
class EVENT_MANAGER
creation make
feature -- Creation
   make, set_focus (focus_widget : WIDGET) is
         -- Creation and initialization with 'focus_widget' as the focus
         require focus_widget_not_void: focus_widget /= Void
         do
             focus := focus_widget
         end -- make, set_focus
feature {ANY} -- Queries
   focus : WIDGET -- The Widget that currently has the focus
feature {ANY} -- Commands
   dispatch (event : EVENT) is
         -- Ask the current head of the responsability chain to handle the event
         do
             focus.handle(event)
             if focus.handled then
                 print("Event dispatched%N")
             else
                 print("Event discarded%N")
             end -- if
         end -- dispatch
invariant
   defined_focus: focus /= Void
end --EVENT_MANAGER
```

In the class WIDGET, we redefine the *handler* relationship to map to an existing one, namely, the *container* relationship. This way, the event will be presented first to the innermost widget, then to its container, and so on up to the window.

```
class WIDGET
inherit
   HANDLER [EVENT]
      rename next_handler as container
      redefine container
      end
feature {ANY}  -- Queries
   container : WIDGET
         -- Co-variant redefinition of the responsibility chain link
feature {ANY} -- Commands
   set_container (new_container : WIDGET) is
```

```
        -- Set a new container WIDGET
    require new_container_not_void: new_container /= Void
    do
      container := new_container
    ensure container = new_container
    end -- set_container
end -- WIDGET
```

The innermost widget, the one with the focus, will receive the new event and either (1) process it if it is interested in it or (2) forward it along the containment path up to the including window. The simplest example of a WIDGET subclass is the following BUTTON.

```
class BUTTON
inherit
  WIDGET
    redefine handle end;
feature {ANY}
  handle (event : EVENT) is
    do
        if event.is_mouse_click then
          handled := True
          print("Button clicked!%N")
        else
          default_handle(event)
        end -- if
    end -- handle
end -- BUTTON
```

Another example of a WIDGET subclass is the class WINDOW, which can contain an embedded WIDGET.

```
class WINDOW
inherit
  WIDGET
    redefine handle end;
feature {ANY}
  add (a_widget : WIDGET) is
    -- Appends a_widget as a direct contained element
    require valid_widget : a_widget /= Void
    do
        a_widget.set_container(Current)
```

```
      end -- add
   handle (event : EVENT) is
      do
         if event.is_close then
            handled := True
            print("Window closed!%N");
         else
            default_handle(event)
         end -- if
      end -- handle
end -- WINDOW
```

To exercise this example, we provide the following root class, which builds a simple WINDOW containing a single BUTTON, and then simulates reading an EVENT stream and dispatching both on an EVENT_MANAGER.

```
class MAIN
creation make
feature -- Creation
   make is
         -- Exercise the 'Responsability Chain' pattern
      local
         button : BUTTON
         window : WINDOW
         manager : EVENT_MANAGER
      do -- Creates a Window containing a Button
         !!button; !!window; window.add(button)
         !!manager.make(button) -- 'button' is supposed to have the focus
         loop_on_events(manager)
      end -- make
   loop_on_events(event_manager : EVENT_MANAGER) is
         -- Event loop
      require
         valid_manager : event_manager /= Void
      do
         from get_next_event until last_event = Void
         loop
            event_manager.dispatch(last_event)
            get_next_event
         end -- loop
         print("Event stream closed%N")
      end -- loop_on_events
   last_event : EVENT
```

```
                        -- last EVENT detected
feature {NONE} -- internal routines
    get_next_event is
            -- Simulates getting a new EVENT from an event stream
        do
            event_index := event_index + 1
            if event_code.valid_index(event_index) then
                !!last_event.make(event_code.item(event_index))
            else
                last_event := Void
            end -- if
        end -- get_next_event
    event_index : INTEGER
            -- Current rank in the event_code list
    event_code : ARRAY[INTEGER] is
            -- A constant ARRAY holding 4 event codes: click, until, click, and close
        once
            Result := <<ec.click,ec.unknown,ec.click,ec.close>>
        end -- event_code
    ec : EVENT_CONST -- Expanded class defining events as const
end -- MAIN
```

If we compile and execute this class as the root of an Eiffel system, we get
the following output:

```
Button clicked!
Event dispatched
Event discarded
Button clicked!
Event dispatched
Window closed!
Event dispatched
Event stream closed
```

# Related Patterns

Chain of Responsibility is often applied in conjunction with Composite (99).
In this case, a component's parent can act as its successor.

# Command (GoF 233)                    (Behavioral)

## Intent

Encapsulate a request as an object, thereby letting you parameterize clients with various requests, queue or log requests, and support undoable operations.

## Structure

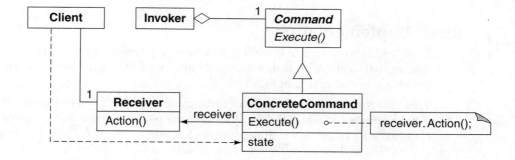

## Collaboration

- The client creates a ConcreteCommand object and specifies its receiver.

- An Invoker object stores the ConcreteCommand object.

- The invoker issues a request by calling Execute on the command. When commands are undoable, ConcreteCommand stores state for undoing the command prior to invoking Execute.

- The ConcreteCommand object invokes operations on its receiver to carry out the request.

The following diagram shows the interactions between these objects. It illustrates how Command decouples the invoker from the receiver (and the request it carries out).

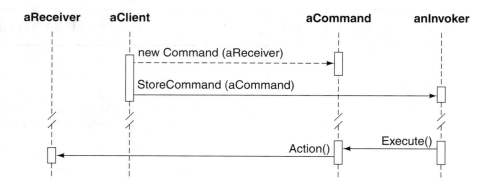

## Eiffel Implementation

By allowing functions to be reifed, this pattern provides a type-safe way of dealing with callbacks, thus subsuming any need to use function pointers, which are not available in Eiffel.

This pattern also provides a way for a class to anonymously expose one of its routines for external use. By hiding the receiver, the pattern allows a class to call a receiver's routine without knowledge of it. A high degree of decoupling is thus possible between the caller and the callee.

The minimal interface specification of a COMMAND follows.

```
deferred class COMMAND
feature {ANY}
   execute is
        -- Should be defined in subclasses to perform the relevant action
      deferred
      end -- execute
end -- COMMAND
```

## Sample Code

We will consider the simple example of a TEXT_EDITOR opened on one file and featuring only two commands: *save* and *quit*.

```
class TEXT_EDITOR
feature {ANY}
   save is
      do
```

```
        print("Text editor is requested to save its buffer.%N")
      end -- save
   quit is
      do
        print("Bye ...%N")
      end -- quit
end -- TEXT_EDITOR
```

Using the Command pattern, we reify the two commands *save* and *quit* as in the class SAVE_COMMAND.

```
class SAVE_COMMAND
inherit COMMAND
creation make
feature {ANY}
   make (editor : TEXT_EDITOR) is
      -- registers client
      require
        editor_not_void : editor /= Void
      do
        client := editor
      ensure
        client_registered : client = editor
      end -- make
   execute is
      -- calls client's save routine
      do
        client.save
      end -- execute
feature {NONE}
   client : TEXT_EDITOR
invariant
   client_not_void : client /= Void
end -- SAVE_COMMAND
```

The class QUIT_COMMAND has exactly the same structure, with its *execute* routine defined to call *client.quit*. Such COMMANDS may be associated to, for example, a BUTTON.

```
class BUTTON
inherit WIDGET
creation set_command
```

```
feature {ANY} -- Creation
  set_command (new_command : COMMAND) is
    -- Register a new COMMAND
    require new_command_not_void: new_command /= Void
    do
      associated_command := new_command
    ensure associated_command = new_command
    end -- set_command
feature {ANY} -- Queries
  associated_command : COMMAND
      -- Command that must be executed when the BUTTON is pressed
feature {ANY} -- Commands
  activate is
    -- Execute the associated_command
    do
      associated_command.execute
    end -- activate
invariant
  associated_command_not_void: associated_command /= Void
end -- BUTTON
```

When triggered, a BUTTON calls the *activate* method and fires the execution of the registered COMMAND. The interface we define for the class BUTTON describes the notion of a *command bearer*. We could abstract this into an INVOKER class and have BUTTON inherit from it. Thus, the only code in BUTTON would be the button-specific aspects of the WIDGET class.

The notion of macro commands can be very easily implemented, using multiple inheritance. Along the lines of the Composite (99) pattern, a MACRO_COMMAND is both a COMMAND and a COMPOSITE [COMMAND].

```
class MACRO_COMMAND
inherit
  COMPOSITE [COMMAND]
  COMMAND
creation make
feature {ANY} -- Creation
  make is
    -- Creation and initialization
    do
      !LINK_LIST[COMMAND]!children.make
    end -- make
```

```
feature {ANY} -- Commands
   execute is
         -- Execute each command of the list in sequence
      local i : INTEGER
      do
         from i := children.lower until i > children.upper
         loop
            children.item(i).execute
            i := i + 1
         end -- loop
      end -- execute
end -- MACRO_COMMAND
```

The application class MAIN will play the client role for this TEXT_EDITOR. MAIN provides the glue among the editor, the buttons, and the commands, including a simple macro command, and then simulates a user clicking on the buttons.

```
class MAIN
creation make
feature {ANY}
   make is
      local
         editor : TEXT_EDITOR
         save_button, quit_button, save_and_quit_button : BUTTON
         save_command : SAVE_COMMAND ; quit_command : QUIT_COMMAND
         save_and_quit_command : MACRO_COMMAND
      do
         -- initializes application components
         !!editor -- Create the editor
         !!save_command.make(editor);!!quit_command.make(editor)
         -- Create the commands
         !!save_and_quit_command.make -- Creates the macro-command
         save_and_quit_command.add(save_command ) -- First command of the macro
         save_and_quit_command.add(quit_command ) -- Last command of the macro
         -- now create 3 buttons: SAVE, QUIT and SAVE&QUIT
         !!save_button.set_command(save_command)
         !!quit_button.set_command(quit_command)
         !!save_and_quit_button.set_command(save_and_quit_command)
         -- Simulate pressing the buttons
         print("Pressing button SAVE: "); save_button.activate
         print("Pressing button QUIT: "); quit_button.activate
```

```
      print("Pressing button SAVE&QUIT: "); save_and_quit_button.activate
    end -- make
  end -- MAIN
```

Compiling this class as the root class of an Eiffel system and executing the resulting program leads to the following output:

```
Pressing button SAVE: Text editor is requested to save its buffer.
Pressing button QUIT: Bye ...
Pressing button SAVE&QUIT: Text editor is requested to save its buffer.
Bye ...
```

## Related Patterns

A Composite (99) can be used to implement macro commands. A Memento (177) can keep the state the command needs to undo its effect. A command that must be copied before being placed on the history list acts as a Prototype (73).

# Interpreter (GoF 243)                    (Behavioral)

## Intent

Given a language, define a representation for its grammar, along with an interpreter that uses the representation to interpret sentences in the language.

## Structure

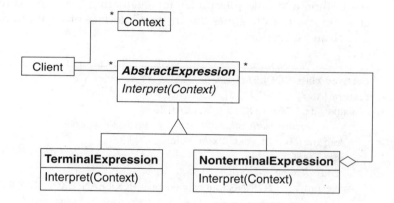

## Collaboration

- The client builds (or is given) the sentence as an abstract syntax tree of NonterminalExpression and TerminalExpression instances. Then the client initializes the context and invokes the Interpret operation.

- Each NonterminalExpression node defines Interpret in terms of Interpret on each subexpression. The Interpret operation of each TerminalExpression defines the base case in the recursion.

- The Interpret operations at each node use the context to store and access the state of the interpreter.

## Eiffel Implementation

When dealing with simple languages, it is common to look for an alternative to a table-driven-generated parser in which semantic interpretation is hard-coded into rules. When the language changes, the whole interpreter needs to be regenerated. Why not try a simple object-oriented approach whereby each notion gets mapped to a class?

The purpose of the Interpreter pattern is to define a class for each syntactic category and to let the syntax tree evaluate itself. Each class derives from an abstract SYNTACTIC_ITEM that provides a method for evaluating the value of the construct. The pattern does not provide a means for building the syntax tree of the sentence to evaluate, even if in simple cases it can be used for both building the tree and evaluating it. In more complex cases, the Builder (63) pattern should be considered, as in the code example given for the Facade (109) pattern.

## Sample Code

We outline a simple interpreter for evaluating boolean expressions. The class BOOLEAN_EXP defines the abstract interface of what can be done with a boolean expression.

```
deferred class BOOLEAN_EXP
feature {ANY}
   value (ctx : CONTEXT) : BOOLEAN is
       -- Return truth value of Current in the 'ctx' context
     require ctx_not_void: ctx /= Void
     deferred
     end -- value
   replacing (var : STRING; subexpression : BOOLEAN_EXP) : BOOLEAN_EXP is
       -- produces new expression with subexpression replacing 'var'
     require
       var_not_void: var /= Void
       subexpression_not_void: subexpression /= Void
     deferred
     ensure Result_not_void: Result /= Void
     end -- replacing
end -- BOOLEAN_EXP
```

An example of a nonterminal is given by the AND_EXP class, which is composed of two BOOLEAN_EXPs and evaluates to their logical conjunction.

```
class AND_EXP
inherit
   BOOLEAN_EXP
creation make
feature {ANY}
   make (left_hand_side, right_hand_side : BOOLEAN_EXP) is
```

```
                -- Creation and initialization
        require
            left_hand_side_not_void: left_hand_side /= Void
            right_hand_side_not_void: right_hand_side /= Void
        do
            left := left_hand_side;  right := right_hand_side
        end  -- make
feature {ANY} -- Queries
    left, right : BOOLEAN_EXP -- left hand side and right hand side in the expression
    value (ctx : CONTEXT) : BOOLEAN is
            -- Return truth value of Current in the 'ctx' context
            -- by evaluating the logical 'and' value of both sides
        do
            Result := left.value(ctx) and right.value(ctx)
        end -- value
    replacing (var : STRING;  subexpression : BOOLEAN_EXP) : BOOLEAN_EXP is
            -- Produces new expression with subexpression replacing var
        do
            !AND_EXP!Result.make(left.replacing(var,subexpression),
                            right.replacing(var,subexpression))
        end -- replacing
end -- AND_EXP
```

As a simple boolean expression example, let's consider the VARIABLE_EXP.

```
class VARIABLE_EXP
inherit
    BOOLEAN_EXP
creation make
feature -- Creation
    make (a_name : STRING) is
            -- Creation and initialization with a_name as the variable name
        require a_name_not_void: a_name /= Void
        do
            name := a_name
        end -- make
feature {ANY} -- queries
    name : STRING -- The symbolic name of this boolean variable
    value (ctx : CONTEXT) : BOOLEAN is
            -- Return truth value of this variable in the 'ctx' context
        do
            Result := ctx.lookup_value(name)
```

```
        end -- value
    replacing (var : STRING; subexpression : BOOLEAN_EXP) : BOOLEAN_EXP is
            -- Produces new expression with subexpression replacing var
        do
            if var.is_equal(name) then
                Result := clone(subexpression)
            else
                !VARIABLE_EXP!Result.make(name)
            end -- if
        end -- replacing
invariant
    name_not_void: name /= Void
end -- VARIABLE_EXP
```

The expression evaluates simply by a lookup in a CONTEXT object. This context is built over a dictionary that maps symbol names to boolean values, as follows.

```
class CONTEXT
creation make
feature  -- Creation
    make is
            -- Creation and initialization
        do
            !!table.make
        end -- make
feature {ANY} -- queries
    is_defined (var : STRING) : BOOLEAN is
            -- Whether variable 'var' in known in this context
        require var_not_void: var /= Void
        do
            Result := table.has(var)
        end -- is_defined
    lookup_value (var : STRING) : BOOLEAN is
            -- Returns boolean value of variable
        require
            var_defined: var /= Void and then is_defined (var)
        do
            Result := table.at(var)
        end -- lookup_value
    assign (var : STRING; val : BOOLEAN) is
            -- Assign value 'val' to variable name 'var'
```

```
          require var_not_void: var /= Void
          do
              table.put(val,var)
          end -- assign
feature {NONE}
    table : DICTIONARY[BOOLEAN,STRING]
invariant
    table_not_void: table /= Void
end -- CONTEXT
```

We can use the class MAIN as a simple test driver to build two variables *x* and *y* and to evaluate their conjunction in a given evaluation context.

```
class MAIN
creation make
feature {ANY}
    make is
        local
            x, y : VARIABLE_EXP
            ctx : CONTEXT
            expr : AND_EXP
        do
            !!x.make("x"); !!y.make("y") -- Build two variables
            !!expr.make(x,y) -- Build an 'and' expression between both
            !!ctx.make -- Make an evaluation context
            print("Setting x to true,"); ctx.assign("x",true)
            print(" and setting y to false %N"); ctx.assign("y",false)
            print("The value of the expression (x and y) is: ")
            io.put_boolean(expr.value(ctx)); io.put_new_line
            print("Result of replacing y with x in (x and y) is: ")
            io.put_boolean(expr.replacing("y",x).value(ctx)); io.put_new_line
        end -- make
end -- MAIN
```

If we compile and execute this class as the root of an Eiffel system, we get the following output:

```
Setting x to true, and setting y to false
The value of the expression (x and y) is: false
Result of replacing y with x in (x and y) is: true
```

## Related Patterns

The Abstract Syntax tree is an instance of the Composite (99) pattern. Flyweight (121) shows how to share terminal symbols within the Abstract Syntax Tree. Interpreter can use an Iterator (159) to traverse the structure. Visitor (227) can be used to maintain the behavior in each node in the Abstract Syntax Tree in one class.

# Iterator (GoF 257)                    (Behavioral)

## Intent

Provide a way to access the elements of an aggregate object sequentially without exposing its underlying representation.

## Structure

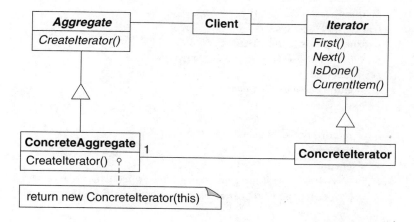

## Collaboration

- A ConcreteIterator keeps track of the current object in the aggregate and can compute the succeeding object in the traversal.

## Eiffel Implementation

A service provided by an aggregate should be accessible without knowledge of its underlying structure; this is the way the service provider is implemented. Nevertheless, the simple need for traversal requires a knowledge of the way to get from one component to the next, which induces tight coupling between a service provider and its customer. The Iterator pattern aims at suppressing this coupling, by providing an abstract interface for traversing aggregates.

An iterator can be used either externally or internally. In the former case, an iterator object is given to the client object, which then takes charge of the effective traversal. In the latter case, the aggregate uses the iterator internally and provides an entry point to apply an operation on each of its components. This approach, very common in LISP, could be used in Eiffel with the aid of the Command (147) pattern. A command object with its execute operation redefined to implement the operation to be performed can be passed along the aggregate.

We use the Eiffel facility for defining routine synonyms to conciliate the definition of the ITERATOR interface from the GoF, with the usual naming standards of Eiffel.

```
deferred class ITERATOR[E]
feature {ANY} -- Queries
   exhausted, is_done : BOOLEAN  is
         -- Whether all elements have been visited
      deferred
      end  -- exhausted, is_done
   item : E is
         -- The current element in the iteration
      require not_exhausted: not is_done
      deferred
      ensure
         -- If not robust, we cannot change the aggregate while traversing it
         robustness: is_robust or else aggregate_state = old(aggregate_state)
      end  -- item
   is_robust : BOOLEAN is
         -- Whether we can insert and delete items in the collection
         -- without interfering with the traversal
      do  -- False by default
      end  -- is_robust
feature {ANY} -- Commands
   start, first is
         -- Go to the aggregate first position: start the iteration
      deferred
      end  -- start, first
   next is
         -- Advance to the next element
      require not_exhausted: not is_done
      deferred
      end  -- next
feature {NONE} -- Private
   aggregate_state : INTEGER is
         -- Encoding of the aggregate abstract state that should not
```

```
        -- change if the Iterator is not robust
    deferred
    end -- aggregate_state
end -- ITERATOR
```

Note, however, that within a given project, you are advised to choose one interface subset and to stick with it.

This interface also makes provision for both *robust* and *nonrobust* iterators. An iterator is said to be *robust* when insertions and deletions do not interfere with the traversal. If the iterator is not robust, this should be clearly spelled out in its contract. This is why the feature *item* in our example has a post-condition stating that if it is not robust, the structure of the aggregate cannot be changed while it is being traversed. Nonrobust iterators are the default situation unless special provision is made—for example, by registering the iterator with the aggregate and letting the aggregate sort out the mess.

In the SmallEiffel Standard Library, the class COLLECTION defines an abstract interface for an indexed collection of objects. Such a collection is traversable, using a simple INTEGER index from 'lower' to 'upper'. Items can be added, changed, or removed. Thus, we can define a generic COLLECTION_ITERATOR, valid for all subclasses of the class COLLECTION.

```
class COLLECTION_ITERATOR[E]
inherit ITERATOR[E]
creation make
feature -- Creation
    make (target: like target_collection) is
            -- Creation and initialization
        require target_not_void: target /= Void
        do
            target_collection := target
        end -- make
feature {ANY} -- Queries
    exhausted, is_done : BOOLEAN  is
            -- Whether all elements have been visited
        do
            Result := index > target_collection.upper
        end -- exhausted, is_done
    item : E is
            -- The current element in the iteration
        do
            Result := target_collection.item(index)
```

```
        end -- item
feature {ANY} -- Commands
    start, first is
            -- Go to the aggregate first position: start the iteration
        do
            index := target_collection.lower
        end -- start, first
    next is
            -- Advance to the next element
        do
            index := index + 1
        end -- next
feature {NONE}
    index : INTEGER -- The cursor on the target collection
    target_collection : COLLECTION[E] -- The target collection itself
    aggregate_state : INTEGER is
            -- Encoding of the aggregate abstract state that should not
            -- change if the Iterator is not robust
        do
            Result := target_collection.count -- Gross simplification
        end -- aggregate_state
invariant
    target_collection_not_void: target_collection /= Void
end -- COLLECTION_ITERATOR
```

Since this iterator relies on the indexes provided by its target collection, it is not robust; insertions and deletions might interfere with the traversal. Thus, we define the *aggregate_state*, such as a change in its cardinality, which would violate its contract, and would be detected. This is a good compromise between the extensive equivalence test and the efficiency of the test.

# Sample Code

To show an example of the use of iterator, imagine that we have the following EMPLOYEE class.

```
class EMPLOYEE
creation make_from_number
feature -- Creation
    make_from_number (his_number : INTEGER) is
            -- Create an employee from its his_number
        do
            number := his_number
```

```
        end -- make_from_number
feature {ANY}
    number : INTEGER -- An employee record number
    print_it is
            -- Print a short description of this employee
        do
            std_output.put_string("Employee number ")
            std_output.put_integer(number)
            std_output.put_new_line
        end -- print_it
end -- EMPLOYEE
```

Suppose that we want to iterate over employee lists, both forward and backward. We could define a REVERSE_ITERATOR, going from the last employee to the first, from a COLLECTION_ITERATOR, in which the code for starting, advancing, and detecting the end of the iteration would be redefined.

```
class REVERSE_ITERATOR[E]
inherit COLLECTION_ITERATOR[E]
        redefine exhausted, is_done, start, first, next end;
creation make
feature {ANY} -- Queries
    exhausted, is_done : BOOLEAN is
            -- Whether all elements have been visited
        do
            Result := index < target_collection.lower
        end -- exhausted, is_done
feature {ANY} -- Commands
    start, first is
            -- Go to the aggregate first position: start the iteration
        do
            index := target_collection.upper
        end -- start, first
    next is
            -- Advance to the next element
        do
            index := index - 1
        end -- next
end -- REVERSE_ITERATOR
```

Then, an employee list could be created and traversed both ways, as follows.

```
class MAIN
creation make
feature {ANY}
   make is
         -- builds context of test and run it
      local
         forward : COLLECTION_ITERATOR[EMPLOYEE]
         backward : REVERSE_ITERATOR[EMPLOYEE]
      do
         build_employees_list(5) -- Makes a list of employees
         !!forward.make(employees) -- Create a (forward) iterator on this list
         !!backward.make(employees) -- Create a backward iterator on this list
         print("From first to last:%N")
         print_employees(forward)
         print("From last to first:%N")
         print_employees(backward)
      end -- make
   print_employees (iter : ITERATOR[EMPLOYEE]) is
         -- demonstrate the use of iterators
      do
         from iter.start until iter.is_done
         loop
            iter.item.print_it
            iter.next
         end -- loop
      end -- print_employees
feature {NONE}
   employees : LINKED_LIST[EMPLOYEE]
   build_employees_list (nb : INTEGER) is
         -- build a list with 'nb' members
      local
         i : INTEGER
         emp : EMPLOYEE
      do
         !!employees.make
         from i := 1 until i > nb
         loop
            !!emp.make_from_number(i)
            employees.add_last(emp)
            i := i + 1
         end -- loop
      end -- build_employees_list
end -- MAIN
```

If we compile and execute this class as the root of an Eiffel system, we get the following output:

```
From first to last:
Employee number 1
Employee number 2
Employee number 3
Employee number 4
Employee number 5
From last to first:
Employee number 5
Employee number 4
Employee number 3
Employee number 2
Employee number 1
```

## Related Patterns

An Iterator is often applied to a recursive structure such as Composite (99). A polymorphic Iterator relies on a Factory Method (69) to instantiate the appropriate Iterator subclass. Memento (177) is often used in conjunction with the Iterator pattern, as a kind of *cursor*.

# Mediator (GoF 273)    (Behavioral)

## Intent

Define an object that encapsulates how a set of objects interact. Mediator promotes loose coupling by keeping objects from referring to one another explicitly and lets you vary their interaction independently.

## Structure

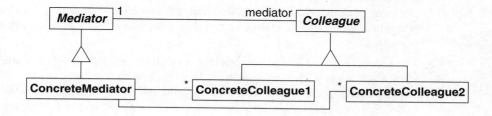

A typical object structure might look like this:

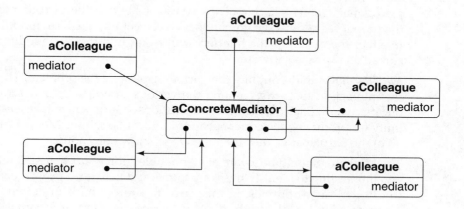

## Collaboration

- Collegues send and receive requests from a Mediator object. The mediator implements the cooperative behavior by routing requests between the appropriate colleague(s).

## Eiffel Implementation

The need for Mediator can arise from two opposite situations. In the first case, analysis identifies the need for a service in an abstract way—for example, selecting a file through a file browser. In this case, the global interaction scheme is identified first. Then, during design, the various items needed to perform the task are identified, such as a browser to move across files, a text field to identify the currently selected file, and various buttons to cancel or to confirm the selection. After the analysis phase, we have only an APPLICATION and a FILE_SELECTOR to which the application delegates the task of selecting the file. During the design phase, the model is enhanced with auxiliary items, such as BROWSER, TEXT_FIELD, and BUTTON, which are connected to the FILE_SELECTOR. Each widget notifies the *Mediator* (here the FILE_SELECTOR) when its state changes. The Mediator is then in charge of updating the appropriate widgets and propagating the notification in a suitable way.

The second case arises in the opposite way; after analysis, a set of items are identified, each with a precise role. In response to interactions, the items have to notify one or several other items and ask them to perform particular tasks. For example, consider a system dedicated to project management. A project consists of tasks, each of which receives a planning estimate made up of a delivery date, the planned work-month effort, and a set of resources consisting of people and time intervals. When a task is selected, it has to update all of the items in charge of displaying all of the components of that task. The same situation holds for every element that captures an aspect of project management. Each tool has to be aware of the others in order to issue the proper requests and commands for a correct update. Each modification in either the model or the interface will result in numerous modifications spread all over the software.

*Mediator* helps in decoupling the various aspects of the problem. This way, the interaction that exists among the various components is described in one place only. Each participant notifies the Mediator, which takes responsibility for producing the correct propagation. Although the Mediator knows all of the participants, they do not have to know one another.

The Mediator should be aware of all possible sources of change. It relies on equality testing to identify the exact source and may need privileged access to call dedicated routines. In this case, all sources have to derive from a common ancestor, although this may not be necessary if identification is based on other tests.

We define an abstract class to reify the Mediator role in this pattern. A MEDIATOR works with COLLEAGUES—represented as a generic formal parameter at this stage—and can be activated and then informed of colleagues' changes.

```
deferred class MEDIATOR [COLLEAGUE] -- COLLEAGUE is a generic formal parame-
ter
feature {ANY}
    activate is
            -- Activate the Mediator's Colleagues
        deferred
        end -- activate
    changed (source : COLLEAGUE) is
            -- Take action to inform dependant of the 'source' change
        require source_not_void: source /= Void
        deferred
        end -- changed
end -- MEDIATOR
```

## Sample Code

We consider a graphical user interface context in which a pop-up window can be displayed to let the user choose a value from a list of values. This pop-up window can be managed by using a DIALOG_DIRECTOR, which is a MEDIATOR subclass specialized to work with this kind of widget.

```
deferred class DIALOG_DIRECTOR
inherit MEDIATOR[WIDGET]
    rename activate as show_dialog end
feature {ANY} -- Queries
    window : WINDOW
    ok, cancel : BUTTON
    entry_list : LIST_BOX
    selected_entry : ENTRY_FIELD
feature {ANY} -- Commands
    show_dialog is
            -- Template Method to open a dialog window made of
            -- a list box, an entry field and 2 buttons labeled "OK" and "CANCEL"
        do
            !!window.make(Current)
            !!ok.make(Current); ok.set_label("OK"); window.add(ok)
            !!cancel.make(Current); cancel.set_label("CANCEL"); window.add(cancel)
            !!entry_list.make(Current); window.add(entry_list)
            !!selected_entry.make(Current); window.add(selected_entry)
            populate_entry_list -- to be customized in subclasses
            window.open
        end -- show_dialog
```

```
feature {NONE} -- Private
  populate_entry_list is
        -- Fill the entry_list contents.
        -- Primitive operation of the 'show_dialog' Template Method above.
      require entry_list_not_void: entry_list /= Void
      deferred
      end -- populate_entry_list
end -- DIALOG_DIRECTOR
```

We take the example of a font selector. The client is a PALETTE, which registers the list of possible fonts in the system and the one that is currently selected.

```
class PALETTE
creation make
feature -- Creation
  make is
      -- initialize possible fonts
      do
        font_names := <<"regular","bold","oblique">>
      end -- end
feature {ANY} -- Queries
  font_names : ARRAY[STRING] -- The available fonts
  selected_font : STRING -- the currently selected font
feature {ANY} -- Commands
  set_font (a_font : STRING) is
      -- select current font
      require
        valid_font : a_font /= Void
      do
        selected_font := a_font
      ensure
        selected_font = a_font
      end -- set_font
end -- PALETTE
```

The selection is managed by a FONT_DIALOG_DIRECTOR, which is responsible for both building the interface and coordinating changes.

```
class FONT_DIALOG_DIRECTOR
inherit
  DIALOG_DIRECTOR
```

```
creation make
feature -- Creation
   make (palette : PALETTE) is
         -- Initialize this Director with palette as its client
      require palette_not_void: palette /= Void
      do
         client := palette
      end -- make
feature {ANY} -- Commands
   changed (w : WIDGET) is
         -- propagates change notification according to the modified widget
      do
         if w = entry_list then
            selected_entry.set_value(entry_list.get_selection)
         elseif w = ok then
            client.set_font(selected_entry.value)
            window.close
         elseif w = cancel then
            window.close
         end -- if
      end -- widget_changed
feature {NONE} -- Private
   client : PALETTE -- The client for which this director works
   populate_entry_list is
         -- Fill the entry_list contents with the client PALETTE contents
      do
         entry_list.set_list(client.font_names)
      end -- populate_entry_list
end -- FONT_DIALOG_DIRECTOR
```

All user interface items, such as Window, Button, Entry Field, and so on, derive from a WIDGET abstract class.

```
deferred class WIDGET
feature {ANY}
   make, make_widget (dir : DIALOG_DIRECTOR) is
      -- registers director
      require dir_not_void: dir /= Void
      do
         director := dir
      ensure director_set: director = dir
      end -- make
   changed is
```

```
         -- calls back director on change notification
      do
         director.changed(Current)
      end -- changed
   handle_mouse (ev : MOUSE_EVENT) is
      -- reaction to mouse event is to be defined in subclasses
      deferred
      end -- handle_mouse
feature {NONE}
   director : DIALOG_DIRECTOR
invariant
   has_director: director /= Void
end -- WIDGET
```

Each particular widget has to define the way it reacts to mouse events. The common behavior of all widgets is the *changed* routine implemented by WIDGET, which calls back the DIALOG_DIRECTOR. The code for our four widgets follows, starting with WINDOW, a WIDGET able to contain other widgets.

```
class WINDOW
inherit
   WIDGET
      redefine make end
creation make
feature {ANY}
   make (dir : DIALOG_DIRECTOR) is
         -- initialize child list
      do
         make_widget(dir)
         !!items.make -- initialize the list of contained widgets
      end -- make
   handle_mouse (ev : MOUSE_EVENT) is
            -- React to mouse event
      do
         print("Window receives an event%N")
         curpos := ev.pos
         changed
      end -- handle_mouse
   add (w : WIDGET) is
         -- add a child widget to the window
      do
```

```
            items.add_last(w)
        end -- add
    open is
            -- Simulate opening the window
        do
            print("Opening window%N")
        end -- open
    close is
            -- Simulate closing the window
        do
            print("Closing window%N")
        end -- close
feature {NONE}
    s_list : LINKED_LIST[STRING]
    curpos : INTEGER
    items : LINKED_LIST[WIDGET]
invariant
    items_not_void : items /= Void
end -- WINDOW
```

A BUTTON is a simple WIDGET that can only be clicked:

```
class BUTTON
inherit
    WIDGET
creation make -- inherited from WIDGET
feature {ANY} -- Queries
    label : STRING -- The label on the button
feature {ANY} -- Commands
    set_label(new : STRING) is do label := new end -- set_label
    handle_mouse (ev : MOUSE_EVENT) is
            -- React to mouse event
        do
            print("Button "); print(label); print(" clicked%N")
            changed
        end -- handle_mouse
end -- BUTTON
```

A LIST_BOX is a WIDGET displaying a list of strings and holding a cursor on the currently selected one.

```
class LIST_BOX
inherit
  WIDGET
creation make  -- inherited from WIDGET
feature {ANY}  -- Queries
  available_choices : COLLECTION[STRING]
        -- The STRINGs available in the LIST_BOX
  current_choice : INTEGER
        -- The index of the currently selected STRING in the available_choices
  get_selection : STRING is
        -- return the selected item if any, or Void if none
    require has_model: available_choices /= Void
    do
        if available_choices.valid_index(current_choice)  then
            Result := available_choices.item(current_choice)
        end -- if
    end -- get_selection
feature {ANY} -- Commands
  set_list (new : like available_choices) is
        -- Assign list_box content
    require new_not_void: new /= Void
    do
        available_choices := new
    end -- set_list
  handle_mouse (ev : MOUSE_EVENT) is
        -- registers mouse position and notifies change
    do
        print("List Box receives an event%N")
        current_choice := ev.pos
        changed
    end -- handle_mouse
end -- LIST_BOX
```

An ENTRY_FIELD is a simple WIDGET used to enter a string.

```
class ENTRY_FIELD
inherit
  WIDGET
creation make
feature {ANY} -- Queries
  value : STRING -- the content of the ENTRY_FIELD
feature {ANY} -- Commands
```

```
set_value (v : STRING) is
    -- Assign 'v' to 'value'
    do
        print("The value of this Entry_Field becomes: ")
        io.put_string(v); io.put_new_line
        value := v
    end -- set_value
handle_mouse (ev : MOUSE_EVENT) is
    -- propagates change
    do
        print("Entry Field receives an event%N")
        changed
    end -- handle_mouse
end -- ENTRY_FIELD
```

Each of these widgets extracts the necessary information from the mouse event to update itself. The widget then notifies the DIALOG_DIRECTOR that it has changed. Knowing the origin of the change, the DIALOG_DIRECTOR is able to perform the necessary calls to keep the whole system consistent.

Our example is exercised by the driver class MAIN, which simulates mouse events.

```
class MAIN
creation make
feature {ANY}
    make is
            -- initialize application components and simulates the occurrence of 2
            -- mouse events: one on the entry_list and then one on the OK button.
        local
            director : FONT_DIALOG_DIRECTOR
            palette : PALETTE
            ev : MOUSE_EVENT
        do
            !!palette.make
            !!director.make(palette)
            director.show_dialog -- Display the PALETTE window
            -- simulates the occurrence of an event on the font_list
            director.entry_list.handle_mouse(new_event(2))
            -- simulates the occurrence of another event on the OK button
            director.ok.handle_mouse(new_event(1))
        end -- make
```

```
feature {NONE} -- Private
    new_event(code: INTEGER) : MOUSE_EVENT is
            -- Factory method to create new mouse events
        do
            !!Result.make(code)
        ensure Result_not_void: Result /= Void
        end -- new_event
end -- MAIN
```

If we compile and execute this class as the root of an Eiffel system, we get the following output:

```
Opening window
List Box receives an event
The value of this Entry_Field becomes: bold
Button OK clicked
Closing window
```

## Related Patterns

Facade (109) unlike Mediator, abstracts a subsystem of objects to provide a more convenient interface. Its protocol is unidirectional; that is, Facade objects make requests of the subsystem classes but not vice versa. In contrast, Mediator enables cooperative behavior that colleagues don't or cannot provide, and the protocol is multidirectional.

It is worth noting the differences between Observer (187) and *Mediator*. Although they both receive notification of changes, Observer does so through an abstract mechanism allowing the source of notification to be independent of its observers. When using Mediator, the source has to know its mediator. On the other hand, this makes it possible for the mediator to easily define appropriate reactions for each stimulus.

# Memento (GoF 283)  (Behavioral)

## Intent

Without violating encapsulation, capture and externalize an object's internal state so that the object can be restored to this state later.

## Structure

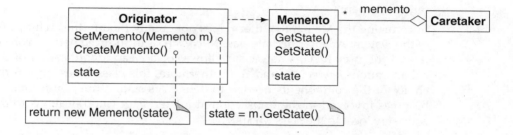

## Collaboration

- A caretaker requests a memento from an originator, holds it for a time, and passes it back to the originator, as the following interaction diagram illustrates:

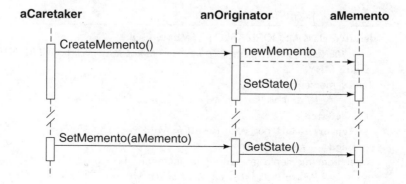

Sometimes the caretaker won't pass the memento back to the originator, because the originator might never need to revert to an earlier state.

- Mementos are passive. Only the originator that created a memento will assign or retrieve its state.

## Eiffel Implementation

Identification of the Memento pattern may come easily at the implementation stage. An object A has to be reset to a previous state by an object B. Nevertheless, this may be obscured by B's just storing some attribute values of A. The main point to check is that B never modifies these values before returning them to A.

Introducing the Memento pattern does not greatly modify the architecture of the system. An intermediate class MEMENTO is introduced between object A and the user B. This new class allows for a clean identification of the collaboration between A and B. Furthermore, this class hides from B the choice of the components needed to define A's state. If more information becomes involved in the transaction at a later stage, modifications to the code stay local to the class MEMENTO.

Memento simplifies design in one particular case: when B needs to remember the state of objects from a heterogenous set. The Memento pattern makes it possible for B to use a common protocol for interacting with the various classes in the set.

Of particular concern here is visibility. It is clear that MEMENTO needs privileged access to internal information belonging to its target object. Features that could have been declared with visibility *NONE* become lifted to a MEMENTO-dedicated interface.

The class MEMORIZABLE defines a common interface for all classes that can give out mementos of their state

```
deferred class MEMORIZABLE [T ->MEMENTO]
    -- The generic formal parameter T is constrained to conform to MEMENTO
feature {ANY}
  new_memento : T is
      -- Factory Method to produce a snapshot of the Current state
    deferred
    ensure Result_not_void: Result /= Void
    end -- new_memento
  set_from_memento (m : like new_memento) is
      -- Return to the state described in the MEMENTO 'm'
```

```
        require m_not_void: m /= Void
        deferred
        end -- set_from_memento
end -- MEMORIZABLE
```

In this case, MEMENTO simply registers its origin in the *make* routine.

```
deferred class MEMENTO
feature {MEMORIZABLE} -- Only MEMORIZABLE subclasses can create & access
MEMENTOs
    make (m : MEMORIZABLE [like Current]) is
            -- Creation and initialization of a Memento of 'm' state
        require m_not_void: m /= Void
        deferred
        end -- make
end -- MEMENTO
```

A common problem is that the state we are interested in remembering is often distributed among multiple objects. Using this pattern makes it very easy to implicitly create a graph of related mementos, one for each object that participates in the definition of the overall state. The problem is to synchronize all of these partial states. When we reset one state, we have to collect all of the valid partial states. The task can quickly grow more difficult than saving each state as a whole. This is the approach we follow here.

## Sample Code

As an example, imagine a class CONSTRAINT_SOLVER that is assigned the responsibility of preserving the relative position of a set of graphics so that when you move one of the graphics components in the set, all of the others get moved with the same vector. Here is the interface.

```
class CONSTRAINT_SOLVER
inherit
    MEMORIZABLE [CONSTRAINT_MEMENTO]
creation make
feature {ANY}
    make is
            -- Creation and initialization
        do
            !!constraint_list.make
        end -- make
```

```
solve (target : GRAPHIC) is
        -- naive implementation of constraint solving
    local
        i, up : INTEGER
        constraint : CONSTRAINT
    do
        print("Solving constraints%N")
        from i := constraint_list.lower; up := constraint_list.upper until i > up
        loop
            constraint := constraint_list.item(i)
            i := i + 1
            if constraint.is_about(target) then
                constraint.repairs_from(target)
            end -- if
        end -- loop
    end -- solve
add_constraint (g1, g2 : GRAPHIC) is
        -- defines a new constraint
    require
        valid_origin : g1 /= Void
        valid_extremity : g2 /= Void
    local
        constraint : CONSTRAINT
    do
        !!constraint.make(g1,g2)
        constraint_list.add_last(constraint)
    end -- add_constraint
remove_constraint(g1, g2 : GRAPHIC) is
    local
        constraint : CONSTRAINT
        index, up : INTEGER
    do
        from index := constraint_list.lower; up :=constraint_list.upper
        until index > up
        loop
            constraint := constraint_list(index)
            if constraint.refers_to(g1,g2) then
                constraint_list.remove(constraint)
            end -- if
            index := index + 1
        end -- loop
    end -- remove_constraint
new_memento : CONSTRAINT_MEMENTO is
        -- Factory Method to produce a snapshot of the Current state
```

```
      do
          !!Result.make(Current)
      end  -- new_memento
  set_from_memento (m : like new_memento) is
          -- Return to the state described in the MEMENTO 'm'
      local i, top : INTEGER
      do
          from i := m.graphics.lower; top := m.graphics.upper
          variant increasing_i: top - i
          until i > top
          loop
              m.graphics.item(i).move_to(m.positions.item(i))
              i := i + 1
          end  -- loop
      end  -- set_from_memento
  feature {CONSTRAINT_MEMENTO}  -- Only a CONSTRAINT_MEMENTO
                                -- can access the following list
  constraint_list : LINKED_LIST[CONSTRAINT]
      end  -- CONSTRAINT_SOLVER
```

On the other side, the associated memento CONSTRAINT_MEMENTO restricts itself to the CONSTRAINT_SOLVER, extracting all necessary information from the solver to register the actual positions of the graphics subject to the solver actions.

```
class CONSTRAINT_MEMENTO
inherit MEMENTO
creation make
feature {CONSTRAINT_SOLVER}
  make (cs : CONSTRAINT_SOLVER) is
          -- register 'cs' state variables
      local i, top : INTEGER
      do
          !!graphics.make; !!positions.make
          from i := cs.constraint_list.lower; top := cs.constraint_list.upper
          until i > top
          loop
              append_constraint(cs.constraint_list.item(i))
              i := i + 1
          end  -- loop
      end  -- make
  graphics : LINKED_LIST[GRAPHIC]
  positions : LINKED_LIST[POINT]
```

```
feature {NONE}
   append_constraint (co : CONSTRAINT) is
      require valid_constraint: co /= Void
      do
         append_graphic(co.first)
         append_graphic(co.second)
      end -- append_constraint
   append_graphic (g : GRAPHIC) is
      require valid_graphic: g /= Void
      local point : POINT
      do
         if not graphics.fast_has(g) then
            graphics.add_last(g)
            !!point.make(g.pos.x, g.pos.y)
            positions.add_last(point)
         end -- if
      ensure graphics.fast_has(g)
      end -- append_graphic
invariant
   graphics_initialized: graphics /= Void
   positions_initialized: positions /= Void
end -- CONSTRAINT_MEMENTO
```

We now illustrate how the Memento pattern relieves the CONSTRAINT_ SOLVER of the need to recompute its graphics positions when a command gets aborted. The MOVE_COMMAND is an example of the pattern Command (147):

```
class MOVE_COMMAND
inherit COMMAND
creation make
feature {ANY}
   make (target_graphic : GRAPHIC; delta : POINT; cs : CONSTRAINT_SOLVER) is
         -- Creation and initialization
      require target_graphic_not_void: target_graphic /= Void
      do
         target := target_graphic
         vector := delta
         constraint_solver := cs
      ensure
         target_not_void: target /= Void
         constraint_solver_not_void: constraint_solver /= Void
      end -- make
```

```
    execute is
            -- Make this command execute itself
        do
            print("Now moving...%N")
            -- First, save the CONSTRAINT_SOLVER state
            saved_state := constraint_solver.new_memento
            -- Actually move
            target.move(vector)
            -- And finally, solve the constraints
            constraint_solver.solve(target)
        end -- execute
    unexecute is
            -- Undo previous command execution
        do
            print("Undoing last move%N")
            constraint_solver.set_from_memento(saved_state) -- Restore to previous state
        end -- unexecute
feature {NONE}
    target : GRAPHIC
    vector : POINT
    saved_state : CONSTRAINT_MEMENTO
    constraint_solver : CONSTRAINT_SOLVER
        end -- MOVE_COMMAND
```

The objects managed are instances of the class GRAPHIC.

```
class GRAPHIC
creation make
feature {ANY}
    make is
            -- Creation and initialization
        do
            !!pos.make(0,0)
        end -- make
feature {ANY} -- Queries
    pos : POINT -- Current position
feature {ANY} -- Commands
    move (delta : POINT) is
            -- simulate a move specified by a vector
        require delta_not_void: delta /= Void
        do
            pos.translater(delta.x,delta.y)
        end -- move
```

```
move_to (new_pos : POINT) is
    -- simulate a move specified by a new position
    require new_pos_not_void: new_pos /= Void
    do
        pos.copy(new_pos)
    end -- move_to
print_position(name : STRING) is
    require name_not_void: name /= Void
    do
        print("Position of "); print(name)
        print(" is: x =  "); io.put_integer(pos.x)
        print(" y = "); io.put_integer(pos.y); io.put_new_line
    end -- print_position
end -- GRAPHIC
```

The CONSTRAINT we define between them remembers their reference and initial relative positions.

```
class CONSTRAINT
creation make
feature
    make (g1, g2 : GRAPHIC) is
        -- Creates a constraint between the two graphics
        require
            valid_origin: g1 /= Void
            valid_extremity: g2 /= Void
        do
            first := g1; second := g2
            dx := g2.pos.x - g1.pos.x; dy := g2.pos.y - g1.pos.y
        end -- make
feature {ANY} -- Queries
    first, second : GRAPHIC -- The two GRAPHICs linked by the constraint
    refers_to (g1, g2 : GRAPHIC) : BOOLEAN is
        -- is constraint between g1 and g2 ?
        do
            Result := (((g1 = first) and (g2 = second)) or
                        ((g2 = first) and (g1 = second)))
        end -- refers_to
    is_about (g1 : GRAPHIC) : BOOLEAN is
        -- is g1 part of this constraint ?
        do
            Result := ((g1 = first) or (g1 = second))
        end -- is_about
```

```
    satisfied : BOOLEAN is
            -- Whether the constraint is satisfied or not
        do
            Result := ((second.pos.x - first.pos.x) = dx)  and
                ((second.pos.y - first.pos.y) = dy)
        end -- satisfied
feature {ANY} -- Commands
    repairs_from (g1 : GRAPHIC) is
            -- move other part to satisfy constraint
        do
            if g1 = first then repair_from_origin else repair_from_end end -- if
        end -- repair_from
feature {NONE} -- Private
    repair_from_origin is
            -- move second to satisfy constraint
        local destination_point : POINT
        do
            !!destination_point.make(first.pos.x + dx, first.pos.y + dy)
            second.move_to(destination_point)
        end -- repair_from_origin
    repair_from_end is
            -- moves first to satisfy constraint
        local detination_point : POINT
        do
            !!detination_point.make(second.pos.x - dx, second.pos.y - dy)
            first.move(detination_point)
        end -- repair_from_end
    dx, dy : INTEGER
end -- CONSTRAINT
```

Constraints can be tested for satisfaction and asked for repairs to be performed, stating which part is supposed to be correct. To illustrate the whole example, we use the following simple driver class.

```
class MAIN
creation make
feature {ANY} -- Creation
    make is
        local
            cs : CONSTRAINT_SOLVER
            move : MOVE_COMMAND
            p0, p1 : POINT
        do
```

```
        !!t1.make; !!t2.make -- Make the graphics at 0,0
        !!p0.make(1,2); t2.move(p0) -- Move t2 to 1,2
        !!cs.make; cs.add_constraint(t1,t2) -- Set up the constraints
        !!p1.make(10,10) -- Initialize a moving vector
        !!move.make(t1,p1,cs) -- Make the MOVE command
        print("Position before moving%N"); print_position
        move.execute
        print("Position after moving%N"); print_position
        move.unexecute
        print("Position after undoing%N"); print_position
      end -- make
  feature {ANY} -- Queries
    t1, t2 : GRAPHIC
  feature {ANY} -- Commands
    print_position is
        -- Print position of both GRAPHICs
      do
        t1.print_position("t1"); t2.print_position("t2")
      end -- print_position
  end -- MAIN
```

If we compile and execute this class as the root of an Eiffel system, we get the following output:

```
Position before moving
Position of t1 is: x =  0 y = 0
Position of t2 is: x =  1 y = 2
Now moving...
Solving constraints
Position after moving
Position of t1 is: x =  10 y = 10
Position of t2 is: x =  11 y = 12
Undoing last move
Position after undoing
Position of t1 is: x =  0 y = 0
Position of t2 is: x =  1 y = 2
```

# Related Patterns

Command (147) can use Memento to maintain state for undoable operations. Mementos can also be used in an Iterator (159).

# Observer (GoF 293)        (Behavioral)

## Intent

Define a one-to-many dependency among objects so that when one object changes state, all of its dependents are notified and updated automatically.

## Also Known As

Dependents, Publish-Subscribe

## Structure

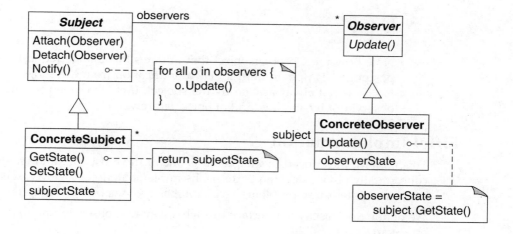

## Collaboration

- ConcreteSubject notifies its observers whenever a change occurs that could make its observers' state inconsistent with its own.

- After being informed of a change in the concrete subject, a ConcreteObserver object may query the subject for information. ConcreteObserver uses this information to reconcile its state with that of the subject.

  The following interaction diagram illustrates the collaborations between a subject and two observers.

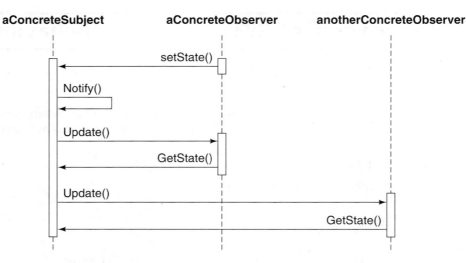

Note how the Observer object that initiates the change request postpones its update until it gets a notification from the subject. Notify is not always called by the subject. It can be called by an observer or by another kind of object entirely.

## Eiffel Implementation

This pattern, introduced in Chapter 1, is one of the most well-known and conceptually obvious design patterns. Its implementation, however, sets a number of interesting problems because it has a wide range of variants.

We define the OBSERVER interface in such a way that observing more than one SUBJECT is possible.

```
deferred class OBSERVER
feature
   update (s : SUBJECT) is
        -- update the observer's view on 's'
      require not_void: s /= Void
      deferred
      end -- update
end -- OBSERVER
```

Indeed, the parameter passed to *update* allows the OBSERVER to know which one of its various subjects did change. However, since often an OBSERVER observes only one SUBJECT, we provide a special case of OBSERVER, called

Mono_Observer, which records only one subject as an attribute and does not bother to look it up when *update* is called.

```
deferred class MONO_OBSERVER
inherit
  OBSERVER
      redefine update end;
feature -- Creation
  make (s : like subject) is
        -- Creation and initialization
      require s_not_void: s /= Void
      do
        subject := s
        subject.attach(Current)
      end -- make
feature {ANY} -- Queries
  subject : SUBJECT
feature {ANY} -- Commands
  update (s : like subject) is
        -- take actions because 's' did change state
      do
        check s_is_my_subject: s = subject end -- check
        update_observer
      end -- update
  update_observer is deferred end
      -- real action, no check needed on the subject identity
  detach is
        -- detach from its subject
      do
        subject.detach(Current)
        subject := Void
      end -- detach
invariant
  subject_observer: subject /= Void implies subject.is_attached_to(Current)
end -- MONO_OBSERVER
```

This Mono_Observer uses a subject attribute whose type should be (co-variantly) specialized in subclasses; see the class Analog_Clock later in this chapter.

A Subject has features to be attached to and detached from an Observer, as well as features for checking its attachment status. A Subject also provides an abstract definition of *notify*.

```
deferred class SUBJECT
feature -- Queries
   is_attached_to (o : OBSERVER) : BOOLEAN is
      -- Whether o belongs to the observers
      require o_not_void: o /= Void
      deferred
      end -- is_attached_to
feature -- Commands
   attach (o : OBSERVER) is
         -- add 'o' to the observers
      require
         o_not_void: o /= Void
         not_yet_attached: not is_attached_to(o)
      deferred
      ensure attached: is_attached_to(o)
      end -- attach
   detach (o : OBSERVER) is
         -- remove 'o' from the observers
      require o_not_void: o /= Void
      deferred
      ensure not_attached: not is_attached_to(o)
      end -- detach
   notify is
         -- Send an update message to each observer
      deferred
      end -- notify
end -- SUBJECT
```

SUBJECT has two implementations. The simpler one makes it store references to its observers; that is, the SUBJECT has a collection of OBSERVERS.

```
class AUTONOMOUS_SUBJECT
inherit
   SUBJECT
feature -- Queries
   is_attached_to (o : OBSERVER) : BOOLEAN is
      -- Whether o belongs to the observers
      do
         Result := observers.fast_has(o) -- identity comparison
      end -- is_attached_to
feature -- Commands
   attach (o : OBSERVER) is
```

```
              -- add 'o' to the observers
         do
              observers.add_last(o)
         end -- attach
    detach (o : OBSERVER) is
              -- remove 'o' from the observers
         do
              observers.remove(observers.fast_index_of(o))
         end -- detach
    notify is
              -- Send an update message to each observer
         local
              i : INTEGER
         do
              from i := observers.lower until i > observers.upper
              loop
                  observers.item(i).update(Current)
                  i := i + 1
              end -- loop
         end -- notify
feature {NONE} -- Private
    observers : COLLECTION[OBSERVER]
              -- the collection holding the observers. Can be instantiated
              -- with either make_array_of_observers or make_list_of_observers
    make_array_of_observers is
              -- Factory method to instanciate observers as an ARRAY
         do
              !ARRAY[OBSERVER]!observers.make(1,0)
         ensure observers_initialized: observers /= Void
         end -- make_array_of_observers
    make_list_of_observers is
              -- Factory method to instanciate observers as a LINKED_LIST
         do
              !LINKED_LIST[OBSERVER]!observers.make
         ensure observers_initialized: observers /= Void
         end -- make_list_of_observers
invariant
    observers_initialized: observers /= Void
end -- AUTONOMOUS_SUBJECT
```

Note that we use two Factory Methods to help concrete subclasses instantiate the collection as either an ARRAY or a LINKED_LIST, depending on its memory requirements and the dynamics of the OBSERVER attachment and detachment. Also, if the observers are capable of modifying the collection as it is iterated, it may be necessary to clone the collection before the actual notification takes place. (See the discussion on robust iterators in the Iterator (159) pattern.)

On the other hand, if the update semantics are more complex, it may be necessary to reify the relationship between SUBJECTS and OBSERVERS, that is, to transform the relationsip into a concrete object. Let us call this object a CHANGE_MANAGER. The responsibilities of a CHANGE_MANAGER are to

- Map a subject to its observers and provide an interface to maintain this mapping. Now neither the subjects nor the observers have to maintain references to each other.

- Define a particular update strategy. For example, if an operation involves changes to several interdependent subjects, the CHANGE_ MANAGER is able to make sure that the observers are notified only after all of the subjects have been modified, to avoid notifying observers more than once.

- Update all dependent observers at the request of a subject.

Let us call MANAGED_SUBJECT a subject making use of such a CHANGE_ MANAGER. Since a CHANGE_MANAGER is typically implemented as a Singleton (79), the MANAGED_SUBJECT is both a SUBJECT and a SINGLETON_ ACCESSOR.

```
deferred class MANAGED_SUBJECT
inherit
   SUBJECT
   SINGLETON_ACCESSOR
      rename singleton as change_manager redefine change_manager end;
feature -- Queries
   is_attached_to (o : OBSERVER) : BOOLEAN is
      -- Whether o belongs to the observers
      do
         Result := change_manager.is_registered(Current,o)
      end -- is_attached_to
feature -- Commands
   attach (o : OBSERVER) is
      -- add 'o' to the observers
      do
         change_manager.register(Current,o)
      end -- attach
   detach (o : OBSERVER) is
```

```
                    -- remove 'o' from the observers
            do
                change_manager.unregister(Current,o)
            end  -- detach
        notify is
                -- Send an update message to each observer
            do
                change_manager.notify(Current)
            end  -- notify
    feature {NONE} -- Private
        change_manager : CHANGE_MANAGER is
                -- Singleton instance of a CHANGE_MANAGER
            once
                !!Result.make
            end  -- change_manager
    invariant
        change_manager_initialized: change_manager /= Void
    end -- MANAGED_SUBJECT
```

## Sample Code

The following example uses this design pattern to implement the relationship between a CLOCK_TIMER and its (multiple) graphical representations. CLOCK_TIMER is a concrete SUBJECT for storing and maintaining the time of day.

```
class CLOCK_TIMER
inherit
    AUTONOMOUS_SUBJECT
creation make
feature -- Creation
    make (initial_time : INTEGER) is
            -- Creation and initialization with a time offset (in seconds)
        require positive_initial_time: initial_time >= 0
        do
            time := initial_time
            make_array_of_observers
        ensure
            time_initialized: initial_time\\86400 = 3600*hour + 60*minute + second
        end  -- make
feature {ANY} -- Queries
    hour : INTEGER is
            -- the current hour
```

```
        do
            Result := (time//3600)\\24
        end -- hour
    minute : INTEGER is
            -- the current minute
        do
            Result := (time//60)\\60
        end -- minute
    second : INTEGER is
            -- the current second
        do
            Result := time\\60
        end -- second
feature {ANY} -- Commands
    tick is
            -- Called by the internal timer to provide an accurate time base
            -- Call 'notify' to inform observers of the change
        do
            time := time + tick_interval; notify
        end -- tick
feature {NONE} -- Private
    time : INTEGER -- Elapsed time since initialization, in seconds
    tick_interval : INTEGER is 5 -- Number of seconds between ticks
invariant
    correct_time: time\\86400 = 3600*hour + 60*minute + second
end -- CLOCK_TIMER
```

Now we can define classes such as ANALOG_CLOCK or DIGITAL_CLOCK to graphically display the time.

```
class ANALOG_CLOCK
inherit
    MONO_OBSERVER
        rename update_observer as draw redefine subject end;
creation make -- Inherited, with its signature automatically redefined (co-variantly)
feature {ANY} -- Commands
    draw is
            -- Draw the clock according to the new status of subject
        do
            io.put_string("Analog display of: ")
            io.put_integer(subject.hour); io.put_character(':')
            io.put_integer(subject.minute); io.put_character(':')
            io.put_integer(subject.second); io.put_new_line
```

```
       end -- draw
feature {ANY} -- Queries
    subject : CLOCK_TIMER
end -- ANALOG_CLOCK
```

```
class DIGITAL_CLOCK
inherit
   MONO_OBSERVER
      rename update_observer as draw redefine subject end;
creation make -- Inherited, with its signature automatically redefined (co-variantly)
feature {ANY} -- Commands
   draw is
         -- Draw the clock according to the new status of subject
      do
         io.put_string("Digital display of: ")
         io.put_integer(subject.hour); io.put_character(':')
         io.put_integer(subject.minute); io.put_character(':')
         io.put_integer(subject.second); io.put_new_line
      end -- draw
feature {ANY} -- Queries
   subject : CLOCK_TIMER
end -- DIGITAL_CLOCK
```

The following class MAIN can then be used as a root class to exercise our example.

```
class MAIN
creation
   make
feature -- Creation
   make is
         -- Creation and initialization
      local
         clock_timer : CLOCK_TIMER
         analog_clock : ANALOG_CLOCK
         digital_clock : DIGITAL_CLOCK
         i : INTEGER
      do
         !!clock_timer.make(33333)
         !!analog_clock.make(clock_timer)
         !!digital_clock.make(clock_timer)
```

```
        from i := 1 until i > 3
        loop
          clock_timer.tick  -- Make the clock_timer tick
          i := i + 1
        end -- loop
      end -- make
end -- MAIN
```

If we compile and execute this class as the root of an Eiffel system, we get the following output:

```
Analog display of: 9:15:38
Digital display of: 9:15:38
Analog display of: 9:15:43
Digital display of: 9:15:43
Analog display of: 9:15:48
Digital display of: 9:15:48
```

Another example of this class is provided by Ted Velkoff (velkoff@erols. com), who implemented the Observer design pattern as a library of reusable components in Eiffel. This library was developed by using ISE Eiffel 4.0, Professional Edition for Windows 95, with backend C compilation performed by Microsoft Visual C++ 4.0. The library is available at http://www. eiffel-forum.org/archive/velkoff/index.htm.

## Related Patterns

By encapsulating complex update semantics, the CHANGE_MANAGER acts as a Mediator (167) between subjects and observers. The CHANGE_MANAGER may use the Singleton (79) pattern to make it unique and globally accessible.

# State (GoF 305)                    (Behavioral)

## Intent

Allow an object to alter its behavior when its internal state changes. The object will appear to change its class.

## Structure

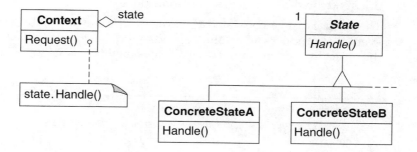

## Collaboration

- Context delegates state-specific requests to the current ConcreteState object.

- A context may pass itself as an argument to the State object handling the request. This lets the State object access the context if necessary.

- Context is the primary interface for clients. Clients can configure a context with State objects. Once a context is configured, its clients don't have to deal with the State objects directly.

- Either Context or the ConcreteState subclasses can decide which state succeeds another and under what circumstances.

## Eiffel Implementation

During analysis, some objects appear to behave differently, depending on their states. This is particularly true when it comes to communication protocols with external objects. The situation also arises with objects whose life cycles are split into well-delineated phases. UML analysis method even recommends drawing statechart diagrams to make explicit the state-dependent behavior of relevant objects (see Section 1.2.2).

As long as the current state of an object does not alter the way it responds to external stimuli, it is not worth doing more than registering its state as a set of attributes. In the other cases, we have to model the automaton defined by the object life cycle. Simply stated, this is a two-dimensional array representing an application from a set of pairs *(event,state)* to the set of states. A state could be defined as a set of values assigned to the internal data stored in the object. However, as our only stated concern is the modification of behavior, let us define a state as a complete set of responses to the stimuli an object may receive. As for event, we make the assumption that it can be modeled as a method call. If we consider the object interface, some routines induce state changes, whereas others do not; some behave differently in different states, and some do not.

The general case can be stated as follows: A routine call can be viewed as an event that produces an action, depending on the current state and leaving the object in another state. This leads to something of the following form.

```
myroutine is
        -- The engine that makes the automaton move between states
    do
        if  state = s1 then
            if condition1 then
                state := s1.t1; do_action1 -- Change state and do an action
            else
                state := s1.t2; do_action2 -- Change state and do an action
            end -- if
        elseif state = s2 then
            if condition2 then
                state := s2.t1; do_action3 -- Change state and do an action
            else
                state := s2.t2; do_action4 -- Change state and do an action
            end -- if
        end   -- if
    end -- myroutine
```

This seems simple to write but tends to lead to code that would be difficult to maintain. The behavior corresponding to a given state, as well as the chain of states, are scattered among the various methods. Adding or modifying a state requires modifying a lot of code and checking consistency all over the code. Locality of modification is lost. This is usually a sign of a bad design: The various aspects of the one thing have not been identified and gathered together.

Getting back to our automaton model, we notice that we have a double dispatch problem: the transition to be fired—the method to be called—depends on both the states and the events. One solution uses polymorphism to implement one of these dispatches. The idea of the State pattern is to reify the notion of *state* and to dynamically choose the method to call according to the state's dynamic type, using dynamic binding.

Let C be a class and *m1, m2, . . . , mk* the methods it uses to handle the events *e1, e2, . . . , ek* it may receive. This is very close to the analysis model. Now we will derive the solution as follows. Objects of class C will forward event handling to a delegate whose abstract interface is defined by the class C_STATE. A subclass of C_STATE will be defined for each possible state of C. The interface of C_STATE will provide one routine for each event to handle, these routines being redefined in its subclasses. The code for the routine *m1* of class C then becomes the following.

```
m1 is
      -- Handle the occurrence of an event e1
   do
      state.m1  -- Delegate to state: The action is state dependent
   end  -- m1
```

The routine *m1* from the relevant C_STATE subclass then usually calls back on C to execute the action associated with this transition and to change C's current state. C_STATE thus needs to have privileged access to C, easily implemented in Eiffel by using restricted exportation clauses.

## Sample Code

In our code example, MAILER defines a public interface for sending and receiving user messages, such as e-mail, regardless of its connection status with the network. When the network connection is available, the messages are simply forwarded to it. If it is disconnected, outgoing messages are buffered in the mailer for subsequent transmission when the network connection is restored (see the following State diagram). MAILER defines two other interfaces: one for external service implementation, whose access is restricted to NETWORK objects; and the other one for state management, whose access is restricted to MAILER_STATE objects. Thus, external and internal aspects of the MAILER class are clearly delineated.

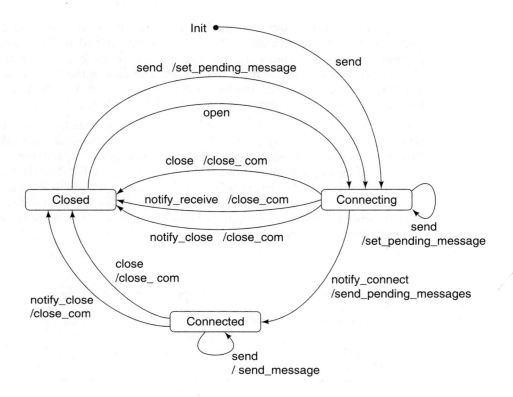

---

```
class MAILER
creation make
feature {ANY} -- Creation
    make is
            -- Creation and Initialization
        do
            -- Creates incoming and outgoing message queues
            !!incoming_queue.make; !!pending_queue.make
            -- Create the 3 possible states of a Mailer
            !!connecting.make(Current); !!connected.make(Current);
                                        !!closed.make(Current)
            -- The initial state is 'closed'
            state := closed
        end -- make
feature {ANY} -- Public Queries
    last_message : STRING -- Last message received
feature {ANY} -- Public Commands
    send (m : STRING) is
            -- try to forward the message 'm' to the network
```

```
        require valid_message: m /= Void
        do
            print("Trying to send the message: ")
            io.put_string(m); io.put_new_line
            state.send(m)
        end -- send
    receive_next_message is
            -- Try to get an incoming message
        do
            io.put_string("Trying to receive a message%N")
            if incoming_queue.empty then
                last_message := Void
            else
                last_message := incoming_queue.first
                incoming_queue.remove_first
            end -- if
        end -- receive_next_message
    open is
            -- try to open a network connection
        do
            state.open
        end -- open
    close is
            -- try to close the network connection
        do
            state.close
        end -- close
feature {NETWORK} -- Only a NETWORK object may call these features
    notify_connect is
            -- connection is open
        do
            io.put_string("Connection is opened%N")
            state.notify_connect
        end -- notify_connect
    notify_close is
            -- connection has been closed
        do
            io.put_string("Connection is closed%N")
            state.notify_close
        end -- notify_close
    notify_received is
            -- a message just arrived
        do
            io.put_string("a message has been received%N")
            state.notify_receive
```

```
        end -- notify_receive
feature {MAILER_STATE} -- Queries restricted to Mailer_State objects
    connecting : CONNECTING -- A Mailer_State
    connected : CONNECTED -- Another Mailer_State
    closed : CLOSED -- A third Mailer_State
    pending_message : STRING -- head of the pending_queue
    incoming_message : STRING -- head of the incoming_queue
feature {MAILER_STATE} -- Features that are called back by Mailer_State objects
    set_state(s : MAILER_STATE) is
            -- select next state
        require valid_state: s /= Void
        do
            state := s; s.init_state
        end -- set_state
    set_pending_message(m : STRING) is
            -- register a message to send
        require valid_message: m /= Void
        do
            pending_queue.add_last(m)
        end -- set_pending_message
    get_next_pending_message is
            -- extract a message from sending queue and put it in pending_message
        do
            if pending_queue.empty then
                pending_message := Void
            else
                pending_message := pending_queue.first
                pending_queue.remove_first
            end -- if
        end -- get_next_pending_message
    set_incoming_message(m : STRING) is
            -- register a message to send
        require valid_message: m /= Void
        do
            incoming_queue.add_last(m)
        end -- set_incoming_message
    get_next_incoming_message is
            -- extract a message from sending queue and put it in incoming_message
        require has_incoming_message: not incoming_queue.empty
        do
            incoming_message := incoming_queue.first
            incoming_queue.remove_first
        end -- get_next_incoming_message
feature {NONE}
```

```
    state : MAILER_STATE
    pending_queue : LINKED_LIST[STRING]
    incoming_queue : LINKED_LIST[STRING]
invariant
    valid_state: state /= Void
end  -- MAILER
```

The role of MAILER_STATE is simply to define the common interface to specific MAILER states and to permit them to register their client.

```
deferred class MAILER_STATE
feature {MAILER} -- Commands for Mailer usage only
    make (m : MAILER) is
        require m_not_void: m /= Void
        do
            mailer := m
        end -- make
    send (message : STRING) is
        require message_not_void: message /= Void
        deferred
        end -- send
    open is deferred end
    close is deferred end
    init_state is deferred end
    notify_connect is deferred end
    notify_close is deferred  end
    notify_received is deferred  end
feature {NONE}
    mailer : MAILER
invariant
    mailer_not_void: mailer /= Void
end -- MAILER_STATE
```

We use CONNECTED to illustrate a specific state implementation.

```
class CONNECTED
inherit
    MAILER_STATE
creation make
feature {ANY}
    send (message : STRING) is
        do
```

```
            print("Effective send while connected%N")
            send_message(message)
         end -- send
      open is
         do
            print("Already open%N")
         end -- open
      close is
         do
            print("Trying to close while open: closing%N")
            mailer.set_state(mailer.closed)
         end -- close
      init_state is
            -- send pending messages
         do
            print("Initializing connected state: sending pending messages%N")
            from mailer.get_next_pending_message until mailer.pending_message = Void
            loop
               send_message(mailer.pending_message)
               mailer.get_next_pending_message
            end -- loop
         end -- init_state
      notify_connect is
         do
            print("Connect notification received while connected%N")
         end -- notify_connect
      notify_close is
         do
            print("Reception of close while open: closing%N")
            mailer.set_state(mailer.closed)
         end -- notify_close
      notify_received is
         do
            print("Reception of a message while open %N")
            mailer.set_incoming_message("A brand new message")
         end -- notify_received
   feature {NONE}
      send_message (m : STRING) is
         require valid_message: m /= Void
         do
            print("Sending message "); print(m); io.put_new_line
         end -- send_message
end -- CONNECTED
```

Connecting and Close are very similar in structure to Connected. They differ only as the state diagram suggests.

In the following example, the class Main simulates a user sending and receiving messages through a mailer over a network. A Network is used to emulate peer notifications.

```
class MAIN
creation make
feature {ANY}
   make is
       -- Creation and initialization
      do
          !!net.make;   !!mailer.make(net)
          simulate_a_session
      end -- make
feature {NONE}
   mailer : MAILER
   net : NETWORK
   simulate_a_session is
          -- issues various commands to the mailer and the network
          -- to simulate a session
      do
          mailer.send("Hello world") -- Sending while the mailer is not connected
          net.notify_connect
          mailer.receive_next_message
          if mailer.last_message /= Void then
             print("Reception of : "); print(mailer.last_message); io.put_new_line
          else
             print("Sorry, no message for you%N")
          end -- if
          mailer.send("Second message") -- Sending while the mailer is connected
          mailer.close
      end -- simulate_a_session
invariant
   mailer_not_void: mailer /= Void
   net_not_void: net /= Void
end -- MAIN
```

If we compile and execute this class as the root of an Eiffel system, we get the following output:

```
Trying to send the message: Hello world
Trying to send while closed: connecting
```

```
Initializing connection
Waiting for connection
Connection is opened
Connect notification while connecting: opened
Initializing connected state: sending pending messages
Sending message Hello world
Trying to receive a message
Sorry, no message for you
Trying to send the message: Second message
Effective send while connected
Sending message Second message
Trying to close while open: closing
Initializing closed: closing
Closing  connection
```

## Alternative Implementation

Returning to the earlier discussion of double dispatch, we could have used MESSAGE instead of STATE as the first dispatch, redefining a *receive* method in each MESSAGE subclass. Doing so can be interesting when messages are not closely related to actions; the drawback is that manual coding of the dispatch is required.

To go one step further, we could dispatch on both messages and states, redefining the *receive* method in each STATE. It is possible be even more flexible while relieving the need for many specific classes. But first, let us go back to the automaton, the abstract model of our design. Instead of abstracting application specifics and trying to plug an automaton into an object, let us try to abstract the automaton and plug in the object-specific parts.

We make concrete classes out of automaton, state, transition, guard, and actions. The AUTOMATON defines the set of possible states, and a new class, SESSION, records the current state of one execution of our automaton. Each state records the set of possible outgoing transitions, which in turn record their associated guard, target state, and action. To describe our application using this model, we just need to

- Map the behavior of our class to the state graph
- Use the pattern Command (147) to expose the necessary routines of the object as *actions* or *guards*

In this alternative implementation, the class STATE is turned into a concrete class.

```
class STATE
creation make
feature {ANY} -- Creation
   make (a_name : STRING) is
         -- initialize state with a name
      require valid_name: a_name /= Void
      do
         !!transitions.make
         name := a_name
      end -- make
feature {ANY} -- Public Queries
   name : STRING
   fireable (mess : STRING; a_session : SESSION) : LINKED_LIST[TRANSITION] is
         -- returns list of fireable transitions
      require valid_message: mess /= Void
      local
         trans : TRANSITION
         i : INTEGER
      do
         !!Result.make
         from i := transitions.lower until i > transitions.upper
         loop
            trans := transitions.item(i)
            print("    State: testing transition # "); io.put_integer(i)
            print(" with mess =  "); print(trans.trigger); io.put_new_line
            if trans.trigger.is_equal(mess) and then trans.passes(a_session) then
               Result.add_last(trans)
            end -- if
            i := i + 1
         end -- loop
      end -- fireable
feature {ANY} -- Public Commands
   add_transition (tr : TRANSITION) is
         -- add a new transition from this state
      require valid_transition: tr /= Void
      do
         transitions.add_last(tr)
      end -- add_transition
feature {NONE}
   transitions : LINKED_LIST[TRANSITION]
end -- STATE
```

An object is attached to a SESSION, which registers the current state. States are linked through TRANSITIONS to which actions and guards get attached. This makes it easier to observe and to allow for runtime behavior modification.

```eiffel
class SESSION
creation make
feature {ANY} -- Creation
   make (st : STATE) is
        -- Creation and Initialization
      require
        valid_initial_state: st /= Void
      do
        current_state := st
      end -- make
feature {ANY} -- Public Queries: the execution context
   current_state : STATE
feature {ANY} -- Public Commands
   fire (mess : STRING) is
        -- fires the transition triggered by mess
      require
        valid_message : mess /= Void
      local
        possible_transitions : LINKED_LIST[TRANSITION]
        selected_transition : TRANSITION
      do
        print("Reception of "); print(mess)
        print(" for state: "); print(current_state.name); io.put_new_line
        possible_transitions := current_state.fireable(mess,Current)
        print(" Possible transitions: ")
        io.put_integer(possible_transitions.count); io.put_new_line
        if possible_transitions.count > 0 then
           selected_transition := select_transition(possible_transitions)
           if (selected_transition /= Void) then
              print("triggering actions and moving to state: ")
              io.put_string(selected_transition.next.name); io.put_new_line
              current_state := selected_transition.next
              selected_transition.fire(Current)
           end -- if
        end -- if
      end -- fire
feature {NONE} -- internal routines
```

```
select_transition (possible : LINKED_LIST[TRANSITION]) : TRANSITION is
        -- select one of the fireable transitions
    do
        Result := possible.first -- here simply take the first one
    end -- select_transition
invariant
    current_state_defined: current_state /= Void
end -- SESSION
```

TRANSITION plays a major role in the automaton machinery. First, it provides services for adding guards and actions. Second, it deals with message management, deciding whether the transition is fireable, by examining the guards. If all guards pass, it fires all registered actions in sequence.

```
class TRANSITION
creation make
feature {ANY} -- Creation
    make (m : STRING; next_state : STATE) is
            -- Creation and Initialization
        require next_state_not_void: next_state /= Void
        do
            next := next_state; trigger := m
            !!actions.make; !!guards.make
        ensure
            has_next: next = next_state
            has_trigger: trigger = m
        end -- make
feature {ANY} -- Public Queries
    next : STATE
    trigger : STRING
    actions : LINKED_LIST[ACTION]
    guards : LINKED_LIST[GUARD]
feature {ANY} -- Public Commands
    add_guard (g : GUARD) is
        require valid_guard: g /= Void
        do
            guards.add_last(g)
        end -- add_guard
    remove_guard (g : GUARD) is
        require valid_guard: g /= Void
        do
            guards.remove(g)
```

```
      end -- remove_guard
  add_action (a : ACTION) is
    require valid_action: a /= Void
    do
      actions.add_last(a)
    end -- add_action
  remove_action (a : ACTION) is
    require valid_action: a /= Void
    do
      actions.remove(a)
    end -- remove_action
  fire (a_session : SESSION) is
      -- Execute the set of actions associated with this transition
    local
      index : INTEGER
    do
      from index := actions.lower until index > actions.upper
      loop
        actions.item(index).execute(a_session)
        index := index + 1
      end -- loop
    end -- fire
  passes (a_session : SESSION) : BOOLEAN is
      -- Whether all guards are evaluated to True
    local
      index : INTEGER
    do
      print("Testing transition guards%N")
      from Result := True; index := guards.lower
      until not Result  or index > guards.upper
      loop
        Result := Result and guards.item(index).passes(a_session)
        index := index + 1
      end -- loop
      print("Result = "); io.put_boolean(Result); io.put_new_line
    end -- passes
end -- TRANSITION
```

We use the MAILER example again to illustrate this second approach. Instead of being hard-coded, the automaton is now described within the class MAILER. The public interface is the same as in the previous example. The main difference lies in the *configure_automaton* routine.

```
class MAILER
inherit NETWORK_CLIENT
creation make
feature {ANY} -- Creation
   make (net : NETWORK) is
         -- Creation and Initialization
      require
         valid_network : net /= Void
      do
         -- Creates incoming and outgoing message queues
         !!incoming_queue.make; !!pending_queue.make
         !!com.make(net,Current); !!session.make(configure_automaton)
      end -- make
feature {ANY} -- Public Queries
   last_message : STRING -- Last message received
feature {ANY} -- Public Commands
   send (m : STRING) is
         -- try to forward the message 'm' to the network
      require valid_message: m /= Void
      do
         pending_queue.add_last(m); session.fire("send")
      end -- send
   receive_next_message is
         -- Try to get an incoming message
      do
         if incoming_queue.empty then
            last_message := Void
            session.fire("receive")
         else
            last_message := incoming_queue.first
            incoming_queue.remove_first
         end -- if
      end -- receive_next_message
   open is do session.fire("open") end -- open
   close is do session.fire("close") end -- close
   com : CONNECTION
feature {NETWORK} -- Only a NETWORK object may call these features
   notify_connect is do session.fire("notify_connect") end -- notify_connect
   notify_close is do session.fire("notify_close") end -- notify_close
feature {ACTION}
   pending_queue : LINKED_LIST[STRING]
   incoming_queue : LINKED_LIST[STRING]
feature {NONE}
   session : SESSION
```

```
configure_automaton : STATE is
    -- Configure the states, guards, and transitions of the automaton
    local
        idle_state, connecting, connected, closed : STATE
        flush : FLUSH_ACTION
        read : READ_ACTION
        open_net : OPEN_ACTION
        query_open : QUERY_OPEN
        close_net : CLOSE_ACTION
        query_close : QUERY_CLOSE
        tr1, tr2, tr3, tr4, tr5, tr6, tr7, tr8 : TRANSITION
    do
        -- first create the states
        !!idle_state.make("idle"); !!connecting.make("connecting")
        !!connected.make("connected")
        -- selection of initial state
        Result := idle_state
        -- Then create the actions
        !!flush.make(Current); !!read.make(Current)
        !!open_net.make(Current); !!close_net.make(Current)
        !!query_open.make(Current); !!query_close.make(Current)
        -- And finally create transitions
        -- NB: transitions to current state without action are declared only for clarity
        -- Transitions starting from the state: idle_state
        !!tr1.make("send",idle_state); idle_state.add_transition(tr1)
        tr1.add_action(query_open)
        !!tr2.make("receive",idle_state); idle_state.add_transition(tr2)
        tr2.add_action(query_open)
        !!tr3.make("open",connecting); idle_state.add_transition(tr3)
        tr3.add_action(open_net)
        -- Transitions starting from the state: connecting
        !!tr4.make("notify_connect",connected)
        tr4.add_action(flush); connecting.add_transition(tr4)
        -- Transitions starting from the state: connected
        !!tr5.make("send",connected); tr5.add_action(flush)
        connected.add_transition(tr5)
        !!tr6.make("receive",connected)
        tr6.add_action(read); connected.add_transition(tr6)
        !!tr7.make("notify_close",idle_state); connected.add_transition(tr7)
        !!tr8.make("close",idle_state); connected.add_transition(tr8)
        tr8.add_action(close_net)
    end -- configure_automaton
end -- MAILER
```

Let us take a look at the OPEN_ACTION as an example of an action that strictly follows the Command (147) pattern.

```
class OPEN_ACTION
inherit ACTION
creation make
feature {ANY} -- Creation
   make (m : MAILER) is
         -- Creation and Initialization
      do
         mailer := m
      end -- make
   execute (a_session : SESSION) is
         -- execute an 'open' action
      do
         mailer.com.open
      end -- execute
feature {NONE}
   mailer : MAILER
end -- OPEN_ACTION
```

## Related Patterns

State objects can be shared by using the Flyweight (121) pattern. State objects are often Singleton (79). They are also often associated with Command (147).

# Strategy (GoF 315)                    (Behavioral)

## Intent

Define a family of algorithms, encapsulate each one, and make them interchangeable. Strategy lets the algorithm vary independently from clients that use it.

## Structure

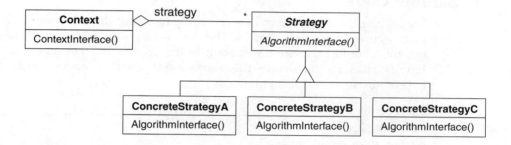

## Collaboration

- Strategy and Context interact to implement the chosen algorithm. A context may pass all data required by the algorithm to the strategy when the algorithm is called. Alternatively, the context can pass itself as an argument to Strategy operations. That lets the strategy call back on the context as required.

- A context forwards requests from its clients to its strategy. Clients usually create and pass a ConcreteStrategy object to the context; thereafter, clients interact with the context exclusively. There is often a family of ConcreteStrategy classes for a client to choose from.

## Eiffel Implementation

The idea behind the Strategy pattern is that instead of using conditional statements to choose among various implementations of a given service, we take the action out of the object and construct a class from it. Strategy has the same structure as the pattern State (197). But whereas State deals with an object's life cycle, Strategy focuses more on configuration. The choice among the various possible actions does not depend on the object itself but on the context in which it is used.

Good indications for the appropriate use of Strategy are algorithms whose form varies according to external object state. Another sign is classes whose only difference lies in the way they provide a given service. Breaking intuitive object boundaries should not result from the designer's mood. Strategy expresses the dual nature of the particular service.

Defining the proper level of interface to the algorithm is central in using Strategy well. The interface definition should be kept at a sufficiently high level of abstraction to allow multiple implementations. The effective implementation of the algorithm may require additional information. In this case, it will require privileged access to the class.

## Sample Code

We use the Strategy pattern here to enable us to use the same interface to print figures on various devices. The device may vary from time to time, but this should be made transparent to the application that manipulates figures. Thus, FIGURE defines the interface and relies on DEVICE subclasses to provide correct implementations.

```
class FIGURE
creation make_default, make
feature {ANY} -- Creation
  make_default is
       -- build a default square
    do
       !!points.make
       points.add_last(new_point(1,1))
       points.add_last(new_point(1,5))
       points.add_last(new_point(5,1))
       points.add_last(new_point(5,5))
    end -- make_default
  make (pts : COLLECTION[POINT]) is
       -- make figure from COLLECTION of points
    require pts_not_void: pts /= Void
    local index : INTEGER
    do
       !!points.make
       from index := pts.lower until index > pts.upper
       loop
         points.add_last(pts.item(index))
         index := index + 1
       end -- loop
    end -- make
```

```
feature {ANY} -- Queries
   device : DEVICE -- Where the figure must be drawn
feature {ANY} -- Commands
   set_device (d : DEVICE) is
         -- define current figure device
      require device_not_void : d /= Void
      do
         device := d
      ensure
         device = d
      end -- set_device
   move (dx, dy : INTEGER) is
         -- translate coordinates from vector
      local index : INTEGER
      do
         from index := points.lower
         until index > points.upper
         loop
            points.item(index).move(dx,dy)
            index := index + 1
         end -- loop
      end -- move
   draw is
         -- produce output suitable to describe figure to current device
      require device_set: device /= Void
      local
         index : INTEGER
         p : POINT
      do
         if points.count > 1 then
            p := points.item(points.lower)
            from index := points.lower + 1
            until index > points.upper
            loop
               device.draw_line(p,points.item(index))
               p := points.item(index)
               index := index + 1
            end -- loop
            device.draw_line(p,points.item(points.lower))
         elseif points.count = 1 then
            device.draw_point(points.item(points.lower))
         end -- if
      end -- draw
feature {NONE} -- Private
```

```
new_point (x,y : INTEGER) : POINT is
    -- Factory method to create a new POINT
  do
    !!Result.make(x,y)
  ensure created: Result /= Void
  end -- new_point
points : LINKED_LIST[POINT]
invariant
  initialized : points /= Void
end -- FIGURE
```

The class Device defines an interface for drawing a point and a line and for moving.

```
deferred class DEVICE
feature {ANY}
  move_to (x,y : INTEGER) is
      -- set current position
    deferred
    end -- move_to
  draw_line (p1, p2 : POINT) is
      -- emit commands to draw a line from p1 to p2
    deferred
    end -- draw_line
  draw_point (p1 : POINT) is
      -- emit commands to draw a point
    deferred
    end -- draw_point
end -- DEVICE
```

We define two concrete subclasses. The first emulates a PostScript device.

```
class PRINTING_DEVICE
inherit
  DEVICE
feature {ANY} -- Commands
  move_to (x,y : INTEGER) is
    do
      io.put_integer(x); io.put_character(' '); io.put_integer(y)
      io.put_string(" move%N")
    end -- move_to
  draw_line (p1, p2 : POINT) is
```

```
        do
            io.put_integer(p1.x); io.put_character(' '); io.put_integer(p1.y)
            io.put_character(' ')
            io.put_integer(p2.x); io.put_character(' '); io.put_integer(p2.y)
            io.put_string(" stroke%N")
        end  -- draw_line
    draw_point (p1 : POINT) is
        do
            io.put_integer(p1.x); io.put_character(' '); io.put_integer(p1.y)
            io.put_string(" stroke%N")
        end  -- draw_point
end  -- PRINTING_DEVICE
```

The second subclass emits traces to simulate graphical device interaction.

```
class DRAWING_DEVICE
inherit
    DEVICE
feature {ANY}  -- Commands
    move_to (x,y : INTEGER) is
        do
            io.put_string("Moving to ")
            io.put_integer(x); io.put_character(' '); io.put_integer(y)
            io.put_new_line
        end  -- move_to
    draw_line (p1, p2 : POINT) is
        do
            io.put_string("Drawing a line from ")
            io.put_integer(p1.x); io.put_character(' '); io.put_integer(p1.y)
            io.put_string(" to ")
            io.put_integer(p2.x); io.put_character(' '); io.put_integer(p2.y)
            io.put_new_line
        end  -- draw_line
    draw_point (p1 : POINT) is
        do
            io.put_string("Drawing a point at ")
            io.put_integer(p1.x); io.put_character(' '); io.put_integer(p1.y)
            io.put_new_line
        end  -- draw_point
end  -- DRAWING_DEVICE
```

Choosing between the two strategies can be exercised as follows.

```
class MAIN
creation make
feature {ANY}
  make is
    local
      printer : PRINTING_DEVICE
      display : DRAWING_DEVICE
      figure : FIGURE
    do
      !!printer; !!display
      !!figure.make_default -- Make it a square
      figure.set_device(display); figure.draw -- Draw it on the Display
      figure.move(3,5); figure.draw -- Move it and redraw it
      figure.set_device(printer); figure.draw -- Now print it
    end -- make
end -- MAIN
```

If we compile and execute this class as the root of an Eiffel system, we get the following output:

```
Drawing a line from 1 1 to 1 5
Drawing a line from 1 5 to 5 1
Drawing a line from 5 1 to 5 5
Drawing a line from 5 5 to 1 1
Drawing a line from 4 6 to 4 10
Drawing a line from 4 10 to 8 6
Drawing a line from 8 6 to 8 10
Drawing a line from 8 10 to 4 6
4 6 4 10 stroke
4 10 8 6 stroke
8 6 8 10 stroke
8 10 4 6 stroke
```

## Related Patterns

Strategy objects often make good Flyweights (121).

# Template Method (GoF 325)    (Behavioral)

## Intent

Define the skeleton of an algorithm in an operation, deferring some steps to subclasses. Template Method lets subclasses redefine certain steps of an algorithm without changing the algorithm's structure.

## Structure

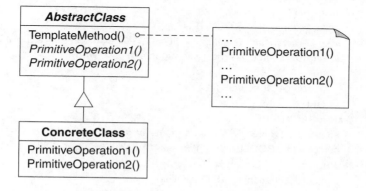

## Collaboration

- ConcreteClass relies on AbstractClass to implement the invariant steps of the algorithm.

## Eiffel Implementation

Very often, a subclass needs to redefine only some aspects of a service provided by its superclass. Instead of rewriting all of the code in each subclass, it is common to split the initial implementation into various subparts that can be easily customized by heirs.

In complex environments, general services available from a collection of classes must respect a predefined call sequence. The best way to guarantee a proper call sequence is to define it in an abstract class through the use of the Template Method. This pattern describes the general strategy for solving a problem, leaving the tactical steps to be customized in ad hoc subclasses. In Eiffel, the responsibilities of the tactical steps should be specified by using Design by Contract. Because a contract associated with a routine—pre- and post-conditions—must be respected even if the routine is redefined (that is, the contract is inherited), we can constrain the semantics of the various tactical steps in the Template Method.

## Sample Code

We consider a simple example of a software installation problem. In an abstract class SOFTWARE, the feature *install* defines the sequence of actions needed to achieve correct installation of a software system independent of the low-level details of these actions.

```
deferred class SOFTWARE
feature {ANY} -- Creation (useful for concrete subclasses)
  make (source_file: STRING) is
        -- Create and initialize the SOFTWARE with the 'source_file' archive
     require source_file_not_void: source_file /= Void
     do
        source := source_file
     end -- make
feature {ANY} -- Queries
  source : STRING -- Where the source of the software is stored
  completed : BOOLEAN -- Whether the install was successful
feature {ANY} -- Commands
  install (destination_dir: STRING) is
     -- Template Method for installing a SOFTWARE
     require destination_dir_not_void: destination_dir /= Void
     do
        print("Starting generic software installation.%N")
        completed := False
        if not is_valid(source) then
           io.put_string(source); print(": invalid source file%N")
        else
           prepare_directory(destination_dir)
           if completed then
             install_files(source,destination_dir)
             if completed then
                build(destination_dir)
                if completed then
                   print("Software installation completed.%N")
                end -- if
             end -- if
           end -- if
        end -- if
     end -- install
```

```
      run (command_name : STRING) is
              -- run this software under the name 'command_name'
          require installation_completed: completed
          deferred
          end -- run
  feature {NONE} -- Hooks for customizing the 'install' Template Method
      is_valid (filename : STRING) : BOOLEAN is
              -- Whether file whose name is 'filename' is valid
          require filename_not_void: filename /= Void
          deferred
          end -- is_valid
      prepare_directory (directory : STRING) is
              -- check for directory existence, creating it if needed
          require directory_not_void: directory /= Void
          deferred
          ensure ready_directory: completed implies is_valid(directory)
          end -- prepare_directory
      install_files(source_file, destination_dir: STRING) is
              -- Unpack the source into the destination_dir
          require
              valid_source_file: is_valid(source_file)
              valid_destination_dir: is_valid(destination_dir)
          deferred
          end -- install_files
      build (destination_dir : STRING) is
              -- Finish the installation by calling whatever command is appropriate
          require
              valid_destination_dir: is_valid(destination_dir)
          deferred
          end -- build
  end -- SOFTWARE
```

A specific subclass can fill in the detail—for example, installing software onto a UNIX computer in a standard way by providing concrete implementations for the features *is_valid*, *prepare_directory*, *install_files*, and *build*, as follows.

```
class UNIXSOFT
inherit SOFTWARE
creation make
feature {ANY} -- Commands
  run (command_name : STRING) is
          -- run this software under the name command_name
```

```
        do
            print("Running "); print(command_name); io.put_new_line
        end -- run
feature {NONE} -- Queries
    is_valid (filename : STRING) : BOOLEAN is
            -- Whether file whose name is 'filename' can be read
        do
            Result := file_exists(filename)
        end -- is_readable
    prepare_directory (directory : STRING) is
            -- check for directory existence, creating it if needed
        do
            if is_valid(directory) then
                completed := True
                print("Directory "); print(directory);
                print(" already existing. Reusing it.%N")
            else
                print("Creating destination directory "); print(directory)
                launch_system_command(<<"mkdir ",directory>>)
                get_last_system_command_status
                if completed then
                    print("Done.%N")
                else
                    print("Failed.%N")
                end -- if
            end -- if
        end -- prepare_directory
    install_files(source_file, destination_dir: STRING) is
            -- Unpack the source_file into the destination_dir
        do
            print("Untaring "); print(source_file)
            print(" into "); print(destination_dir); io.put_new_line
            launch_system_command(<<"tar xvf ",source>>)
            get_last_system_command_status
            if completed then
                print("Done.%N")
            else
                print("Failed.%N")
            end -- if
        end -- install_files
    build (destination_dir : STRING) is
            -- Finish the installation by calling whatever command is appropriate
        do
            print("Running make in "); print(destination_dir); io.put_new_line
```

```
            launch_system_command(<<"cd ",destination_dir,"; make">>)
            get_last_system_command_status
            if completed then
                print("Done.%N")
            else
                print("Failed.%N")
            end -- if
        end -- build
feature {NONE} -- Internals
    get_last_system_command_status is
        -- Set the boolean variable 'completed' according
        -- to the status of the last system command
        do
            completed := True -- Simulate actual call
        end -- get_last_system_command_status
    launch_system_command (arg : ARRAY[STRING]) is
            -- Concatenate the strings in the array and use the result
            -- as a command for the underlying system
        require arg_not_void: arg /= Void
        local
            command : STRING
            i : INTEGER
        do
            !!command.make(80)
            from i := arg.lower until i> arg.upper
            loop
                command.append_string(arg.item(i))
                i := i + 1
            end -- loop
            print("   -->"); print(command); io.put_new_line -- Simulate execution
        end -- launch_system_command
end -- UNIXSOFT
```

UNIXSOFT can be manipulated as follows.

```
class MAIN
creation make
feature {ANY}
    make is
        local
            soft : SOFTWARE
        do
            !UNIXSOFT!soft.make("mysoft.tar")
```

```
        soft.install(".")
        if soft.completed then
            soft.run("mysoft")
        end -- if
    end -- make
end -- MAIN
```

If we compile and execute this class as the root of an Eiffel system, we get the following output:

```
Starting generic software installation.
Directory . already existing. Reusing it.
Untaring mysoft.tar into .
    -->tar xvf mysoft.tar
Done.
Running make in .
    -->cd .; make
Done.
Software installation completed.
Running mysoft
```

## Related Patterns

Factory Methods (69) are often called by Template Methods. Template Methods use inheritance to vary part of an algorithm. Strategy (215) use delegation to vary the entire algorithm.

# Visitor (GoF 331)                              (Behavioral)

## Intent

Define a general interface to apply various computations to a set of classes without modifying them each time.

## Structure

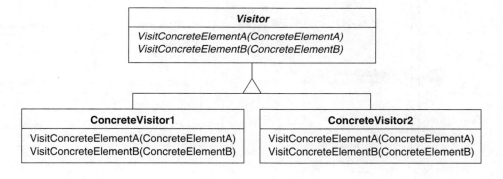

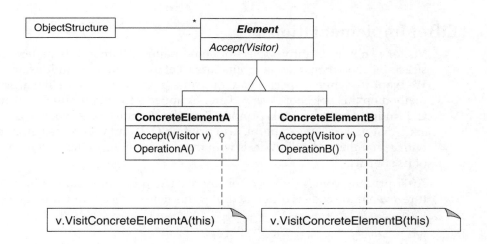

## Collaboration

- A client that uses the Visitor pattern must create a ConcreteVisitor object and then traverse the object structure, visiting each element with the visitor.

- When an element is visited, it calls the Visitor operation that corresponds to its class. The element supplies itself as an argument to this operation to let the visitor access its state, if necessary.

The following interaction diagram illustrates the collaboration among an object structure, a visitor, and two elements:

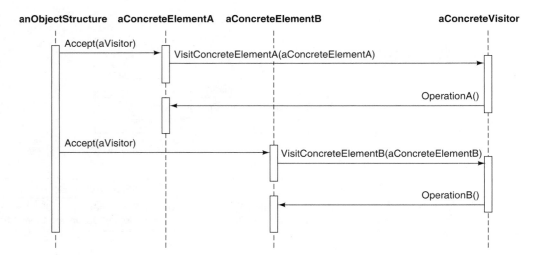

## Eiffel Implementation

Visitor is not an intuitive object-oriented pattern. Rather, this pattern abstracts behavior beyond class boundaries. Let us consider a simple example. We want to define a special way of printing an object. We define a print method on this object of class A. Later, A appears to be composed of B and C. Printing A now requires printing B and in circumstances when A is in a state that makes C meaningful, also printing C. B and C become equipped with a *print* method, and A deals with the proper calling of the *print* method of its subparts.

After printing comes the need for saving. The problem is similar in structure, even if the code is different. But is this new service an intrinsic quality of our object? Adding more and more routines to an object makes its interface complex. Identifying the object semantics that look at its interface becomes more difficult.

Of course, the two general services print and save can be inherited, but what happens if you need, for example, to provide two kinds of printing services? Sometimes, we feel that we can't forecast how many forms of processing we may need to apply on a set of related classes. We need a general mechanism that will make it easier to add new services later.

The principle of separation of concerns leads us to the Visitor design pattern. Let each class define its real interface and equip it with the means of receiving commands. Since we want a uniform interface on each class of our set and an action to be performed according to the type of each class, we define a set of entry points, one for each class in the set. We thus define the notion of VISITOR and provide each class in our set with a routine *accept*, taking VISITOR as a parameter. In turn, our VISITOR defines three methods: *visitA*, *visitB*, and *visitC*.

The proper traversal of the set could be the responsibility of either the traversed items or the VISITOR. In the former case, all visitors would traverse in the same way, which might be a little too rigid. Sometimes, for example, you need to do an action before going deeper in the traversal (often called a preaction); sometimes, *after* it (postaction). You might even need to do both.

When the traversal code is located inside the visitor, it gets full control of the traversal at the expense of having to fiddle with the set internal structure. Furthermore, the traversal logic becomes duplicated in every visitor. See the class NODE_VISITOR discussed with the pattern Facade (109) for an illustration of this policy.

The solution we propose to this problem is to have the traversal code located inside the visited object but encapsulated in its own routine *visit_ children*. Then, any visitor may (or may not) call back *visit_children* on the visited object, performing any needed preactions and postactions.

A particular abstract visitor needs to be defined for each set. If a new class is added, all visitors will need to gain a new entry point. It is thus better to wait for a stabilized structure before designing visitors. The base VISITOR class may provide a default implementation for every class visited. This way, concrete visitors not interested in a particular operation may just omit it from their interface.

Visitors often need privileged access to the object they visit. Once again, we can deal with this problem by leveraging the restricted exportation clauses available in Eiffel.

## Sample Code

We return to the example of the classes EQUIPMENT and COMPOSITE_ EQUIPMENT, modeling such computer parts as drive, bus, chassis, cabinet, and so on. (see the pattern Composite (99)). We modify the class EQUIPMENT so that it features a deferred routine *accept (v : EQUIPMENT_VISITOR)*. The class EQUIPMENT_VISITOR is defined as follows.

```
deferred class EQUIPMENT_VISITOR
feature {ANY} -- Commands
  visit_bus (b : BUS) is deferred end
  visit_cabinet (c : CABINET) is deferred end
  visit_card (c : CARD) is deferred end
  visit_chassis (c : CHASSIS) is deferred end
  visit_floppy_disk (fd : FLOPPY_DISK) is deferred end
end -- EQUIPMENT_VISITOR
```

According to the preceding discussion, the class COMPOSITE_EQUIPMENT is augmented with the definition of a routine for visiting its children: It inherits the routine *accept* from EQUIPMENT.

```
deferred class COMPOSITE_EQUIPMENT
inherit
  COMPOSITE [EQUIPMENT]
  EQUIPMENT
    redefine make end;
feature -- Creation
  make (its_name : STRING) is
    -- Creation and initialization of the children as an ARRAY
    do
      name := its_name
      !ARRAY[EQUIPMENT]!children.make(1,0)
    end -- make
  make_with_list  (its_name : STRING) is
    -- Creation and initialization of the children as a LINKED_LIST
    do
      name := its_name
      !LINKED_LIST[EQUIPMENT]!children.make
    end -- make_with_list
feature {ANY} -- Queries
  net_price : REAL is
      -- Sum the net prices of the subequipment
    local
```

```
        i : INTEGER
    do
        from i := children.lower until i > children.upper
        loop
            Result := Result + children.item(i).net_price
            i := i + 1
        end -- loop
    end -- net_price
discount_price : REAL is
    do
        Result := net_price * 0.9
    end -- discount_price
power : REAL is 0.0 -- Should be a computation
feature {EQUIPMENT_VISITOR} -- Commands restricted to EQUIPMENT_VISITOR
    visit_children (v : EQUIPMENT_VISITOR) is
            -- Makes v visit the current piece of equipment.
        local
            i : INTEGER
        do
            from i := children.lower until i > children.upper
            loop
                children.item(i).accept(v)
                i := i + 1
            end -- loop
        end -- visit_children
invariant
    filiation: parent /= Void implies parent.has(Current)
end -- COMPOSITE_EQUIPMENT
```

Because the traversal responsibility remains in the visitor, a concrete piece of equipment, such as CHASSIS, just defines the routine *accept* in order to call back the relevant visitor routine.

```
class CHASSIS
inherit COMPOSITE_EQUIPMENT
creation make, make_with_list -- inherited creation methods
feature {ANY} -- Public queries
    length, width : REAL -- in centimeters
feature {ANY} -- For Visitors
    accept (v : EQUIPMENT_VISITOR) is
            -- Makes v visit the current piece of equipment.
        do
            v.visit_chassis (Current)
```

```
     end -- accept
end -- CHASSIS
```

It then becomes the visitor's responsibility to call the CHASSIS traversal routine *visit_children*.

To illustrate the pattern, we create two visitors. The first one is dedicated to inventorying the content of a piece of EQUIPMENT. This visitor goes through each component and produces a formatted output representation of the equipment.

```
class INVENTORY_VISITOR
inherit EQUIPMENT_VISITOR
feature {ANY} -- Commands
   visit_bus (b : BUS) is
      do
         io.put_string("%N   - ")
         b.visit_children(Current)
         io.put_string("plugged into a "); io.put_string(b.name)
      end -- visit_bus
   visit_cabinet (c : CABINET) is
      do
         io.put_string(c.name); io.put_string(" containing ")
         c.visit_children(Current)
         io.put_new_line
      end -- visit_cabinet
   visit_card (c : CARD) is do io.put_string(c.name); io.put_string(", ") end
   visit_chassis (c : CHASSIS) is
      do
         io.put_string("a "); io.put_string(c.name)
         io.put_string(" made of:")
         c.visit_children(Current)
      end -- visit_chassis
   visit_floppy_disk (fd : FLOPPY_DISK) is
      do
         io.put_string("%N   - "); io.put_string(fd.name)
      end -- visit_floppy_disk
end -- INVENTORY_VISITOR
```

The second visitor is used to obtain the total price of a piece of equipment, including everything contained within it.

```
class PRICING_VISITOR
inherit EQUIPMENT_VISITOR
feature {ANY} -- Queries
    total : REAL
        -- Sum of the net_prices of simple equipment
feature {ANY} -- Commands
    visit_bus (b : BUS) is do b.visit_children(Current) end
    visit_cabinet (c : CABINET) is do c.visit_children(Current) end
    visit_card (c : CARD) is do  total := total + c.net_price end
    visit_chassis (c : CHASSIS) is do c.visit_children(Current) end
    visit_floppy_disk (fd : FLOPPY_DISK) is do total := total + fd.net_price end
end -- PRICING_VISITOR
```

The driver class MAIN just has the two visitors visit a newly built hypothetical PC:

```
class MAIN
creation make
feature -- Creation
    make is
        -- Creation and initialization
    local
        e : EQUIPMENT
        visitor1 : PRICING_VISITOR
        visitor2 : INVENTORY_VISITOR
    do
        e := new_equipments
        -- Display the various component names in e with an INVENTORY_VISITOR
        io.put_string("Equipment made of: ")
        !!visitor2; e.accept(visitor2)
        -- Compute the price of e with a PRICING_VISITOR
        !!visitor1; e.accept(visitor1)
        io.put_string("Its price is ")
        io.put_real(visitor1.total); io.put_new_line
    end -- make
feature {NONE}
    new_equipments : EQUIPMENT is
        -- Factory Method to create pieces of EQUIPMENT
    local
        cabinet : CABINET
        chassis : CHASSIS
        bus : BUS
```

```
        e : EQUIPMENT
    do
        !!cabinet.make("PC Cabinet")
        !!chassis.make_with_list("PC Chassis") -- use a list representation
        cabinet.add(chassis)
        !!bus.make("MCA Bus")
        !CARD!e.make("16Mbs Token Ring"); bus.add(e)
        chassis.add(bus)
        !FLOPPY_DISK!e.make("3.5 Floppy"); chassis.add(e)
        Result := cabinet
    end -- new_equipment
end -- MAIN
```

If we compile and execute this class as the root of an Eiffel system, we get
the following output:

```
Equipment made of: PC Cabinet containing a PC Chassis made of:
   - 16Mbs Token Ring, plugged into a MCA Bus
   - 3.5 Floppy
Its price is 90.000000
```

## Related Patterns

Visitors can be used to apply an operation over an object structure defined
by the Composite (99) pattern. Visitors may be applied to do the interpretation, as in the Interpreter (153) pattern, as well as to do the code generation
in a compiler, as in our code example for the Facade (109) pattern.

# PART III

# Building on Design Patterns

# Chapter 6

# Application to Software Configuration Management

Using a solid software configuration management (SCM) system is mandatory for establishing and maintaining the integrity of the elements of a software project throughout its life cycle. Even with the help of sophisticated tools (see Leblang, 1994; Mosley et al., 1996), handling the various dimensions of SCM can be a daunting (and costly) task for many projects (Adams, 1995; Ray, 1995). This chapter builds on creational design patterns to simplify SCM. First, we show how the notion of *variants* can be reified into language-level objects. Then, we discuss how newly available compilation technology can enhance performance (memory footprint and execution time) by inferring which classes are needed for a specific configuration and optimizing the generated code accordingly. We illustrate this idea with a small case study representative of properly designed OO software system.

This chapter is based on a paper presented at the 20th International Conference on Software Engineering (Jézéquel, 1998b).

## 6.1 Introduction

Using a solid SCM system (Leblang and Levine, 1995; Tichy, 1994) is a basic requirement in the Software Engineering Institute's (SEI) capability maturity model (CMM), a process-based quality management model for assessing the level of an organization's software development (Humphrey, 1989):

> The purpose of Software Configuration Management is to establish and maintain the integrity of the products of the software project throughout the project's software life cycle.

Software Configuration Management involves identifying the configuration of the software (i.e., selected software work products and their descriptions) at given points in time, systematically controlling changes to the configuration, and maintaining the integrity and traceability of the configuration throughout the software life cycle. The work products placed under software configuration management include the software products that are delivered to the customer (e.g., the software requirements document and the code) and the items that are identified with or required to create these software products (e.g., the compiler).

A software baseline library is established containing the software baselines as they are developed. Changes to baselines and the release of software products built from the software baseline library are systematically controlled via the change control and configuration auditing functions of software configuration management.

This key process area covers the practices for performing the software configuration management function. The practices identifying specific configuration items/units are contained in the key process areas that describe the development and maintenance of each configuration item/unit.

There are, however, a number of interpretations of the exact meaning of *software configuration management*. In this chapter, we focus on the management of software development projects with respect to the dimensions identified in Estublier and Casallas (1995):

- Targeting environmental differences, such as multiple platforms

- Supporting multiple versions and controlling the status of code

- Having multiple developers work on the same code at the same time

Following terminology widely used in the software engineering community (Mackay, 1995), we define **variants** of configuration items as implementations that remain valid at a given instant in time, created to handle environmental differences (logical versioning). We term **revisions** as the steps a configuration item goes through over time (historical versioning), whether to handle new features, to fix bugs, or to support permanent changes to the environment—for example, operating system upgrades, if the old one is no longer supported. Variants and revisions provide a two-dimensional view into the repository, with variants incrementing along one axis as required and revisions incrementing through time on the other.

**Versions** of configuration items are understood by the SCM community to be synonymous with either revisions or variants (Tichy, 1992). Therefore, a version of a single configuration item denotes an entry in the two-dimensional view of the repository, reached from an origin through a path of revisions and variants.

A third dimension is brought in when concurrent development activities, or cooperative versioning, are enabled: At a given time, concurrent activities may have a cooperative version of the same object (Estublier and Casallas, 1995). Since many developers may be authorized to modify the same version at the same moment, each of them is in fact provided with a copy of the item, in much the same way that shared virtual memory pages can be updated by using weak-consistency algorithms in distributed systems (Li, 1986).

Some attempts to apply the OO paradigm to the SCM problem have tried to implement a classical SCM with the help of OO technology (Ambriola and Bendix, 1989; Bendix, 1992; Gallagher and Berman, 1993; Oquendo, 1992; Render and Campbell, 1991). Our approach consists of altering the (object-oriented) design in such a way that some aspects of the SCM (the variability dimension) are vastly simplified.

Creational design patterns can then be used to provide the necessary flexibility for describing and selecting relevant configurations within the object-oriented implementation language, thus benefiting from the better security implied by static typing checked by the compiler. SCM could then be implemented with much simpler, less costly tools; only revisions would need to be dealt with. Alternatively, SCM could make full-featured tools easier to use, thus attacking one of the perceived drawbacks of off-the-shelf SCM tools: their difficult learning curve (Adams, 1995; Dart and Krasnov, 1995). The performance results we cite are obtained with freely available software (the SmallEiffel compiler). Since the source code of our case study is also freely available the results are easily reproduced and checked. (See Appendix D for this book's Web site.) We also discuss the interests, limitations, and drawbacks of our approach. Finally, we present related works and draw conclusions on the perspective opened by our approach.

## 6.2 Software Configuration Management

### 6.2.1 Variants in Software Systems

The reasons that a given software design may have different implementations, all valid at a given instant in time, are manifold. However, the basic idea is to be able to handle *environmental* differences, which we can classify as follows:

- **Hardware level:** Most software systems must be able to drive various hardware devices, such as multimedia or network interface boards. Many real-time systems even use esoteric peripherals. These are often devices produced in limited quantities, and it is not unusual for instances of ostensibly the same model to behave differently and to require differences in the drivers. As an extreme example, consider the case cited in Gentleman (1989) of three installations of a program that used a LED array, similar to a sports scoreboard, as an output device. Although the three LED arrays were the same part number from the same supplier, the timing parameters and control codes were different for each LED array!

- **Heterogeneous distributed systems:** More and more applications, especially in the real-time domain, are implemented on distributed systems having more than one processor type and thus have to handle such things as task allocation and functionality distribution and, eventually, differences in binary formats.

- **Specificities in the target operating systems:** Some system calls have syntax and/or semantics peculiar to a specific operating system (OS). Even more complicated are the cases when seemingly close abstractions—for example, I/O handles in Win32 and file descriptors in UNIX—must, in fact, be dealt with by using considerable differences in programming style (Win32 proactive I/O versus UNIX reactive I/O). Note also that functions whose names exist in only a subset of the supported systems cannot be linked in with a general-purpose version configurable at runtime.

- **Compiler differences:** Poorly standardized languages obtaining different interpretations in different compilers.

- **Range of products:** For marketing reasons, it is often useful to be able to propose a range of products instead of a single "one-model-fits-all" product. For instance, one approach is to make various levels of functionality available: demo, shareware, retail, and premium versions. Also in this category are the variants developed specifically for an important client.

- **User GUI preferences:** Look-and-feel and other aspects of the graphical user interface.

- **Internationalization:** Dealing with various languages and ways of handling country specificities, such as date and time formats, money representation, and so on.

Managing all of the combinations of these variability factors can soon become a nightmare. Consider the case of software for a medium-sized switch, such as the Alcatel E-10, in the telecommunications domain. The source code for this switch is in the order of a million lines. Due to the many versions of the switch tailored to fit the specificities of each country, its configuration software also reaches the million-lines mark.

## 6.2.2  Traditional Solutions

One of the early, most primitive "solutions" to these problems was to patch the executable program at installation time to take particular variants into account. One of the most striking examples of this approach was the word processor Wordstar under the CP/M operating system, cited in Gentleman (1989). To cope with the widely different characteristics of printers and CRT terminals on CP/M systems, in addition to accommodating individual user preferences, this program came with a configuration tool and scripts. Running the configuration tool modified configuration data in the executable image of the word processing program. Various scripts provided consistent sets of answers, corresponding to common configurations, to questions asked by the installation tool.

Device drivers are one example of configurability common to almost all operating systems. The actual binding can take place in source code, at link time, at boot time, or on demand at runtime, with kernel-loadable modules as in Win32, Linux, or Solaris OS.

A widely used technique for making small real-time programs configurable is the static configuration table. Data structures are provided for things that might differ in various installations of the program, and the installer is responsible for providing appropriately initialized instances for a specific installation. Sometimes, configuration records are not directly prepared as initialized records in the programming language of the system but rather are produced as database entries or are expressed as sentences in a grammar, with a tool provided to generate from these the programming language records the system will use. This can be particularly useful when several programs need to be implemented for the same configuration. Static configuration tables are not entirely satisfactory, however. They rarely provide for error checking; indeed, because they are purely declarative, with no language-defined semantics, they can make constraint verification and consistency checking, as well as error checking, difficult. The tables make an implicit assumption of an associated library that keeps variant units of code, yet there is no assistance in managing or manipulating that library.

For larger systems, one of the most popular approaches uses conditional compilation, or assembly, implemented, for example, with a pre-processor. C programmers are familiar with the cpp tool, invoked as a first pass of the C compiler, that allows the following kind of code to be written:

```
#ifdef unix
#ifdef solaris
#define xx 5
#else
#define xx 3
#endif
```

```
#else
#define xx 1
#endif
```

Despite the help of sophisticated tools, such as the GNU autoconfig, this kind of code can rapidly become difficult to maintain (Ray, 1995). For example, to add support for a new OS, one needs to review *all* of the written code, looking for relevant #ifdef parts.

## 6.2.3  Using SCM Tools

Traditionally, SCM is implemented with check-in/check-out control of sources—and sometimes binaries—and the ability to perform builds, or compiles of the end products. Other functions, such as *process management*, or control of the software development activities, will not be considered here.

Modern SCM tools have evolved from academic prototypes to full-strength industrial products. Most of them now keep track of all of the changes to files in secure, distributed repositories, as well as support parallel development by enabling easy branching and merging. These tools provide version control of not only source code but also binaries, executables, documentation, test suites, libraries, and so on. Examples of such tools are Adele (Belkhatir and Melo, 1994) or ClearCase (Allen et al., 1995).

For instance, ClearCase provides each developer with multiple consistent, flexible, and reproducible workspaces. It uses *views*, similar to the views concept in databases, to present the appropriate versions of each file and directory for the specific task at hand. Views are defined by configuration specifications consisting of a few general rules. Rules may be as simple as *"the versions that were used in the last release"* or can be more complex when particular sets of bug fixes and features need to be combined. Views are dynamic; they are continually updated by reevaluating the rules that define them. Newly created versions can thus be incorporated into a view automatically and instantly. Views allow team members to strike a balance between shared work and isolation from destabilizing changes.

The main drawbacks of these sophisticated tools are that they are very costly to use and have a steep learning curve. Furthermore, even when these two problems are overcome, their underlying three-dimensional model of the repository does not provide an easy framework to mentally handle the complexity of large software developments (Adams, 1995, Dart and Krasnov, 1995). Therefore, their use is still not as pervasive as it could be.

## 6.3 Case Study: The Mercure Software System

Mercure is a model of a communication software system that sends, receives, and relays "messages" from a set of network interfaces connected to the distributed-memory parallel computer, a set of loosely coupled CPUs, on which it runs. Mercure is inspired by a real-world telecommunication software system, an SMDS (switched multimegabits data service) server whose design and implementation have been described in Jézéquel, 1996a, 1996b, and 1998a. Mercure is basically an oversimplification of this software, having retained only configuration management–related issues. Mercure must handle the following variability factors (as defined in Section 6.2.1):

- **Hardware level:** Mercure must support a wide range of network interface boards—for ATM, Ethernet, FDDI, ISDN, X25, and so on—from various manufacturers. Let us call $V_i$ the number of supported boards. Since new hardware continually pops up, there must be an easy way to add support for it in future releases of Mercure.

- **Heterogeneous distributed systems:** Since Mercure is to be run on such a system, provision must be made to deal with heterogeneous code generation and task distribution. Some processors are specialized for relaying messages (switching), others for computing routes, others for network management (billing, accounting, configuring, and so on), and still others for dealing with persistent databases. Let us call $V_p$ the considered number of specialized processors.

- **Range of products:** Various levels ($V_n$) of functionality must be provided in the domain of network management.

- **User preferences for GUIs:** Various ($V_g$) look-and-feels must be available.

- **Internationalization:** Support for $V_l$ languages must be available.

Considering that a given variant of the Mercure software might be configured with support for any number of the $V_i$ network interfaces and $V_l$ languages and one of $V_p$ kinds of processors, one of the $V_n$ levels of network management, and one of the $V_g$ GUIs, the total number of Mercure variants is:

$$V = V_p \times V_n \times V_g \times 2^{V_i + V_l - 2}$$

For $V_i = 16$, $V_p = 4$, $V_n = 8$, $V_g = 5$, $V_l = 24$, this formula gives more than several trillion possible variants (43,980,465,111,040, to be precise).

## 6.3.1 Object-Oriented Modeling of Variants

If we use an object-oriented analysis and design approach, it is natural to model the commonalities among the variants of Mercure in an abstract way, expressing the differences in concrete subclasses. Consider, for example, the case of the network interface boards. Whatever the interface, we must be able to poll for incoming messages, to read them into memory buffers, to send outgoing messages, and to set various configuration parameters. Accordingly, this abstract interface, which is valid for all kinds of network interface boards, could be expressed as the following Eiffel deferred class.

```eiffel
deferred class NETDRIVER
feature -- Queries
    is_msg_available : BOOLEAN is deferred end
    last_msg : MESSAGE
            -- Storing last msg retrieved from network
    address: INTEGER
            -- Model the IO address
    manager : MANAGER
            -- The network management entity where I report events
feature -- Actions
    configure (new_address: INTEGER; new_manager: like manager) is
        -- Initialize the driver to be at a given address
        require
            new_manager_not_void: new_manager /= Void
            valid_address: new_address /= 0
        deferred
        ensure configured: manager = new_manager and address = new_address
        end -- configure
    read_msg is
            -- read a MESSAGE from the network and store it in last_msg
        require msg_available: is_msg_available
        deferred
        ensure msg_received: last_msg /= Void
        end -- read_msg
    send (msg: like last_msg) is
        require msg_not_void: msg /= Void
        deferred
        end -- send
invariant
    valid_address: address /= 0
    valid_manager: manager /= Void
end -- NETDRIVER
```

The idea underlying this kind of object-oriented design is that a method, such as *read_msg* in the class NETDRIVER, has an abstractly defined behavior—read an incoming message from the lower-level network interface and store it in a buffer—and several differing concrete implementations, defined in proper subclasses, such as NETDRIVER1, NETDRIVER2 . . . NETDRIVERN. This way, the method can be used in a piece of code independently of the actual type of its receiver—that is, independently of the configuration, or on which kind of interface board we read a message.

```
process_a_driver (driver: NETDRIVER) is
    -- Poll and process 'driver'
  require driver_not_void: driver /= Void
  local
    outgoing_address : INTEGER
  do
    if driver.is_msg_available then
      driver.read_msg
      outgoing_address := routing(driver.last_msg)
      if drivers.valid_index(outgoing_address) then
        forward(drivers.item(outgoing_address),driver.last_msg)
      end -- if
    end -- if
  end -- process_a_driver
```

Dealing with multiple variants is thus moved from the implementation realm, where it is usually handled by means of conditional compilation and complex CM tools, to the problem domain, or analysis and design realm, meaning that it can be handled fully within the semantics of the OO design and implementation language. This way, it can be subject to both compiler verification and semantic-based *safe* optimizations.

In the past, indeed, handling this kind of issue in an object-oriented way had a major drawback for many applications: performance. Since the choice of the proper method to call would have to be delayed until runtime, we had to pay the price overhead of dynamic binding. This overhead could be prohibitive for some real-time or performance-driven applications; with Smalltalk, for example, the inheritance hierarchy had to be searched, and even with C++, the handling of dynamic binding through a *vtable* used to provoke cache misses. Fortunately, object-oriented compiler technology has made tremendous progress in the last few years, as explained in the next section.

Figure 6.1 presents a class diagram of the Mercure software, using the UML (Unified Modeling Language) object-model notation. (On this diagram, only a rather flat inheritance hierarchy is suggested; however, it is evident that the

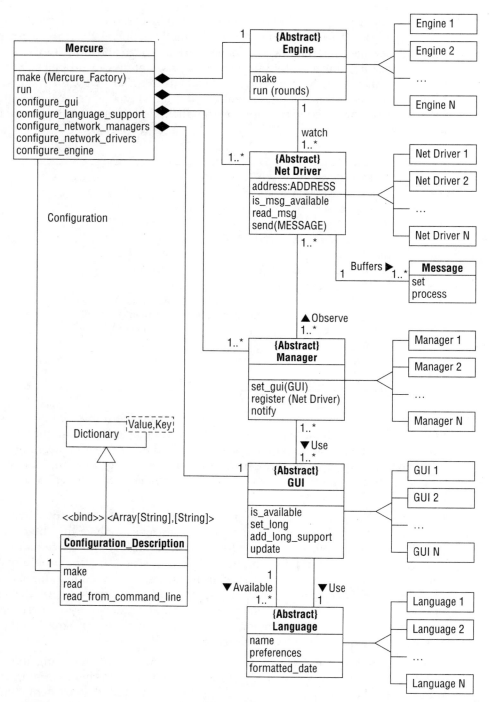

**Figure 6.1** Class diagram modeling the Mercure software in UML

designer should factor the commonalities among subclasses in an inheritance graph as deep as required.)

A Mercure system is an instance of the class MERCURE, aggregating

- A GUI that encapsulates the user preference variability factor. A GUI has itself a collection of supported languages, among them the currently selected language.

- A collection of MANAGERS representing the range of functionality available

- A collection of NETDRIVERS encapsulating the network interfaces of this instance of Mercure

- An ENGINE that encapsulates the work that Mercure has to do with its NETDRIVERS on a particular processor of the target distributed system

```
class MERCURE
creation
   make
feature -- Creation
   make (mf : MERCURE_FACTORY) is
      -- Creation and initialization
      require mf_not_void: mf /= Void
      local timer : TIMER
      do
         !!timer.start
         !!configuration.read
         configure_gui(mf)
         configure_language_support(mf)
         configure_network_managers(mf)
         configure_network_drivers(mf)
         configure_engine(mf)
         run
         timer.stop
         io.put_double_format(timer.elapsed_time, 3); io.put_new_line
      end -- make
feature {ANY} -- Queries
   gui : GUI
   engine : ENGINE
   managers : ARRAY[MANAGER]
   netdrivers : ARRAY[NETDRIVER]
feature {ANY} -- Commands
   run is
         -- process the net drivers for the number of times
```

```
                  -- specified in the configuration
        do
            if configuration.has(" -run") then
                engine.run(configuration.value_at(" -run",1))
            end  -- if
        end  -- run
    feature {NONE}  -- Private
        configuration : CONFIGURATION_DESCRIPTION
                  -- Describing the dynamic configuration
                  -- i.e. how many network interfaces have been probed, etc.
        configure_gui (mf : MERCURE_FACTORY) is
            -- select one GUI type according to the command line
        do
            if configuration.has(" -gui") then
                gui := mf.new_gui(configuration.value_at(" -gui",1))
            else
                gui := mf.new_gui(0)
            end  -- if
        ensure gui_not_void: gui /= Void
        end  -- configure_gui
    -- ...
```

## 6.3.2  Applying Creational Design Patterns

With this design framework, configuration management can be programmed
*within* the target language; it boils down to simply creating the class instances relevant to a given configuration. However, some care has to be taken in programming the creation of these objects to ensure that the design is flexible enough.
A good approach is to use the *creational patterns* discussed in Chapter 3. In our
simple case, we use an *Abstract Factory* (called MERCURE_FACTORY) to define an
interface for creating Mercure variants (see Figure 6.2).

```
deferred class MERCURE_FACTORY
feature  -- Creation
    make is
        -- Branch to the Mercure entry point
        -- passing itself as the actual FACTORY
    local
        mercure : MERCURE
    do
        !!mercure.make(Current)
    end  -- make
```

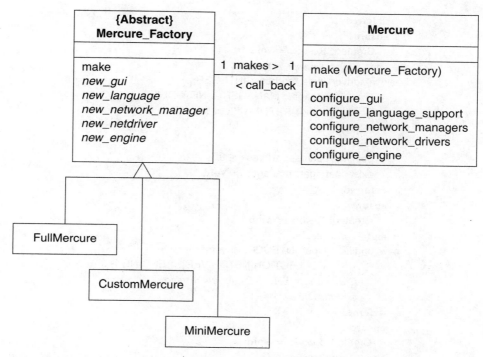

**Figure 6.2** Class diagram modeling the Mercure software in UML

```
feature -- Abstract Factory methods called back by Mercure to build itself
   new_gui  (type: INTEGER) : GUI is
         -- Create a new GUI subclass instance,
         -- according to 'type'
      deferred
      ensure
         Created: Result /= Void
      end -- new_gui
   new_language (type: INTEGER) : LANGUAGE is
         -- Create a new LANGUAGE subclass instance,
         -- according to 'type'
      deferred
      ensure
         Created: Result /= Void
      end -- new_language
   new_network_managers (type: INTEGER) : MANAGER is
         -- Create a new MANAGER subclass instance,
         -- according to 'type'
```

```
        deferred
        ensure
           Created: Result /= Void
        end -- new_network_managers
     new_netdriver (type, address: INTEGER;
                        manager: MANAGER) : NETDRIVER is
           -- Create a new NETDRIVER subclass instance,
           -- according to 'type'
        require
           positive_address: address > 0
           exist_manager: manager /= Void
        deferred
        ensure
           Created: Result /= Void
        end -- new_netdriver
     new_engine  (type: INTEGER; drivers:
                        COLLECTION[NETDRIVER]) : ENGINE is
           -- Create a new ENGINE subclass instance,
           -- according to 'type'
        deferred
        ensure
           Created: Result /= Void
        end -- new_engine
  end -- MERCURE_FACTORY
```

In the preceding listing, we can see that the class MERCURE_FACTORY features one Factory Method, encapsulating the procedure for creating an object, for each of our five variability factors. The Factory Methods are parameterized to let them create various kinds of products, that is, variants of a type, depending on the dynamic Mercure configuration selected at runtime. These Factory Methods are abstractly defined in the class MERCURE_FACTORY and given concrete implementations in the subclasses, called *concrete factories*. A concrete factory starts by creating a MERCURE instance, which calls back to the concrete factory to configure its components (see Figure 6.3).

Building a variant of the Mercure software consists of implementing the relevant concrete factory. By restricting at compile time—that is, in the source code of a concrete factory—the range of products that a Factory Method can dynamically create, we can choose to build specialized versions of the general-purpose Mercure software. Following is an example of a concrete factory that statically restricts the configuration: only eight network drivers, five languages, and five processor types are supported, as well as only one network manager and one GUI.

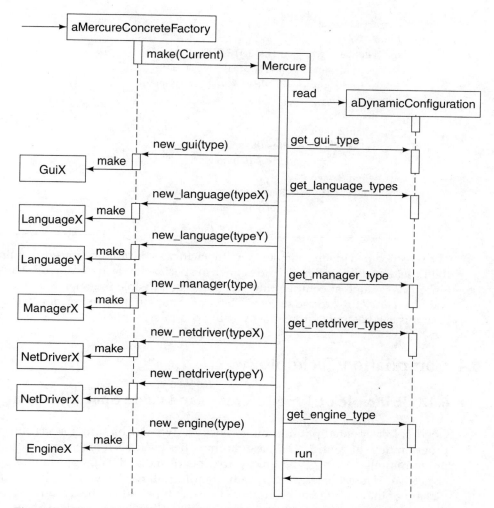

**Figure 6.3** Dynamic configuration of the Mercure software (UML sequence diagram)

```
class CUSTOMMERCURE
inherit
    MERCURE_FACTORY
creation
    make
feature -- Factory methods: concrete definitions
    new_gui (type: INTEGER) : GUI is
            -- Always return a GUI2 object, ignoring 'type'
        do
```

```
        !GUI2!Result
     end -- new_gui
  new_netdriver (type, address: INTEGER;
                 manager: MANAGER) : NETDRIVER is
     -- Create a new NETDRIVER subclass instance
  do
     inspect type
     when 2 then
        !NETDRIVER2!Result.configure(
                 address*10,manager)
     when 3 then
        !NETDRIVER3!Result.configure(
                 address*10,manager)
```

The selection of a given concrete Mercure factory as the application entry point—
the Eiffel *root class*—allows the designer to specify the desired Mercure variant.
Since this is done at compile time, it should be possible to generate executable
code *specialized* toward the selected Mercure variant. In the next section, we show
how this can be done automatically, using compiler technology.

## 6.4 Compilation Technology

### 6.4.1 Principle of Type Inference and Code Specialization

Good object-oriented programming relies on dynamic binding for structuring a
program flow of control; OO programming has even been nicknamed "caseless
programming." Most of the time, a routine, or method call, applies to a given
object, called *target* or *receiver*. Dynamic binding allows delaying the choice of the
version of the routine until runtime: The exact type, called the dynamic type, of
the receiver need not be known at compile time. Whenever more than one version
of a routine might be applicable, dynamic binding ensures that the most directly
adapted to the target object is selected. In statically typed languages, such as C++,
Eiffel, Java, and Ada 95, a receiver's type, called the receiver's static type, must
be declared beforehand. Then, the receiver's dynamic type must be a subtype of
its static type.

In this context, the main goal of the compilation techniques based on *type inference* consists of *statically* computing the set of types a *receiver* may assume at a
given point in the program's execution. In the most favorable case, this set is a
singleton, and thus the routine can be statically bound and even in-lined. In less
favorable cases, the set may contain several types. However, the compiler is still
able to compute the reduced set of routines that are potentially concerned and

to generate specialized code accordingly, with an *if-then-else* block or a switch on the possible dynamic types of the receiver, for example. In either case, the cost of the conceptual dynamic dispatch can be mostly optimized out.

## 6.4.2  The SmallEiffel Compiler

SmallEiffel is a free Eiffel compiler distributed under the terms of the GNU General Public License as published by the Free Software Foundation (see Section B.2.1 for more details on SmallEiffel and how to get it). The SmallEiffel compiler uses a simple type inference mechanism to translate Eiffel source code to C code. The computation of a specific version of an Eiffel routine is not done for all of the target's possible types, only for those that *exist* at runtime. As a consequence, it is first necessary to know which points of an Eiffel program may be reached at runtime and then to remove those that are unreachable.

## 6.4.3  Living and Dead Code in SmallEiffel

Remember that in Eiffel, the programmer specifies the entry point of an application by singling out a specific class, the root class, along with one of its creation procedures (A creation procedure corresponds to a class constructor in C++ terminology.) When a program is run, a single instance of the root class is created (the root object), and the specified creation procedure is called.

The SmallEiffel compilation process computes which parts of the Eiffel source code may or may not be reached from the application root, without doing any data flow analysis. The result of this first computation is thus completely independent of the order of instructions in the compiled program. With respect to conditional instructions, we assume that all alternatives may be executed. Starting from the application root, the SmallEiffel algorithm recursively computes the **living code**, or code that may be executed. Code that can never be executed is called **dead code**. Living-code computation is closely linked to the inventory of classes that may have instances at runtime; see Collin, Colnet, and Zendra (1997) for more details.

By analogy a **living class** is one for which at least one instantiation instruction is in living code. Conversely, a **dead class** is one for which no instance may be created in living code.

## 6.4.4  Specialized Code Generation in SmallEiffel

Code is generated for living types only. An object is classically represented by a structure (C `struct`) whose first field is the number that identifies the corresponding living type (corresponding to the C++ RTTI).

A dynamic type set can thus be represented as a set of integers. Referring back to the example of using a NETDRIVER (see Section 6.3.1), we see that the code generated for the routine *read_msg* has the following structure:

```
void  XrNETDRIVERread_msg(void *C){ /* C represents the receiver */
  int id=((T0*)C)->id; /* the Dynamic Type Identifier, aka RTTI */
  switch (id) {
    /* call read_msg defined in NETDRIVER1, whose RTTI is 123 */
    case 123: rNETDRIVER1read_msg((NETDRIVER1*)C); break;
    /* call read_msg defined in NETDRIVER2, whose RTTI is 124 */
    case 124: rNETDRIVER2read_msg((NETDRIVER2*)C); break;
    ...
    case 138: rNETDRIVER16read_msg((NETDRIVER16*)C); break;
  }
}
```

Depending on the knowledge the compiler has on the possible dynamic types of the NETDRIVER, the number of branches in the switch can be reduced, or the switch itself could even be replaced by a sequence of **if-then-else**. If the dynamic type set for the receiver is a singleton (for example, NETDRIVER5 whose ID is 127), SmallEiffel further specializes the generated code by optimizing out the runtime type test completely and substituting the call to XrNETDRIVERread_msg by a direct call to rNETDRIVER5read_msg.

# 6.5  Performance Results

## 6.5.1  Experimental Conditions

Let us compare three versions of Mercure for the effect of the specialization of the code generation.

- **FullMercure:** The general-purpose version of the program, including all of the configurable parts. Thus, *any one* of the trillions of combinations can be dynamically chosen at runtime: All calls to the variant methods must be dynamically bound.

- **CustomMercure:** A restricted version of the program, including support only for eight different network drivers, five languages, and five processor types. Only one network manager and one GUI are available, thus allowing some method calls to be statically bound. (See the class CUSTOMMERCURE, listed on page 251).

- **MiniMercure:** A minimal version of the software, with only one of each configurable part available. Support is included only for ENGINE1, GUI2, LANGUAGE3, MANAGER4, and NETDRIVER5. This limited support would, theoretically, allow every method to be statically bound; thus, the resulting code could have the same structure as, for example, the #ifdef-based preprocessor method.

```
class MINIMERCURE
inherit
    MERCURE_FACTORY -- reduce the scope of factory methods
        redefine new_gui, new_language, new_network_managers,
                new_netdriver, new_engine end;
creation
    make
feature -- Factory methods. Redefine for configuration specialization
    new_gui  (type: INTEGER) : GUI2 is
            -- Create a new GUI subclass instance, according to 'type'
        do
            !!Result
        end -- new_gui
    new_language (type: INTEGER) : LANGUAGE3 is
            -- Create a new LANGUAGE subclass instance, according to 'type'
        do
            !!Result
        end -- new_language
    new_network_managers (type: INTEGER) : MANAGER4 is
            -- Create a new MANAGER subclass instance, according to 'type'
        do
            !!Result.make
        end -- new_network_managers
    new_netdriver (type, address: INTEGER; manager: MANAGER) : NETDRIVER5 is
            -- Create a new NETDRIVER subclass instance, according to 'type'
        do
            !!Result.configure(address*10,manager)
        end -- new_netdriver
    new_engine  (type: INTEGER; drivers: COLLECTION[NETDRIVER]) : ENGINE1 is
            -- Create a new ENGINE subclass instance, according to 'type'
        do
            !!Result.make(drivers)
        end -- new_engine
end -- MINIMERCURE
```

**Table 6.1**
Compile-Time Statistics

| Version | Eiffel LOC (config.) | Eiffel LOC (user) | Eiffel LOC (total) | Type inference Score | C LOC (generated) |
|---|---|---|---|---|---|
| FullMercure | 96 | 2,903 | 10,056 | 93.29% | 7,135 |
| CustomMercure | 60 | 1,421 | 8,574 | 96.79% | 3,839 |
| MiniMercure | 36 | 713 | 7,866 | 7,866% | 2,639 |
| HelloWorld | — | 6 | 4,478 | 100.00%% | 189 |

These three variants use exactly the same software baseline. The only difference is that a different Mercure concrete factory is selected as the root class, the class containing the entry point of the application. (See Figure 6.2.)

## 6.5.2  Compilation

In this section, we compare compile-time statistics for the Mercure software to the minimal "Hello, world!" program (see Table 6.1). We display the number of Eiffel lines of code (LOC) for describing the configuration—the number of LOC of the relevant Mercure concrete factory—the number of LOC written by the programmer, and the total number of lines in all of the classes needed by the application, including the libraries.

The type inference score is the proportion of dynamic calls that could be replaced by direct call at compile time. This proportion ranges from 93 percent to more than 99 percent; the SmallEiffel compiler (version -0.87) has been able to early bind nearly all of the conceptually dynamic binding in the MiniMercure version.

The last column shows the size of the generated C code. Note that it includes the SmallEiffel runtime system, whose size may be approximated by the "Hello, world!" one. The small size of the code generated for the MiniMercure version illustrates the ability of the SmallEiffel compiler to take advantage of its knowledge of the living types to efficiently specialize generated C code: Only code relevant to the specific variant of the Mercure software is generated.

## 6.5.3  Memory Footprint and Runtime Performance

All versions have exactly the same dynamic behavior, because the dynamic configuration we choose for the Mercure and CustomMercure variants is the one selected at compile time in MiniMercure. That is, we give the configuration as a set of command line parameters:

**Table 6.2**
Runtime Statistics on Linux

| Version | Footprint | Run Time | Speed-up |
|---------|-----------|----------|----------|
| FullMercure | 82,544 | 1.319 | 0% |
| CustomMercure | 40,512 | 1.159 | 12.1304% |
| MiniMercure | 26,880 | 1.086 | 17.6649% |

**Table 6.3**
Runtime statistics on SPARC/Solaris

| Version | Footprint | Run Time | Speed-up |
|---------|-----------|----------|----------|
| FullMercure | 116152 | 0.486 | 0% |
| CustomMercure | 57696 | 0.433 | 10.9053% |
| MiniMercure | 38824 | 0.413 | 15.0206% |

```
-run 10000 -engine 1 -gui 2 -lang 3 -manager 4 -netdriver '5 5 5 5 5 5 5 5'
```

Their output is thus exactly the same.

The results presented in Tables 6.2 and 6.3 were attained on a PC 486 system running Linux 1.2.13 (and GCC 2.7.0, optimization level -O3) and on a SPARC running Solaris 5.0 (and GCC 2.7.2.1, optimization level -O3).

Note that because all three variants have the same dynamic behavior—they do exactly the same thing—their use of dynamic memory is also identical. Despite the system's being designed for a fully dynamic configuration, the compiler is able to use type inference to detect what is, in fact, configured statically in specialized versions of Mercure factories to generate code nearly as compact and efficient as if it had been written statically from the beginning. For example, in the MiniMercure case, the call to the pure virtual routine *read_msg* from the class NETDRIVER has been compiled to a direct call to rNETDRIVER5read_msg, the version defined in the class NETDRIVER5. If we look in the generated code, we can check that it has even been in-lined in the context of the caller. More generally, the generated code has the same structure as the one that would have been obtained with, for example, the #ifdef-based preprocessor method. The performance differences between MiniMercure and FullMercure represent the maximum price that the designer would have to pay for trading time and space performances for dynamic configuration capabilities. But what is much more interesting is that with *exactly the same software baseline*, the designer can easily choose the tradeoff between these two properties by selecting the relevant concrete factory.

## 6.6 Discussion

Our approach to SCM problems has a number of drawbacks as well as advantages.

- It forces some SCM issues, such as variant management, to be dealt with during the software design phase. But our conviction is that it belongs there because it makes the notion of a product family much more concrete. There is one concrete factory for each variant of the product and no longer a need to understand the variations among variants in terms of "diff" listings.

- A compiler is able to do type inference only if it has access to the full code. It is clear that in our approach, we cannot deal efficiently with libraries of classes compiled in .o or .a forms. However, .o and .a UNIX formats are not very usable in an OO context, lacking type information. They were used in the past to solve a number of problems that are now dealt with on another level.

  - **Enforcing modularity for procedural programs:** This has now been superseded by OO concepts.

  - **Speed of compilation:** Although this still holds for small programs, it is well known that large C++ compilations spend most of their time in link editing. So having .o or .a files no longer reduces the overall edit/compile/link/test time. With respect to medium-size programs, for example, it takes only 10 seconds on a Pentium Pro 200 to have SmallEiffel compile itself (50,000 LOC).

  - **Source protection:** Having access to the full code does not mean full *source* code, because the source can be precompiled in a "distributable" format, such as Java *.class* formats or Eiffel "precompiled" formats from some vendors. Alternatively, sophisticated encryption technology could be used to protect the source code.

- Our approach does not remove the need for classical configuration management tools. We still have to deal with *revisions*, such as new features and bug fixes, and, possibly, concurrent development activities. However, concurrent development activities are minimized by the fact that a variant part is typically small and located in its own file: Someone responsible for a product variant would not have to interfere with other people's modifications, and conversely. Thus, in our experience, a simple tool, such as RCS (Revision Control System) or CVS (Concurrent Versions System), equipped with automatic symbolic naming of versions, should be enough for many sites.

- Programming the concrete factories to specify the configuration is straightforward but quite tedious. This could easily be generated by, for example, a simple Tcl/Tk shell that would also encapsulate the call to the compiler and thus could retrieve the name of all of the files used in the compilation. On the basis of this information, a snapshot of the full configuration, including the compiler, linker, and so on, could be assigned a symbolic version name and stored in a repository, using RCS, for example.

- Doing all of the configuration in the target language eliminates the need to learn and to use yet another complex language used just for the configuration management—for example, the various existing module interconnection languages, as in Adele (Belkhatir and Melo, 1994), Proteus, Floch, 1995), and so on.

## 6.7  Bibliographic Notes

The idea presented in this chapter can be seen as an application of ideas circulating in the "partial-evaluation" community for years. Indeed, it can be seen as taking advantage of the fact that the types of configurable parts have bounded static variations; that is, the sets of possible types are known at compile time. Thus the partial-evaluation community's *The Trick* (see Jones, 1990) can be applied to specialize the general program at compile time.

Because this partial evaluation deals only with the computation of dynamic type sets, it is also clearly related to the domain of type inference. Ole Agesen's (1996) Ph D. thesis contains a complete survey of related work. Reviewed systems range from purely theoretical ones (Vitekn, Horspool, and Uhl, 1992) to systems in regular use by a large community (Milner, 1978) via partially implemented systems (Suzuki, 1981; Suzuki and Tarada, 1984) and systems implemented on small languages (Graver and Johnson, 1990; Palsberg and Schwartzback, 1991). Using Agesen's (1996) classification, the SmallEiffel compiler's algorithm can be qualified as **polyvariant**, which means that each feature may be analyzed multiple times, and **flow insensitive**, or no data flow analysis. The SmallEiffel algorithm deals with both *concrete types* and abstract types. The Cartesian product algorithm (CPA) (Agesen, 1995) is a more powerful one. However, the source language of CPA, unlike Eiffel, is not statically typed; it handles prototypes (no classes) and allows dynamic inheritance. On the other hand, the late-binding compilation technique we described for Eiffel can be applied to any class-based language forbidding the dynamic creation of classes.

Related work from the SCM point of view has already been extensively discussed in this chapter. In this section, we have restricted ourselves to approaches trying to leverage the object-oriented or object-based technologies. Our idea of designing the application in such a way that the SCM is simplified is not new (Bendix, 1992; Gallagher and Berman, 1993). But previous works needed a dedicated tool to handle the SCM. Since in our approach the SCM is done *within* the OO programming language, there is no need for such an ad hoc tool: The compiler itself handles all of the work.

## 6.8 Conclusion

This chapter set out to illustrate the ability of creational design patterns to simplify software configuration management by reifying the *variants* of an object-oriented software system into language-level objects. The chapter also showed that newly available compilation technology makes this proposal attractive with respect to performance (memory footprint and execution time) by inferring which classes are needed for a specific configuration and optimizing the generated code accordingly. This approach opens the possibility of leveraging the good modeling capabilities of OOL (Object-Oriented Languages) to deal with fully dynamic software configurations while being able to produce space- and time-efficient executables when the program contains enough static configuration information. For example, in the most favorable cases, the SmallEiffel compiler is able to infer the type of the receiver in up to 100 percent of the cases and thus to optimize out the dynamic-binding overhead.

# Chapter 7

# Combining Patterns for Building User Interfaces

There are many ways of building user interfaces. Although tools exist for designing of the purely graphical part, the programmer is often left without much support for linking graphics elements to the applicative part. Starting from the Model-View-Controller (MVC) model, we propose a systematic approach to derive an implementation from an interface specification.

## 7.1 Problem and Strategies

### 7.1.1 Building a Model

#### 7.1.1.1 A User Perspective

When using a software product, we ask for services, which we access through the user interface. A graphical interface consists of a set of items we can interact with to trigger actions and to display information. We don't know how it's achieved, and we don't want to know. We just want the interface to be easy to use, react quickly, and give the kind of result we expect. Even if we are not very keen on software engineering, we ask for a clear separation between interface and implementation. All we can and want to comment on is the interface.

There is obviously an aesthetic aspect to the computer interface problem. The developer must be able to deal with the appearance as a problem per se. The layout, the shape, and the widgeting itself should be easy to modify. The only way to grant such a possibility is a clear separation between program and interface.

The second part is the ergonomics aspect. We don't speak here about bells and whistles glittering everywhere on a screen. The subject is the user, who had a life before the product. We must learn the way the user used to work, in order to identify the concepts underlying his or her perception. We have to capture the kind of interactions he or she expects. What the software is supposed to do is one thing, how the user perceives it and uses it is something nearly independent. In other words, between the application and the user interface lies something that, to some extent, captures the user perception of the application. The interface is not directly plugged into the core system but rather just observes the application and reacts to its changes.

Sometimes we introduce new concepts that are built from the basic notions found in the system to help the user figure out what is going on. These notions are deduced from analyzing the user perception. They use the same mechanisms as the graphical interface to reflect the core application. From a user perspective, they become part of the core application and the interface is linked to them in the same way. From now on, we will label **Model** what the user interface describes. The interface is a projection of this model on a computer screen, and we will try to define a way of building that projection.

Let's remember that writing huge manuals is not the best way to help a user. If we try to evaluate the quality of a proposed interface, we could say that we are close to our aim when the user easily recognizes the meaning and use of what he or she sees. This is the first level of interaction. For further observing the way we can work with the software, a good metaphor is to consider action, or sequences of actions, as sentences in a particular language. We can propose predefined sentences, but we know that the user will want to define new ones, combining existing ones, or even introducing new concepts from the application domain notions. At the architectural level, the system is never finished but continuously evolves in the user's hands to fit his or her needs more precisely. Thus, we must be able to record actions and to compose them. Then we reify them: That is, we turn the concept into an object.

### 7.1.1.2  Displays and Modifications of Application Data

So far, our model is three-tiered. The lowest part consists of the problem domain concepts. We build on top of that a second layer, consisting of derived notions we want to present to the user. These two layers comprise the model of the application, providing all of information and services offered to the user. The interface is the third layer, which we build on top of the other two layers.

When building an interface, our first concern is to provide a consistent view of our model. Any modification of our model has to be reflected in any associated presentation. For instance, suppose that I am working on a spreadsheet. If I set the value of an integer to 3, I want to see the integer field in the form set to 3 and I want to see the pie chart redrawn accordingly. As soon as the model changes, all attached presentations have to update their displays accordingly.

In some situations, however, such immediate reactions are not welcome. These cases are related mainly to complex or lengthy calculations and validity control. Every interaction does not produce a correct and definitive model state. The users can change their minds or ask to undo previous actions. This implies either deferred notification until user confirmation or command storing with a recovery mechanism. Validity control is also an issue: Input (data or order) may be inappropriate in the current context. It is better to prevent such situations, but it is not always convenient. Instead of calling for modification, we end up calling for a modification request. The modification has to be allowed before being performed.

Another aspect that impacts heavily on system design is the transformation of data induced by the view we want to present. Many modeling items may participate via complex transformations to a single user interface component. On the other hand, elementary data items may vary too quickly for an accurate display refresh. In such situations, we must provide for buffering transformations and delaying update.

Starting from this set of constraints, we will try to elaborate a strategy that could help us in setting up interfaces. Let's begin with common practices and see what we might gain from studying them.

## 7.1.2  The Interface Builder Approach

- **Drawing the picture:** An interface builder is often used to deal with the interface problem. This kind of tool allows the designer to concentrate on the graphical part of the problem, instead of underlying application constraints.

  Such a freedom is a major quality factor. As we said earlier, we want to show what the user has in mind when using our tool. The interactive drawing of the graphical part should reflect the user model of the problem. First results, even hand drawings, can form a basis for further discussions and refinements. Now we have to give life to these elements.

- **Building and connecting:** Once we have assembled various graphical components to form a complete interface, we may produce the corresponding code in the toolkit we chose. What we obtain is a set of software elements with predefined interaction points. Some allow for graphical modifications; others provide items that should be redefined or extended to describe application reactions to graphical state changes.

At this stage, we have two worlds, completely independent even if semantically related: the application model and the graphics. Each subset in the graphical part is the expression of a user point of view. It is time to link them together.

At this point, two problems arise. The first one is to keep the applicative part independent from its various representations. If we use a simple solution, consisting of mutual calls from both parts, we introduce graphical knowledge in the applicative part. This will result in a lot of pieces of code scattered about. As a consequence, verifying the correct interaction will require a search throughout applicative code, which is usually error prone. Furthermore, modification of the applicative part results in moving and rewriting the connectivity. Finally, modifying the interface will produce changes in the applicative code, which is highly undesirable.

The second problem comes from the loss of control on the views we define. As a very general model of the problem, we obtain an applicative part; several views, or projections, in the graphics space; and the related graphic components. The former approach leaves us without any tool to identify and then document, control, and modify these views. This is a common situation. When an aspect of a problem is not clearly identified and, more, reified in the solution, it tends to dissolve in the whole application, leading to "stiff" software. It is clearly a lesson learned from the pattern community: Simple calls and references are a low level of description when it comes to object cooperation. Naming these links and uses and defining canonical implementation is a key step toward software quality.

## 7.1.3 Modal or Nonmodal Interaction: Responsibility versus Forbidding

Another important aspect of interaction style we want to promote is the production of nonmodal software. In **modal** software, the application always stays in a state defined by the user's previous actions. In such a state, some actions are allowed; others are not. This situation results from the need to protect the system from undesirable, possibly fatal, actions. To limit necessary controls, designers define a set of states, each one giving access to a subset of actions and forbidding access to others. Thus, by registering the current state of the user, we can easily constrain user actions to those that are easy to control. This defines a graph of correct-use paths in the software and is very comforting for the programmer.

Unfortunately, this leads to complex interactions and asks a lot from the user. The user has to remember previous actions or may get stuck in a path in which the desired action is unreachable. The user then has to go back to the place where he or she took the wrong way. This looks a little bit like a maze, and the only way to get out of this maze is to carefully read the manual.

What we expect, on the contrary, is a stateless system. The choices the user is offered are always the same. Of course, a user who destroys an object will not be able to display it again. But the reason for this lies in the application semantic, not in the interface design.

Any controls have to be legitimized by the application. The integrity of the model should be granted by the model itself. A benefit of this **nonmodal approach** is that we don't need to spread it in the graphical components. If we offer users a set of choices that are consistent with model intrinsic states, we reduce user's memory efforts and give users a chance to gain deeper understanding of the system and make its behavior predictable, which is highly desirable.

Leaving this control in the model prevents exposing system internals. If the system changes, validity controls are modified accordingly, without further impacts on the interface.

## 7.1.4  A Consistent Interface from Uniform Mechanisms

### 7.1.4.1  *Defining Responsibilities and Isolating Them into Objects*

As we have noticed before, scattering behavior and control in numerous parts of the system is not the best way to keep a firm grip on the whole. By contrast, relying on a set of predefined components is a very secure way to guarantee a consistent interface, particularly in large software systems.

What we need is a palette of predefined coupling styles between an application and its interface. If the models of connection are properly defined, they could provide a firm basis during the analysis phase. Then, supported by a set of implementation schemes, they would ease the design and allow a unique confidence level in the implementation.

### 7.1.4.2  *Identifying Complex Tasks and Assigning Them Patterns*

Before going further into analysis, let's summarize the problem we are interested in. Suppose that we start with an applicative model that exists on its own. We want to build an interface to display this model and interact with it. Our aim is to minimize modification in the applicative part. We want to display and modify application properties, be notified of changes, and be able to trigger application services. When defining this interface, we select some properties of our model and combine and transform other properties to obtain the level of information we want to present to our user. These new notions are introduced to fill the gap that may exist between the applicative model and the user perception. These notions are built on top of the application model and should not interfere with it. The same holds for the graphics. What we want to display and how we choose to display it do not depend on the application. To keep the display accurate and leave the application free from any graphical code, we have to provide some general mechanisms that can bind them together.

## 7.2 Models and Designs

### 7.2.1 Two Worlds and a Bridge: From Application to Interface

#### 7.2.1.1 *The MVC Architecture*

The common architectural approach to deal with the user interface problem is the famous **Model-View-Controller (MVC)** approach, which was made popular by the Smalltalk environment (Goldberg and Robson, 1983). MVC was a good definition of the problem and proposed a clear solution. The applicative part of the application is kept independent from the interface, and a general mechanism is proposed to bind the graphic to the model without introducing graphical knowledge into the model. Reaction to an input can depend on both the model and the graphic. A *Controller* is introduced to define such a reaction. According to Buschmann et al. (1996), we can define the responsibilities of each component as follows:

- **Model**, the core application part,
  - Provides the functional core of the application
  - Registers dependent views and controllers
  - Notifies dependent components about data changes
- **View,** the graphical component of the interface,
  - Creates and initializes its controllers
  - Displays information to the user
  - Implements the update procedure to keep itself accurate
  - Retrieves data from the model
- **Controller,** the decision-making part of the application,
  - Accepts user inputs as events
  - Translates events to service requests for the model or display requests for the view
  - Implements indirect graphical update procedures if required.

The application driver creates the model and the view and then it initializes the view with the model. On initialization, the view registers on the model, creates a suitable controller, and initializes it with itself and the model. In turn, the controller registers on the model.

When a model change occurs, the model notifies the view. The view then updates its display and the controller so that it may perform some actions on graphics, such as action inhibitions.

When a user event occurs, the controller notifies the model in an appropriate way such that it can modify its state. In turn, the view is notified so that it can update its display. Finally, the controller is notified so that it can take the appropriate graphics actions.

### 7.2.1.2 A Particular Implementation

Our aim is to define a simple generic and possibly generizable implementation of the MVC architecture. So, the question is how to derive an implementation of an interface for a given model using the MVC approach.

- The model part is clear. It simply provides the basic services and carries the main system notions. What we add is a general mechanism of notification on change.

- The view part is responsible for the visual aspect. In classical MVC, the view part is also in charge of controller creation and update implementation.

- The controller directly receives user input and uses model knowledge to modify interface behavior.

One point to consider is the complexity of the view we will implement. The more complex it is, the bigger the controller is. At one extreme, we could find an application with only one view and one controller. In that case, the controller holds all of the application logic, and the view is totally application specific. Clearly, it is not the best solution for reusability. To remedy that problem, a particular refinement of the MVC model, the **PAC** model, has been developed (Coutaz, 1987). The PAC model (**Presentation-Abstraction-Control**) proposes an implementation of the MVC principle, based on a hierarchy of MVC triads. A first triad is connected to the model and to a lower level of triads, which plays the role of its views. The lowest level implements the graphical views. The responsibility of the intermediate levels is to coordinate the various views.

This model is difficult for us to manipulate in a generic way. Here, the specificity of the application is hard-wired into the composition of the various levels of PACs and in the coding of their control. We can consider PAC as the intermediate approach to the MVC implementation.

At the other extreme, there is a new possibility to explore: the reduction of views to their atomic expression. Each nonstatic element in the interface needs to have its behavior defined. We propose to do that through the use of an object that defines the projection between the applicative model world and the particular graphic. We call this projection a *view*, even though in the MVC model, it is a kind of atomic controller. If it is extreme, this approach gives us some interesting possibilities.

- We can define a taxonomy of the displayers.

- We can define a set of patterns to express the way they communicate with the model.

- We can reuse the patterns through composition.

We will now try to define more precisely what we obtain. We call our approach the **MVG** model, or **Model-View-Graphic**.

Following what we said before, we end up with a three-tier model.

- **Model:** The applicative model holds intrinsic properties and operational abilities that characterize the system. The model comprises a graph of interrelated objects, with the more peripheral ones implementing the concepts identified during analysis or even specification activities. All of the notions the user is aware of lie in the model. The model can be defined on its own with its self-contained semantics.

    In order to be of some use, the model needs to expose some of its properties to the outside world. Some of its components can be observed, and some can be modified; some of its services can be triggered.

- **View**. The views define how we attach graphics to model. Regarding the general notion of projection we attach to views, we could say that they define the intended use of the model. They combine various model aspects and even define by-products. Our purpose is to provide simple, reusable elements that carry the atomic controls sufficient to implement the system interface. As long as there is no need to build temporary objects out of the realm of the application, our simple views are enough to build the system. In the other case, we propose to introduce dedicated elements, or **editors,** to carry out these transformations. *Editors* use observation mechanisms to be linked to the model and are then to be considered as model elements from the interface point of view. Thus, editors can be presented to the user in the same way, building on the set of views.

- **Graphic:** The graphics are the visible part of the system. They also define the interacting schemes between the user and the system and implement the way public parts of the system are accessed by the user. Apart from the underlying components used, our interest will be focused on the protocol of communication they define.

Our resulting triad is a variant of the **Model-View-Controller** architecture. In our case, we put strong restrictions on the role of views and the controller. In our model, we use the term Graphic for the visual part, as we consider only elementary components and their protocol of communication. Our View is the connection between the Graphic and Model components as we want to constrain them to canonical forms of control. We then propose to express these forms of control by a set of patterns. Leaving semantics control in the model and assigning the responsibility of elaborate dependency checking in the editors, we get the opportunity to elaborate a systematic approach and to assemble patterns to form a generic way of composing an interface.

We are now able to define the low level above which an interface is built. This level will also provide a kind of operational description of the model, independent of model semantics.

We consider a model as a set of objects, either atomic or composed, linked to one another and providing services through callable routines. Our notion of atomic objects is biased toward our aim. We consider an object atomic if a graphical component is able to display and modify it. At the beginning of our process, this notion will carry a simple meaning: strings, numbers, Boolean, and the like, will form the set of atomic components.

Displaying a composite object is obtained by the composition of the display of some of its atomic components. Displaying a part of a system is obtained by the composition of the display of some of its objects and the links that bind them together.

## 7.2.2  The Observer: Always the Same; Always Different

### 7.2.2.1  *Principles*

The first goal to achieve is the accurate display of atomic objects' values. We consider a composite object we want to display: say, a phone book with directories and cards made of atomic values we call attributes; or a name and a phone number. (See Figure 7.1.)

As we want the display to keep up with the model value, the first attempt is the use of the Observer (187) pattern. The graphics, here two text fields, will register as observers of the CARD. This means that the model, here the CARD, will be modified in two ways.

- CARD will inherit from OBSERVABLE, thus gaining the interface to register and unregister observers, as well as implementation of the notification mechanism.

- All attribute modifications will get a hook. This is made easier if all changes are made through the disciplined used of a mutator, in which case a simple call to notify has to be added to this routine. In Eiffel, the use of a mutator is mandatory for modifications performed outside the object. For internal

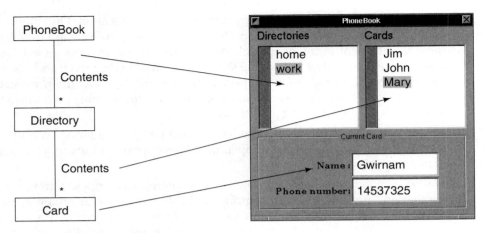

**Figure 7.1** A simple example: Phone Book

modifications, we may adapt our strategy to particular cases. In ordinary cases, this call has to be added after each modification of the attributes.

On the graphics side, let's suppose that we use a particular object library that provides a widget class dedicated to displaying strings. We call TEXTFIELD such a class. We need to define a TEXTFIELD subclass that inherits from OBSERVER and that redefines the *model_has_changed* routine to get the value of the CARD *name* attribute and set the content of the TEXTFIELD accordingly. Moreover, the creation of the graphic should be extended so that it could register on the CARD and get the initial value on opening.

Although functional, this solution is not satisfactory. The main drawback is the increased responsibility put on the graphic's part. The separation of concern is lost. It's not the graphic's role to keep track of the model layout. To solve this problem, we introduce a *view* between model and graphic.

### 7.2.2.2 *Refinement on the Observer*

As we want to keep notifications at a minimum level, we want to make sure that nothing useless is propagated. Useless notifications arise when an object receives an event it is not interested in. In the observer case, this happens when a feature of an object changes and the registration mechanism does not provide for interest declaration at feature level. Thus, observers receive notifications even if the changing item is not part of their concern. To solve this problem, we propose a fine-grained registration mechanism that makes it possible to select which particular object part the observers feel concerned about. On the observer side, a simple *model_has_change* protocol is set.

```
deferred class OBSERVER
feature
   model_has_changed (subject : OBSERVABLE ; feature_id : INTEGER) is
      -- notification entry point
      deferred
      end
   path_has_connected (an_obj, a_target : OBSERVABLE ; feature_id, a_rank
                                    : INTEGER) is
      -- item a_target has been inserted in observed relation
      require
         valid_object : an_obj /= Void
      deferred
      end
   path_has_broken  (an_obj, a_target : OBSERVABLE ; feature_id, a_rank
                                    : INTEGER) is
      -- item a_target has been removed from observed relation
      require
         valid_object : an_obj /= Void
      deferred
      end
end -- OBSERVER
```

The OBSERVABLE class provides all of the necessary services for registering and notifying observers. The *feature_id* parameters carry the *Meta Information* necessary to identify one feature among others in the most abstract way.

There are many ways of doing it. The solution described here is not the simplest. It is possible to identify features through their name and to store the list of observers in a dictionary. In practice, observer lists tend to be short, so the overhead due to hashing overcomes the benefit of O(1) access most of the time.

We use a robust iteration over observers. This is a worst-case solution. A more economical approach is to use a simple iterator providing postcondition to ensure that the traversal was safe. See the Iterator (159) pattern for a description of such an iterator.

Here is the code of our OBSERVABLE.

```
deferred class OBSERVABLE
feature
   init_observer is
      -- build the list of registered observers, initially empty
      do
         !!observers.make
```

```
    ensure
        observers_not_void : observers /= Void
    end -- init_observer
add_observer (observer : OBSERVER; feature_id : INTEGER) is
    -- registers observer on a particular feature defined by feature_id
    require
        obs_not_void : observer /= Void
        initialized : observers /= Void
    do
        observers.add(feature_id,observer)
    end -- add_observer
remove_observer (observer : OBSERVER; feature_id : INTEGER) is
    -- removes observer from the list of feature_id clients
    require
        obs_not_void : observer /= Void
        initialized : observers /= Void
    do
        observers.remove(feature_id,observer)
    end -- remove_observer
notify (feature_id : INTEGER) is
    -- calls model_has_changed on all observers registered on this feature
    require
        initialized : observers /= Void
    local
        original_list, copy_list : LINKED_LIST[OBSERVER]
        i : INTEGER
        observer : OBSERVER
    do
        -- We make a copy of observer list to perform a robust
        -- iteration over it. Notification may have side effects on other
        -- items of the list.
        original_list := observers.for(feature_id)
        if original_list /= Void then
            !!copy_list.from_collection(original_list)
            from i := copy_list.lower
            until i > copy_list.upper
            loop
                observer := copy_list.item(i)
                if original_list.has(observer) then
                    observer.model_has_changed(Current,feature_id)
                end -- if
                i := i + 1
            end -- loop
        end -- if
```

```
    end -- notify
disconnect_notify (removed_item : OBSERVABLE ; feature_id, rank : INTEGER) is
    -- calls path_has_broken on all observers registered on this feature
    require
        initialized : observers /= Void
    local
        original_list, copy_list : LINKED_LIST[OBSERVER]
        i : INTEGER
        observer : OBSERVER
    do
        -- We make a copy of observer list to perform a robust
        -- iteration over it. Notification may have side effects on other
        -- items of the list.
        original_list := observers.for(feature_id)
        if original_list /= Void then
            !!copy_list.from_collection(original_list)
            from i := copy_list.lower
            until i > copy_list.upper
            loop
                observer := copy_list.item(i)
                if original_list.has(observer) then
                    observer.path_has_broken(Current,removed_item,feature_id,rank)
                end -- if
                i := i + 1
            end -- loop
        end -- if
    end -- disconnect_notify
connect_notify (inserted_item : OBSERVABLE ; feature_id, rank : INTEGER) is
    -- calls path_has_connected on all observers registered on this feature
    require
        initialized : observers /= Void
    local
        original_list, copy_list : LINKED_LIST[OBSERVER]
        i : INTEGER
        observer : OBSERVER
    do
        -- We make a copy of observer list to perform a robust
        -- iteration over it. Notification may have side effects on other
        -- items of the list.
        original_list := observers.for(feature_id)
        if original_list /= Void then
            !!copy_list.from_collection(original_list)
            from i := copy_list.lower
            until i > copy_list.upper
```

```
        loop
            observer := copy_list.item(i)
            if original_list.has(observer) then
                observer.path_has_connected(Current,inserted_item,feature_id,rank)
            end -- if
            i := i + 1
        end -- loop
    end -- if
  end -- connect_notify
feature {NONE}
  observers : OBSERVER_LIST
end -- OBSERVABLE
```

The list of list of observers, sorted by items, could be managed by a class like OBSERVER_LIST.

```
class OBSERVER_LIST
creation
    make
feature
    make is
        -- initializes the two lists used to register observers
        do
            !!items.make
            !!observers_lists.make
        ensure
            item_list_not_void : items /= Void
            observers_lists_not_void : observers_lists /= Void
        end -- make
    for (id : INTEGER) : LINKED_LIST[OBSERVER] is
        -- returns observers list dedicated to a particular feature_id
        local
            pos : INTEGER
        do
            if items.has(id) then
                pos := items.fast_index_of(id)
                Result := observers_lists.item(pos)
            end -- if
        end -- for
    add (id : INTEGER ; obs : OBSERVER) is
        -- registers a new observer on some feature_id
        require
            observer_not_void : obs /= Void
```

```
        local
            obs_list : LINKED_LIST[OBSERVER]
        do
            obs_list := for(id)
            if (obs_list = void) then
                !!obs_list.make
                observers_lists.add_last(obs_list)
                items.add_last(id)
            end -- if
            obs_list.add_last(obs)
        end -- add
    remove (id : INTEGER ; obs : OBSERVER) is
        -- take an observer out of the list of observers concerned by
        -- the specified feature_id
        require
            observer_not_void : obs /= Void
        local
            obs_list : LINKED_LIST[OBSERVER]
            pos_item : INTEGER
            pos_obs : INTEGER
        do
            obs_list := for(id)
            if obs_list /= void and obs_list.has(obs) then
                pos_obs := obs_list.fast_index_of(obs)
                obs_list.remove(pos_obs)
                if pos_obs.count = 0 then
                    pos_item := items.fast_index_of(id)
                    observers_lists.remove(pos_item)
                    items.remove(pos_item)
                end -- if pos_obs
            end -- if obs_list
        end -- add
feature {NONE}
    items : LINKED_LIST[INTEGER]
    observers_lists : LINKED_LIST[LINKED_LIST[OBSERVER]]
end -- OBSERVER_LIST
```

---

Now we have to deal with the problem of members' identifications: where to get them and how to declare them. We propose a simple solution, based on the use of a unique number generator ID_GENERATOR accessed through the Singleton (79) pattern and defining a *new_id* routine. See the discussion on Singleton (79) implementation for more details.

To use this, we resort to a special class responsible for carrying the meta-information we need. One such class will be defined for each observable class and itself will be a singleton and an heir of a DESCRIPTOR. This last class encapsulates the use of the singleton ID_GENERATOR. It provides a unique routine, *new_id*, which creates a singleton accessor and calls back *new_id* on it. An example of such a descriptive class looks like the following, taken from our example.

```
expanded class CARD_DESCRIPTOR
inherit
  DESCRIPTOR
feature {ANY} -- Public
  name_id : INTEGER is
     once
        Result := new_id
     end --name_id
  phone_numer_id : INTEGER is
     once
        Result := new_id
     end --name_id
end -- CARD_DESCRIPTOR
```

To be fully operational, the descriptor inheritance hierarchy must match the model classes' inheritance hierarchy. This is mandatory if we want to be able to ask a descriptor for the ID of an inherited attribute. This also guarantees that we obtain the same value from wherever we ask for it.

A simpler approach is possible. Instead of managing feature identifiers, we could have the OBSERVABLE use maps of OBSERVER lists, indexed by the name of the feature. This is made possible by the unambiguity granted by the compiler: no inheritance name clash or overloading. In that case, the observer can just ask to register on a particular feature by giving its name. The cost of hashing decreases when the number of observed features increases.

### 7.2.2.3 *Inserting a View between the Model and the Graphic*

As we don't want to put specific model knowledge in the graphics part, we introduce a special class, a VIEW, between the model and the graphic. The VIEW will be responsible for registering on the model instances. To map a particular item to a particular graphic, we derive a dedicated view class, which will inherit the behavior of both an observer and a graphics client. This is the place for a two-way collaboration: toward a model and toward a graphic. Figure 7.2 illustrates the transformation induced by the view.

The view is the result of two patterns: the Observer (187) pattern and a degenerate form of Observer. In the solution we present here, views can be thought of as

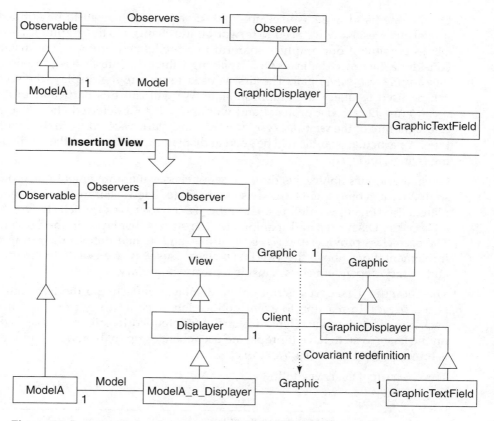

**Figure 7.2** Inserting a view between the model and the graphic

monoobservers. They don't have to select on the observable to decide their be-havior. On the graphics side, they also are monoobservable, in the same fashion. The link from graphic to view is unique in both directions. This could be consid-ered a strong restriction. It is quite possible to design a view with many models and many graphics. We choose not to do it, to keep the atomic aspect we pre-sented while discussing our MVC implementation.

One thing is interesting to note. When a given object participates in two reifi-cations of the same pattern, a simple way to keep things clear is to rename the feature, supporting the protocol. Here, *modelHasChanged* becomes *graphicHas Changed*; thus, the need for switching on the source disappears.

We can define two phases in our approach: (1) abstract the interface of the GRAPHIC and (2) put the model-tracking responsibility onto the VIEW. These two operations are complementary.

On the one hand, we have set up an observation mechanism to be notified of model changes. Now we need to forward these changes to the graphics. This becomes possible if our graphics conform to a predefined protocol. For instance, consider a GRAPHIC dedicated to displaying values. Its interface is composed of a (*set_value*, *get_value*) pair. The first is used to update the display; the second can be used to query the graphical state. We will call this particular protocol a GRAPHIC_DISPLAYER protocol and will assign it to a deferred class. The precise signature of the *set_value/get_value* routines varies according to the graphics type. A particular graphic will be good at displaying integers, another at displaying strings, and so on.

Given a graphics library, we derive a set of classes that implement our protocol so that we can bind them to models via dedicated views. For instance, to manipulate a TEXTFIELD, we define a GRAPHIC_TEXT_DISPLAYER, which derives from a GRAPHIC_DISPLAYER and manipulates the strings displayed in the TEXTFIELD. The base class provides the *get/set* features, and its heir defines their graphical implementations above the TEXTFIELD class. This way, we isolate the platform- and library-dependent classes inside a precise boundary.

The GRAPHIC_DISPLAYER is not only a displayer, reflecting a model value, but also a *trigger*. In reaction to event notification, such as a key press, it will call back a dedicated action. Here, this action is intended to call *graphicHasChanged* on the DISPLAYER to have it propagate user changes up to the model. This action is reified in the DISPLAYER_ACTION class.

The GRAPHIC_DISPLAYER follows.

```
deferred class GRAPHIC_DISPLAYER
inherit GRAPHIC
    redefine client, set_client end;
feature
    set_client (displayer : DISPLAYER) is
        -- attach client view to the graphic
        require
            valid_displayer: displayer /= Void
        do
            client := displayer
            -- register graphicHasChanged as callback through action
            !!action.make(client)
            -- We could use associative map from event to action to be general
        ensure
            client = displayer
        end  -- set_client
    set_content (data : ANY) is
        -- defines new graphical content to be displayed
```

```
            deferred
            end
        client : DISPLAYER
        content : ANY
    feature {NONE}
        action : DISPLAYER_ACTION
        on_event is
            -- react to graphical events
            do
                -- actions should be associated with particular events
                if action /= Void then
                    action.execute
                end -- if
            end -- on_event
    end -- GRAPHIC_DISPLAYER
```

The DISPLAYER_ACTION simply follows the Command (147) pattern and can be implemented as follows.

```
class DISPLAYER_ACTION
inherit
    ACTION
creation
    make
feature
    make (cl : DISPLAYER) is
        -- initializes client
        require
            client_not_void : cl /= Void
        do
            client := cl
        end -- make
    execute is
        -- calls back graphicHasChanged
        do
            client.graphic_has_changed
        end -- execute
feature {NONE}
    client : DISPLAYER
invariant
    client_not_void : client /= Void
end -- DISPLAYER_ACTION
```

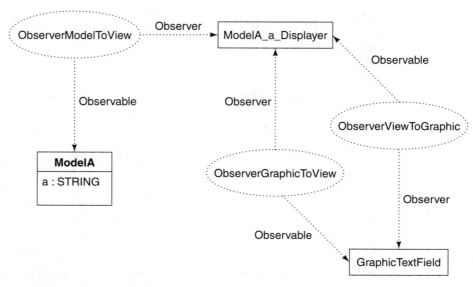

**Figure 7.3** A design with three observers

In fact, we use the Command (147) pattern to produce a degenerate implementation of the Observer (187) pattern. Our model is in fact composed of three observers, as described in Figure 7.3.

The observation of the view from the graphic (*ObserverViewToGraphic*) reduces to almost nothing. The registration is performed on initialization. As soon as the view changes in response to model changes, it propagates via a *setContent* to the graphic. The other way round, the graphic notifies the View of its changes by firing the attached action. This default action calls *graphicHasChanged* on the view. This way, the graphic is not aware of the precise nature of the view to which it is connected.

The role of a view displayer is to bind the graphic to its model. Here again, we have a two-level hierarchy. The general mechanism of being notified of object changes and propagating them to the graphic is dealt with by a DISPLAYER. At a lower level, according to the Observer (187) pattern, the concrete displayers implement the update procedure. If we come back to the Phone Book example, a NAME_DISPLAYER class and a NUMBER_DISPLAYER class are set up. Each knows its model class and the attribute it observes. This knowledge is hard-coded in the *model_has_changed* routine.

The code of the DISPLAYER follows.

```
deferred class DISPLAYER
inherit
  SINGLE_VIEW
    redefine graphic end;
  ATTRIBUTE_OBSERVER
feature
  model_has_changed (subject : OBSERVABLE ; feature_id : INTEGER) is
    -- update graphic according to model change
    do
      update_graphic
    end -- model_has_changed
  graphic_has_changed is
    -- update model according to graphic change
    do
      set_model_value(graphic.content)
    end -- graphic_has_changed
  get_model_value : ANY is
    -- how to get value from model
    deferred
    end -- get_model_value
  set_model_value(a_value : ANY) is
    -- how to set value in model
    deferred
    end -- set_model_value
  open_displayer (a_model : OBSERVABLE) is
    -- register the possibly new model then open and update graphic
    do
      update_graphic
    end -- open_displayer
  close_displayer is
    -- forget model and close graphic
    do
      disconnect
      graphic.close
    end -- close_displayer
  disconnect is
    -- forget model
    do
      model := Void
      graphic.empty
    end -- disconnect
  update_graphic is
```

```
        -- modify graphic content according to model
    do
        graphic.set_content(get_model_value)
    end -- update_graphic
graphic : GRAPHIC_DISPLAYER
end -- DISPLAYER
```

The NAME_DISPLAYER class, which implements the deferred routines, follows.

```
class NAME_DISPLAYER
inherit
  DISPLAYER
    redefine model, open end
feature
  open (card : CARD) is
    -- registers model and opens graphic
    require
      valid_model : card /= Void
    local
      descriptor : CARD_DESCRIPTOR
    do
      connect_model(card)
      model.add_observer(Current,descriptor.name_id)
      open_displayer(card)
    end -- open
  close is
    -- forget model and close graphic
    local
      descriptor : CARD_DESCRIPTOR
    do
      model.remove_observer(Current,descriptor.name_id)
      close_displayer
    end -- close
  get_model_value : STRING is
    -- how to get value from model
    do
      if model /= Void then
        Result := model.name
      else
        !!Result.copy("")
      end --if
    end -- get_model_value
  set_model_value(a_value : STRING) is
```

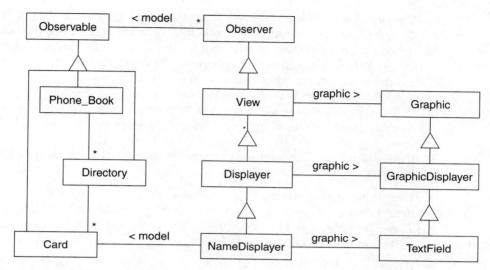

**Figure 7.4** Card name diagram

```
          -- how to set value in model
      do
          if model /= Void then
              model.set_name(a_value)
          end -- if
      end -- set_model_value
   model : CARD
end -- NAME_DISPLAYER
```

The various relationships between these classes are presented in Figure 7.4.

Keeping a display up to date with its model is not the only problem to be addressed. A number of other issues have to be dealt with, including

- **Model instance selection:** The displayer has to register on a particular instance of its model class—the CARD in the previous example. We must define a way to tell the displayer how to reach that instance. Note that the model instance selection may depend on the particular state of other interface elements. For instance, it can be the selected item in a list.

- **Graphic creation and binding:** Views need some graphics knowledge. They have to be linked to the proper graphical instance to make an accurate display possible. If we consider the set of Views on the one hand and the set of Graphics on the other, they form two related graphs. The first one describes the observed objects and how they are linked. It is described by the views and their relationships. The second one describes the composition of the interface, that is, the layout of the various graphics items. Although not directly dependent, these graphs have to respect a number of constraints in order to make the mapping between them possible. Integer displayer views can only be plugged into graphics able to display integers; the same holds for *triggers* and *selectors*, which we will describe later. The set of graphics defines a list of entry points. Each of these points is typed by the protocol it can handle. The same holds for the set of views. Pairing these protocols is the way we map graphics to views.

- **User input management:** When the user clicks on a button, selects an item, or modifies entries, the model should be modified accordingly. These Triggers should be equipped with commands that fire under the particular event-reception situation.

- **Access path tracking:** Models are reached by following a particular path through our system. This path can change over time. Some instances may become unreachable; in that case, the associated displayers should disappear. Or, new objects may be created and registered in observed relationships. The associated displayers have to be provided. To deal with such transformations, we introduce the notion of Path_Observer, which registers over a link between two objects. That is, it registers on the object that is the origin of the link for changes on the relationships that leads to the object on the other end. Thus, it can manage connections and disconnections along that path. If a view has to traverse several relationships to reach its model, all of these links have to be observed. Where should the observation start? When a group of views is opened, a context is provided. Some model instances are provided on opening. We will start observation from these objects.

## 7.2.3  Graphics Creation and Binding

As we mentioned earlier, the dependency between the graph of observations and the composition of the graphical interface is loose. For example, we have a phone book with many cards, and we want to build an interface to examine them. Suppose that we want a window with a list of cards and a frame to display the selected card with two text fields: one for the name and one for the phone number. When we start our application, we open the window on our phone book. That is, when our view is opened, it is opened on a **context**, namely, the instance of the phone book we use. The context is the set of instances we call **root instances**. They define the origin of our graph of observation.

At the same time, the view we have defined will open along with all of the subviews. The graphical part will do the same, and both will connect. Thus, on the one side, we have a view set, defined by a context (root instances), a set of views, and the path from the root instances to the models of the views. On the other side, we have a window with layouts, a list, and text fields.

Since views need to be aware of the graphics they have to connect to (and not the reverse) it is natural to let the views create the graphics. Two approaches are possible.

1. Define an abstract view class for each graphic: displayers and triggers, as well as windows and layouts. Thus, we obtain a direct mapping between graphics and views. Creating a view will create the corresponding graphic and will link them. Graphical resources can be managed at the view level and graphical layout carried out by layout views.

2. Build both sets as a whole and define a mechanism for the views to get the particular graphics they have to link with. The graphics properties and layout are carried by a dedicated class called a GRAPHIC_SET. This class provides suitable entry points for a VIEW_SET to map on. Items in the view set are responsible for the model knowledge. According to this second approach, we obtain the following code for view.

```
deferred class VIEW
feature
  open_view is
    -- propagates open on subviews if any and then open graphics
    do
      graphic.open
    end -- open_view
  close is
    -- the view is used no more; notify dependents
    deferred
    end -- close
  graphic : GRAPHIC
  map (a_graphic : like graphic) is
    -- associate views to their corresponding representations
    require
      valid_graphic : a_graphic /= Void
    do
      graphic := a_graphic
```

```
        graphic.set_client(Current)
    ensure
        graphic_initialized : graphic /= Void
    end  -- map
end  -- VIEW
```

The following discussion presents both approaches but gives detailed description only of the second one, which gives more flexibility. We call the first solution the *simple approach*; the second, the *decoupled approach*.

### 7.2.3.1 The Simple Approach

Direct mapping establishes a one-to-one mapping between views and graphics. For each graphics protocol, we define a subclass of VIEW. Each view carries the knowledge of both its model and its graphic. When a view is created, the associated graphic is created. The graphic attaches the view as its client and receives its properties. When the view is opened, it tries to connect to its model and then updates and displays the graphic. The path followed by the instance to reach its model is hard-coded into the *open* routine, which has to go carefully through each step toward the model. Views are linked in a hierarchy that mimics the graphic composition tree. The same composition tree is used to forward the *open* or *close* requests. To make this mapping possible, we define five graphics categories and thus five view categories.

- **Triggers** are in charge of mapping user input to the triggering of an application service. A trigger view is notified when a particular graphical event occurs. That view stores commands according to their firing event. In response to the notification, all commands registered on that event are executed. Triggers are typically mapped with button or menu items.

- **Displayers** maintain an up-to-date representation of a model property in the corresponding graphic. They register as observers on both the attribute they display and each relationship they traverse to reach their model. As we mentioned before, this path of observation has to start somewhere. When a window is opened, a set of instances, called *root instances*, is passed along. That set defines the context of execution of that window. Those root instances are supposed to be always valid, or nonvoid, instances. From an observation perspective, root instances are considered fixed objects. Singleton object are also good candidates to start an observation path, even if they are not part of the window context. Displayers are also often triggers to support users' modifications. Displayers are typically associated with text fields.

- **Layouts** register which view is a subview of the current one. Layouts provide mechanisms to add or remove a subview. They are also in charge of the open and close propagation.

- **Windows,** a particular case of layouts, also provide the root instances that form the context of the overall view. Roots are those objects we consider to be fixed.

- **Selectors** are the views we use to observe a relationship. A selector, with one model and one subview class, observes a particular relationship on that model. When an object is added to this relationship, the selector creates a new instance of its subview and gives it its rank in the relationship. This information is used to maintain the relative position of the subviews in the relationship. We call it the *route*. For each multiple relationship traversed, the relative rank is stored in the route of the subview. Then, the subview is opened, with the new object as its model. As they can react to an object selection, selectors are also triggers. When a subview is selected by the user, the selector registers the corresponding model object in its *selection* relationship. Selectors are often associated with lists.

### 7.2.3.2 *The Decoupled Approach*

This is the solution we present in more detail. Our motivation when building this solution was to be able to reuse views and graphics independently.

The simple approach was designed to make it possible to generate views from the graphical layout description. As we have seen, with one graphic leading to one view, it is easy to deduce the view classes and the way they are connected. What is left up to the programmer is the description of the connections to the model.

Here, we want to keep views as independent from the graphic as possible. To make it possible, we group views and graphics into two different sets. All graphical information is carried by a GRAPHIC_SET subclass. A concrete graphic set provides entry points to access those graphical components that may be connected to views. On the other hand, a VIEW_SET gathers the views. This class defines a context, a corresponding GRAPHIC_SET, and a mapping between the GRAPHIC_SET entry points and the elements of the VIEW_SET. What was a WINDOW in the former approach becomes a VIEW_SET. In the same way, the subview of a SELECTOR is a VIEW_SET as well. In the simple approach, each view builds its corresponding graphic. Here, only VIEW_SET carries this role. The main abstract classes are described in Figure 7.5.

Each view is associated with a graphic in charge of displaying it. This relationship is redefined for SELECTOR DISPLAYER and VIEW_SET but not implemented for TRUNK, as we will see in the following section. A SINGLE_VIEW is linked to a

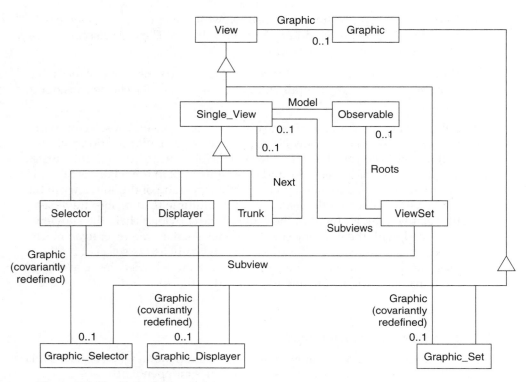

**Figure 7.5** The VIEW_SET model

model that must derive from OBSERVABLE. For a VIEW_SET, we define the working context as a set of instances recorded as *roots*.

On creation, the concrete VIEW_SET creates its subviews; links them to one another, if necessary; creates the GRAPHIC_set chosen for the display; and maps the views to the graphics. Now, the VIEW_SET is ready to receive its working instances for opening.

VIEW_SET code follows.

```
deferred class VIEW_SET
inherit
   VIEW
feature
   init is
      -- create subviews and graphics and bind them together
      -- template method
      do
```

```
                !!subviews.make
                build_subviews
                map(init_graphic)
            end
        disconnect is
                -- model disappeared, notify dependents
            local
                indice : INTEGER
            do
                from
                    indice := subviews.lower
                until
                    indice > subviews.upper
                loop
                    subviews.elem(i).disconnect
                end
            end
        close is
                -- the view is used no more; notify dependents
            local
                indice : INTEGER
            do
                from
                    indice := subviews.lower
                until
                    indice > subviews.upper
                loop
                    subviews.elem(i).close
                end
            end
    feature {NONE}
        init_graphic : GRAPHIC is
            -- build the associated graphic
            deferred
            end
        build_subviews is
            -- build subviews and connect them
            deferred
            ensure
                has_subviews : subviews.count > 0
            end
        subviews : LINKED_LIST[VIEW]
    end -- VIEW_SET
```

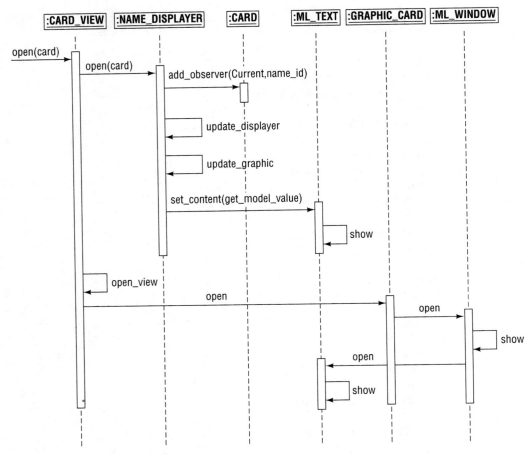

**Figure 7.6** Opening a VIEW_SET

What happens on opening is depicted in Figure 7.6. To make things clearer, we give the code for CARD_VIEW.

```
class CARD_VIEW
inherit VIEW_SET
    redefine build_subviews, map, graphic, init_graphic end
creation
    make
feature
    make is
        do
            init
```

```
            end  -- make
        open(directory : DIRECTORY) is
            -- propagates open on subviews and then open graphics
            do
                selector.open(directory)
                selection_link.open(selector)
                open_view
            end  -- open
        name : NAME_DISPLAYER
        number : NUMBER_DISPLAYER
        selector : CARD_SELECTOR
        selection_link : TRUNK_SELECTOR
        graphic : GRAPHIC_CARD
    feature {NONE}
        build_subviews is
            -- build subviews and connect them
            do
                !!name
                !!number
                !!selector.make
                !!selection_link.make
                subviews.add_last(name)
                subviews.add_last(number)
                subviews.add_last(selector)
                selection_link.add_next(name)
                selection_link.add_next(number)
            end  -- build_subviews
        init_graphic : GRAPHIC_CARD is
            -- build selected graphic representation
            do
                !!graphic.make
                Result := graphic
            end  -- init_graphic
        map (a_graphic : GRAPHIC_CARD) is
            -- associate views to their corresponding representations
            require
                valid_graphic : a_graphic /= Void
            do
                name.map(a_graphic.text_up)
                number.map(a_graphic.text_down)
                selector.map(a_graphic.selector)
            end  -- map
end  -- CARD_VIEW
```

The following code of the associated Graphic_Card uses graphics from a hypothetical library called ML. We use this library to implement a window ML_Window, a text field ML_Text, and a selection list ML_List.

```
class GRAPHIC_CARD
inherit
  GRAPHIC
    redefine open
    end
creation
  make
feature
  make is
    do
      !!window.make
      !!text_up.make
      !!text_down.make
      !!selector.make
      window.add(text_up)
      window.add(text_down)
      window.add(selector)
    end
  open is
    do
      window.open
    end
  close is
    do
      window.close
    end
  show is
    do
      window.show
    end
  hide is
    do
      window.hide
    end
  window : ML_WINDOW
  text_up,text_down : ML_TEXT
  selector : ML_LIST
end -- GRAPHIC_CARD
```

## 7.2.4  Keeping Track of Model Path Changes

An important aspect of both the simple and the decoupled approaches is the ability to register on a path between objects, which provides opportunity to react to structure changes in the model. Often, information becomes of particular interest as soon as corresponding objects get registered in a relationship. An object that goes out of the scope of interest is often removed from some relationships. Observing these relationships is thus a precious hint about the overall model change. When a path is broken, displayers become meaningless, as lists are to be updated. When a new item is inserted in a path, displayers have to be introduced to present this new element. When observing a path, we have to take care of both the item that gets in or out of the relationship and the rank of this changing item.

We explained earlier that we consider that a window opens in a given context. This context is defined by the objects provided to the window as open parameters. We make the assumption that these objects won't disappear while the window is open. These objects are the fixed reference points in our landscape. We call them *roots*. When a displayer opens, it needs to register on each link traversed from a root instance to the object that provides the attribute it observes. If that path is broken, the displayer becomes meaningless. It has to close or to appear insensitive. There are at least two ways of registering that path.

- In the simple approach, each displayer has the registry hard-coded in a *register_path* method, called on the opening. If the displayer can reach its model, it registers it and opens its graphic with the proper content.

- In the decoupled approach, each edge observation is set up by the VIEW_ SET and shared among the views. The graph of observation from the roots to the displayers of this *View_Set* is carried out by instances of the class TRUNK. Each TRUNK is in charge of the observation of one edge in the observation graph that is not displayed. The trunks are chained in a *next* relationship, and displayers are hooked on them, unless they directly observe VIEW_SET *roots*.

Virtually, we could consider that we browse through the graph of object relationships and mark those we are interested in. Thus, we draw the trail of our interest. All marked links get an observer attached, therefore, a cut in that path gets forwarded to the appropriate views. On view opening, the path is followed, and all observers and displayers get their models. Those whose model can't be reached start in an incomplete state, waiting to receive notification of connection.

### 7.2.4.1  Connection Notification

When an item gets inserted in an observed link between two objects, the object that carries the link is an observable and notifies all of the path observers that a new item has been inserted at a particular position. Two situations may occur.

- That item was a missing link in the path to the model of a displayer. In that case, the displayer will be notified directly or via the trunk it is connected to that its connection has been reset and will be able to open on this newly reached model.

- The link is observed by a selector. A new subview will be added to the list managed by that selector. This subview will be opened with the new item as part of its context. In turn, the displayer will open on the newly created model.

In the simple approach, one displayer happens to be observer of many path edges. Thus, when notified, the displayer needs to provide code for determining which portion of the path was modified. It does this by object reference comparison between the object provided by the notification and the various items on its path. Depending on where the connection appeared, the displayer will or will not open its graphic. This is the place where it uses the route information to properly traverse multiple links. The procedure used on opening is quite similar.

When using the decoupled approach, trunks are chained to one another in a *next* relationship up to displayers and selectors. One link propagates information to all its *next* colleagues. The trunk code looks like the following.

```
deferred class TRUNK
inherit
    PATH_OBSERVER
        redefine path_has_connected, path_has_broken
        end
    SINGLE_VIEW
feature
    open_trunk (an_obj, a_target : OBSERVABLE) is
        require
            valid_source : an_obj /= Void
        do
            an_obj.add_observer(Current,relation_id)
            if a_target /= Void then
                open_next(a_target)
            end -- if
        ensure
            trunk_registered_on_source : -- Current declared as observer
        end -- open_trunk
    close  (an_obj : OBSERVABLE) is
        require
            valid_source : an_obj /= Void
        do
```

```
      if model /= Void then
         model := Void
         an_obj.remove_observer(Current,relation_id)
         close_next
      end -- if
   end -- close
path_has_connected (an_obj : like model ; a_target :OBSERVABLE ;
                    feature_id, a_rank : INTEGER) is
   require
      non_multiple_relation : a_rank < 2
   do
      if a_target /= Void then
         open_next(a_target)
      end --if
   end -- path_has_connected
path_has_broken (an_obj :  like model ; a_target :OBSERVABLE ;
                 feature_id, a_rank : INTEGER) is
   require
      valid_object : an_obj /= Void
      non_multiple_relation : a_rank < 2
   do
      close_next
   end -- path_has_broken
add_next(an_obs : SINGLE_VIEW) is
   require
      valid_observer : an_obs /= Void
   do
      next.add_last(an_obs)
   end -- add_next
remove_next (an_obs : SINGLE_VIEW) is
   require
      valid_observer : an_obs /= Void
   local
      i : INTEGER
   do
      if next.has(an_obs) then
         i := fast_index_of(an_obs)
         next.remove(i)
      end -- if
   end -- remove_next
feature {NONE} -- Private
get_target (a_source : like model) : OBSERVABLE is
   -- returns object at the end of the observed relationship
   require
```

```
                valid_source : a_source /= Void
            deferred
            end -- get_target
        open_next(a_target : OBSERVABLE) is
            require
                valid_target : a_target /= Void
            local
                i : INTEGER
            do
                from i := next.lower
                until i > next.upper
                loop
                    next.item(i).open(a_target)
                    i := i + 1
                end -- loop
            end -- open_next
        close_next is
            local
                i : INTEGER
            do
                from i := next.lower
                until i > next.upper
                loop
                    next.item(i).close
                    i := i + 1
                end -- loop
            end -- close_next
        relation_id : INTEGER
        next : LINKED_LIST[SINGLE_VIEW]
    invariant
        next_list_initialized : next /= Void
    end -- TRUNK
```

### 7.2.4.2 Disconnection Notification

The scenario is the same for disconnection. Displayers will get notified that they have lost their model and will close their respective graphics or put them in a disconnected appearance. Selectors will close the corresponding subview, and all depending graphics will get closed.

### 7.2.4.3 The Selector Special Case

The SELECTOR plays a particular role in the framework. It is the only object that dynamically creates and deletes others. Apart from registering its subviews, the selector is responsible for maintaining the mapping between the model rank of an item and its graphics rank. As there is a direct mapping from a view to its graphic, the selector needs to register only the association between the model rank and the subview rank.

In the direct approach, this is obtained by a direct mapping between both ranks. The subview is assigned a route by the selector to provide the necessary information for multiple links traversing at the right index when searching for the model.

In the decoupled approach, the selector uses the Template Method (221) pattern to allow subclasses to perform filtering and sorting before deciding where to insert subviews.

The following scenario describes a SELECTOR initialization. The selector being described is a subview of the current VIEW_SET. The creation of the set triggers the creation of the selector through the *build_subviews* routine. Here, a CARD_SELECTOR is created. The second phase of the set creation is the graphic initialization (*init_graphic*). The graphic set associated with our view set is created. Here, it is a GRAPHIC_CARD. In turn, the creation of the graphic set triggers the creation of all graphical subcomponents. This is when the ML_LIST, our particular graphics selector, is built. At that time, no item is inserted in the selector. This is done when the selector opens. Receiving its model for the first time, it becomes able to determine which subviews to build according to the observed relationship. When built, graphic and views are linked together by calling the *map* routine. This routine is defined by each particular view set. It carries the minimum knowledge of the graphics set, namely, the name of the graphics set features giving access to those graphics components subject to view connection. The resulting interaction is sketched in Figure 7.7. The abstract selector is implemented as follows.

```
deferred class SELECTOR
inherit
  SINGLE_VIEW
     redefine map, graphic  end;
  PATH_OBSERVER
  OBSERVABLE
feature
  map (a_graphic : GRAPHIC_SELECTOR) is
     -- bind graphic to view
     require
       valid_graphic : a_graphic /= Void
     do
       graphic := a_graphic
       graphic.set_client(Current)
     ensure
```

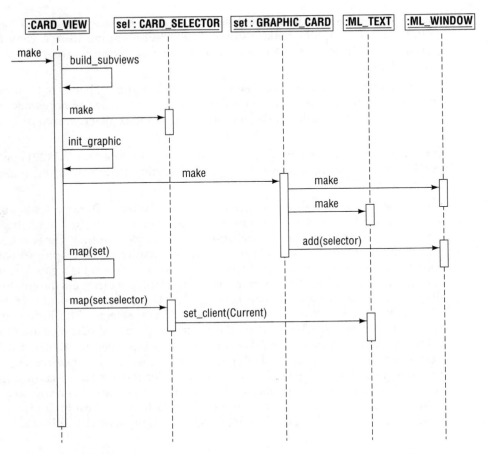

**Figure 7.7** Creating a card selector

```
        graphic_initialized : graphic /= Void
    end -- map
path_has_connected (root : like model; subject :like selection;
                    feature_id , rank  : INTEGER) is
    -- a new item has been inserted in observed relation
    do
        add_subview(subject,rank)
    end -- path_has_connected
path_has_broken (root : like model; subject : likeselection ;
                feature_id , rank  : INTEGER) is
    -- an item has been removed from observed relation
    do
```

```
      if (subject = selection) then
          erase_selection(subject)
      end -- if
      remove_subview(subject,rank)
   end -- path_has_broken
graphic_item_selected (rank : INTEGER) is
   -- update selector according to graphic change
   do
      update_selection(rank)
   end -- graphic_item_selected
graphic_item_deselected (rank : INTEGER) is
   -- update selector according to graphic change
   do
      clear_selection(rank)
   end -- graphic_item_deselected
open_selector (a_model : OBSERVABLE) is
   -- register model open and update graphic
   do
      open_subviews
      update_graphic
   end -- open_selector
close_selector is
   -- forget model and close graphic
   do
      disconnect
      close_subviews
      graphic.close
   end -- close_selector
disconnect is
   -- forget model
   do
      model := Void
      graphic.empty
      close_suviews
   end -- disconnect
update_graphic is
   -- modify graphic content according to model
   do
      graphic.show
   end -- update_graphic
close_subviews is
   -- close all existing subviews
   local
      i : INTEGER
```

```
    do
        from i := subviews.lower
        until i > subviews.upper
        loop
            subviews.get_item(i).close
            i := i + 1
        end -- loop
    end -- close_subviews
open_subviews is
    -- create as many subviews as found
    deferred
    end -- open_subviews
add_subview (model : OBSERVABLE ; rank : INTEGER) is
    -- add a new subview
    require
        valid_model : model /= Void
    deferred
    end -- add_subview
remove_subview (model : OBSERVABLE) is
    -- take specified subview out of subview list
    local
        model_position : INTEGER
    do
        modell_position := get_subview_pos(model)
        if model_position >= 0 then
            subview := subviews.item(model_position)
            subview.close
            graphic.remove_subview(model_position)
            subviews.remove(model_position)
        end -- if
    end -- remove_subview
append_selection(subject : like selection) is
    -- set item as selection
    require
        valid_selection : subject /= Void
    local
        descriptor : SELECTOR_DESCRIPTOR
    do
        selection := subject
        connect_notify(subject,descriptor.selection_id,1)
    end -- append_selection
erase_selection(subject : OBSERVABLE) is
    -- remove item from selection list
    require
```

```
            valid_selection : subject /= Void
        local
            descriptor : SELECTOR_DESCRIPTOR
        do
            selection := Void
            disconnect_notify(subject,descriptor.selection_id,1)
        end  -- erase_selection
    clear_selection(rank : INTEGER) is
        -- remove item selected on graphical position rank from
        -- selection. We suppose mono selection
        local
            old_selection : like subject
            descriptor : SELECTOR_DESCRIPTOR
        do
            old_selection := selection
            selection := Void
            disconnect_notify(old_selection,descriptor.selection_id,1)
        end  -- clear_selection
    update_selection(rank : INTEGER) is
        -- set item in graphic position rank selected. We consider here
        -- that graphic and model rank are identical
        local
            model_list : LINKED_LIST[like selection]
        do
            if model /= Void then
                model_list := get_model_sublist
                if rank >= model_list.lower and
                    rank <= model_list.upper then
                    append_selection(model_list.item(rank))
                end -- if
            end -- if
        end  -- update_selection
    graphic : GRAPHIC_SELECTOR
    selection : OBSERVABLE
    subview : VIEW
    subviews : LINKED_LIST[VIEW]
feature {NONE} -- private part
    init_subview (position : INTEGER)  : VIEW is
        -- creates a new subview and its graphic
        deferred
        end -- init_subview
    get_model_sublist : LINKED_LIST[like selection] is
            -- return the list of objects in the observed relation
        deferred
```

```
        end -- get_model_sublist
    get_subview_position (submodel : OBSERVABLE) : INTEGER is
            -- compute model position according to associated subview
        local
            i : INTEGER
        do
            Result := -1
            from i := subviews.lower
            until i > subviews.upper
            loop
                if subviews.item(i).model = submodel then
                    Result := i
                end -- if
                i := i + 1
            end -- loop
        end -- get_subview_position
invariant
    subviews_list_initialized : subviews /= Void
end -- SELECTOR
```

Once created, the view can be opened, as well as the selector. The view receives its model as parameter and begins to register on the observed relationships. Then the selector will create one subview for each object registered in the observed relation. The subview class is a VIEW_SET. The creation scenario is thus the same as previously. The SIMPLE_CARD_VIEW creates its subviews and the associated graphics and links them together.

The *open* method is redefined in each selector to allow for specialized open routines on the subview set. As described previously, subviews are opened with their appropriate models, and graphics are shown. The resulting interaction is sketched in Figure 7.8. This scenario is based on the following code for CARD_SELECTOR:

```
class CARD_SELECTOR
inherit
    SELECTOR
        redefine
            model, selection, subview, subviews, open  end
creation
    make
feature
    make is
            -- initialize subviews list
```

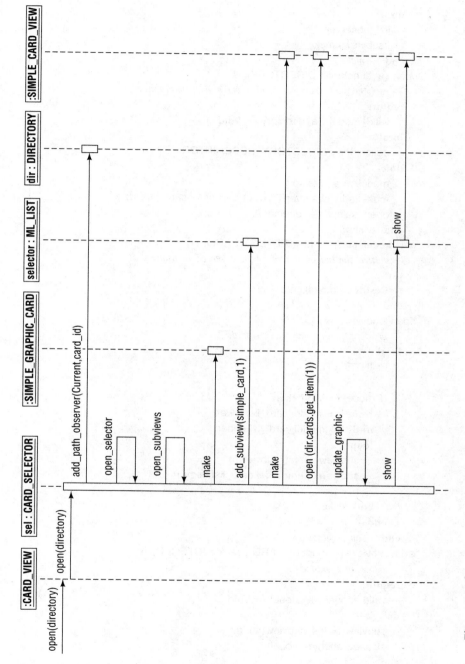

**Figure 7.8** Opening a selector with one subview

```
        do
            init_observer
            !!subviews.make
        end -- make
    open (a_directory : DIRECTORY) is
        -- register model connect as observer and open graphic
        require
            valid_model : a_directory /= Void
        local
            descriptor : DIRECTORY_DESCRIPTOR
        do
            model := a_directory
            model.add_observer(Current,descriptor.card_list_id)
            open_selector(a_directory)
        end -- open
    get_model_sublist : LINKED_LIST[CARD] is
        -- return the list of objects in the observed relation
        do
            Result := model.card_list
        end -- get_model_sublist
    open_subviews is
        -- create as many subviews as cards
        local
            i : INTEGER
        do
            if model /= Void then
                from i := model.card_list.lower
                until i > model.card_list.upper
                loop
                    subview := init_subview(i)
                    subview.open(model.card_list.item(i))
                    i := i + 1
                end -- loop
            end -- if
        end -- open_subviews
    add_subview (a_model : CARD ; rank : INTEGER) is
        -- add a new subview
        require
            valid_model : a_model /= Void
        do
            subview := init_subview(rank)
            subview.open(a_model)
        end -- add_subview
    model : DIRECTORY
```

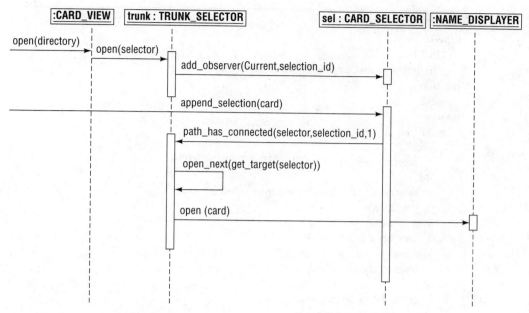

**Figure 7.9** Opening a trunk

```
    selection : CARD
    subview : SIMPLE_CARD_VIEW
    subviews : LINKED_LIST[SIMPLE_CARD_VIEW]
feature {NONE}
    init_subview (position : INTEGER) : SIMPLE_CARD_VIEW is
        -- creates a new subview and its graphic
    do
        !!Result.make
        subviews.force(Result,position)
        graphic.add_subview(Result.graphic,position)
    end -- init_subview
end -- CARD_SELECTOR
```

The TRUNK behavior is based on the same principle. The only difference is that the subview is built on trunk creation. In fact, the subview is under the responsibility of the encapsulating VIEW_SET. If the trunk target, that is, the object at the extremity of the observed relationship, exists, the views declared as *next* to the trunk are opened. If no target can be reached, the attached views open when the target is inserted in the observed relationship. The resulting interaction is depicted in Figure 7.9. Here is the code for TRUNK_SELECTOR.

```
class TRUNK_SELECTOR
inherit
   TRUNK
      redefine model, connect_model, open end
creation
   make
feature
   make  is
      local
         selector_descriptor : SELECTOR_DESCRIPTOR
      do
         relation_id := selector_descriptor.selection_id
         !!next.make
      end -- make
   open (an_obj : SELECTOR) is
      require
         valid_source : an_obj /= Void
      do
         if model /= an_obj then
            connect_model(an_obj)
            open_trunk(an_obj, get_target(an_obj))
         end -- if
      end -- open
   get_target (a_source : like model) : OBSERVABLE is
      require
         valid_source : a_source /= Void
      do
         Result := model.selection
      end -- get_target
   model : SELECTOR
   connect_model (a_model : SELECTOR) is
      do
         model := a_model
      end -- connect_model
end -- TRUNK_SELECTOR
```

## 7.2.5  Triggering Actions: Passing Information Around

A TRIGGER is a view used to fire routine execution. A trigger may be interested in
a list of events. When such an event occurs, the actions registered on this event
are executed. Events are direct notification from the graphic. Actions are object
encapsulation of the notion of callback. They simply follow the Command (147)

pattern. In the most simple cases—a button, for instance—the trigger becomes a SIMPLE_TRIGGER, interested only in one event and directly implementing the command pattern.

On creation, the concrete heirs of the trigger register the desired ACTIONS on the selected events. It may be interesting to extend the trigger protocol by associating a condition with the action execution. A common situation is to make the trigger active only if a particular condition is valid. To achieve this, we can make use of the observation path. Suppose that a boolean feature along that path enables us to tell whether we should activate our trigger. We can observe this feature and set the graphical state accordingly.

Another simple possibility is to hook the trigger into a trunk, by making it a *next view* of that trunk. This way, the trigger will be *opened* (that is, activated) only when an object—say, the target of the command—becomes reachable.

## 7.2.6  Combining and Grouping

We have presented two ways of implementing an atomic notion of controller we called a *View*. The first approach is aimed at direct code generation, so it promotes simplicity at the cost of hindering extensibility. View reuse is of little concern. In the second approach, we define a way of building interfaces from reusable blocks we called VIEW_SET and GRAPHIC_SET. The graphic set is semantics-free, merely defining interaction points that can be bound to appropriate views as needed. As such, it is easily reusable.

There are several ways of making VIEW_SET reusable. The first one is to abstract the meaning of the path it observes. This could be thought of as the type of an object aggregate. Until now, reusable graphics components tended to be limited to simple class, those we called atomic. With this method, we can go a step further. As views are reusable interface for atomic objects, view sets define the interface for groups of objects. As long as the interconnection graph is the same, view sets can be reused, with as many graphics presentations as needed.

The second way comes from the reuse of what we called *editors*. To make this clearer, we consider the example of a browser. In its most basic incarnation, it is the composition of a selector inside another selector. The situation is explained in Figure 7.10.

The purpose of a browser is to display selected parts of a tree. Let's call *subnode* the relationship that defines the tree. The external selector displays the selected nodes in the tree. As this relation is not part of the application, we define an editor object we call RECURSIVE_PATH_OBSERVER, or *RPO*. When opened, the view set is given a simple root, the starting node of the tree. The RPO registers this node as the first element in its *selected* relationship. The external selector displays this relationship, so it builds one subview to display this node. This subview is an

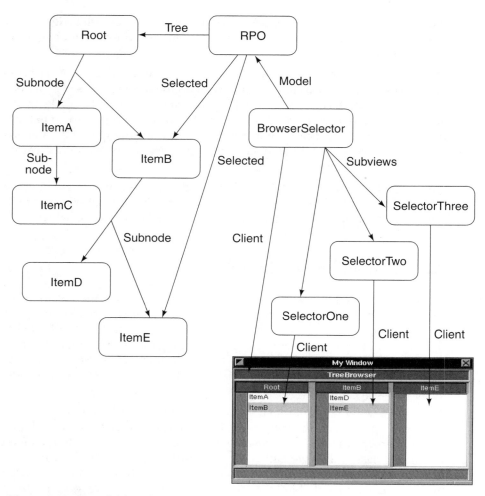

**Figure 7.10**  A model for a browser

internal selector that displays all of the nodes registered in the *subnode* relation of the current node.

When the user selects one node in the inner selector, the items registered in the *selected* relationship with rank equal or greater are discarded. Corresponding inner selectors, losing their model, disappear. Then, the selected item is added to the *selected* relation of the *RPO* at the position corresponding to its selector rank. A new inner selector is added by the external selector to display the subnodes of the newly selected node. The browser behavior is thus obtained by adding and removing nodes in the *selected* relationship of the RPO according to user selection.

This example illustrates how we can build more complex objects from our atomic views by encapsulating view set, editor, and graphics set in a new component, provided we could define a general model, as the tree here does.

The third way of reusing such components consists of adding slight modifications to existing view set by adding or removing displayers.

## 7.2.7  Introducing Control: How to Stay Generic

We have introduced only the main pattern combinations, which are sufficient to build common application interfaces in a disciplined and safe way. We could carry on. We presented the example of the trigger observing a Boolean sensitivity condition or being inserted in a dependency chain. It is easy to build new ones. These kinds of extensions provide simple implementations of the problem they solve. We could think of them as a new pattern, but they are not. They just attach particular semantics to an existing pattern.

As we mentioned before, the model is responsible for keeping its state description up to date. The control could then be deduced from this state observation. Recall that views and graphics could be the model of other views. This leads us to consider the model as a box with lights flickering on its side and knobs and buttons to push and rotate. Having defined a priori protocols of communication, we are in a much better position to produce reusable components.

## 7.2.8  Generating or Reusing: The Limits of Genericity

The first approach we have briefly described has been used in a tool that produces interface and connection to model code from the abstract description of the interface and desired connection. A meta-model carries the description of the model classes and their relationships. Dedicated tools help the user to draw the interface and then to describe the connection from a given graphical component to its model item. From that specification, the descriptions of dedicated classes that implement the relevant patterns are built into the meta-model. When the user is satisfied with the application, the code is generated and compiled and the resulting application launched.

The use of code generation may help in the process of enforcing the use of patterns here. Genericity allows us to abstract the role of an object as long as we don't need to reclaim services from it. The services we may ask for have to be specified by its abstract ancestor. With code generation of patterns, we can abstract a set of objects as long as they maintain a collaboration following a dedicated structure. Working at the language level, we can attach a common semantics to various explicit types, routines with varying numbers of parameters, or features with various names. A routine called *run* in an object of class ALPHA can play the same role and receive the same implementation as a routine called *execute* in an object of class BETA.

What is important to note is the fact that the pattern is the abstraction of the collaboration between a group of objects, not the design model produced or the code itself. Having identified a collaboration as a pattern allows us to choose a suitable implementation of our problem and later on to change that implementation, if needed, without further impact on the rest of our product. There are many ways of implementing a pattern and many ways to translate that particular implementation into code.

A good tool has to propose several implementations of the patterns it deals with. The tool should allow the user to add new implementations and even to describe new patterns. There is a commonly accepted format to describe a pattern. An implementation is best described by the set of abstract classes it defines and an example of concrete classes. The code generation rules could be provided in a language suitable to manipulate meta-information describing previously mentioned classes (Desfray, 1995).

## 7.3  Analysis and Remarks

### 7.3.1  Exposing Properties for Further Uses

Summing up our approach, we now try to abstract some of its salient properties. We require the objects we work with to expose some of their features. An example of such publication is the use of notification on changes. A published feature is one that explicitly provides a hook for connecting external mechanisms. Here, the registration mechanism is that hook. The client is the only one that attaches semantics to that mechanism.

Thus, we are nearly *defining a new language*. The set of published features of an object and the type of hooks involved define the operational type of that object. They are now able to take part in fruitful collaborations.

### 7.3.2  Reifying Collaborations

Beyond relationships, we need to identify collaborations among objects. A collaboration is the use in a defined order of a set of routines and relationships among objects to achieve a particular task. Collaborations are the best places for changes in a system. As soon as objects are rearranged, collaborations need to be reconnected or modified. If they are scattered in code, this quickly becomes painful and unsafe. If that collaboration is to some extent reified in a pattern, all we have to do is reassign the roles or choose a new pattern. In both cases, the specification is clear and the impact easy to forecast.

### 7.3.3 Designing Components; Using Connection Protocols

A great problem in software reuse is the matching of class interfaces. As we saw for graphical interface generation, relying on types is too restrictive. We should instead try is to get rid of this impedance problem through the use of generalized connection mechanisms. We should refrain from specifying a component by a simple list of

```
This class provides a foo routine with one parameter of type
spam that reset the contents of bar
```

We could instead specify a component by describing the connections a user is expected to attach to particular features of defined classes, according to given patterns. Thus, through the use of a dedicated tool or by following a disciplined approach, we could produce the proper code to safely connect components. As the pattern carries the semantics of the collaboration, it is likely to match on both sides if the reused component really fills the system need. Furthermore, being defined this way, the component carries within it its own user guide.

### 7.3.4 Performances Issues

The proposed solution may seem heavy, especially on a small example, but we think that it is a misleading impression. We have not introduced new problems; we have only made them explicit and provided general solutions to solve them. Ad hoc solutions make the economy of the registration mechanism, but they have to provide suitable **if elseif** constructs in order to select the proper reaction on notification. It must be noted that it's not the most time-consuming part of an application. And if it costs more in space, due to these registrations, it is more efficient in execution time, as there are no dedicated tests to perform.

The return in quality, clarity, and confidence in the result—the whole being built on identified and trusted components—far surpasses the increase in memory size. The introduction of many classes does not participate in this increase, as one instance of $N$ classes does not waste more space than $N$ instances of one class.

### 7.3.5 Leaving Room for Evolution

Maybe the most important thing to consider is the ability of our software to evolve. Defining roles and repeating common schemes all along our software help us to get a deeper understanding of its overall structure. Real software is never done in one pass. One release follows another one. If we don't build on well-identified mechanisms, the shape of the software will vanish, and the whole piece will collapse. The use of patterns makes it possible for the shape to change to a new one instead of melting into chaos.

# Appendix A

# Glossary

**Ancestor**   A *class* from which another class—called its heir, or subclass—inherits. In Smalltalk, it is called a *superclass*; in C++, a *base class*.

**Assertion**   Either a comment or a Boolean expression that may be tagged with an identifier. Assertions foster the formalization of the *contract* binding a *routine* caller (the *client*) and the routine implementation (the contractor, or *supplier*).

**Attribute**   A named property of an object, holding a part of its abstract state. It is called a *field* in procedural languages, a *data member* in C++, and an *instance variable* in Smalltalk.

**Class**   A template description that specifies properties and behavior for a set of similar *object*s. It is the implementation of an abstract data type, which defines the data structures, features, and interfaces of software objects.

**Class invariant**   A *class invariant* is a set of *assertion*s characterizing properties that any of its *instance*s must respect both on entering a *routine* (thus strengthening its *precondition*) and on exiting it (thus strengthening its *postcondition*). Compare with **Loop invariant.**

**Client**   An object that uses the services provided by another object, which is called its *supplier*, or *server*.

**Cluster**   A logical construct for grouping classes. An operating system notion, such as a directory, may be used to implement the logical cluster. Clusters provide an intermediate unit of packaging between the entire system and the basic building blocks of classes. Class names must be unique within a cluster.

**Contract**   Governs the relationship between *client* objects and *supplier* objects. It spells out the precise definitions of obligations and benefits for both *clients* and *suppliers* by means of a set of *assertions* that encompass feature *preconditions* and *postconditions* and *class invariants*.

313

**Creation routine**    A *routine* used to create and initialize an *object* (called class constructor in C++ or Java).

**Deferred class**    A class having at least one *deferred feature*. A deferred class (*abstract class* in C++) may not be instantiated. It merely describes the common properties of a group of classes that descend from it.

**Deferred feature**    A specification, made of a name, a *signature*, and *preconditions* and *postconditions*, of a feature but no implementation. (Known as *pure virtual function* in C++.)

**Delegation**    A mechanism by which an object can issue a request to another object in response to a request made to it: The operation is thus delegated. Delegation can be used as an alternative to the module extension aspect of inheritance.

**Design pattern**    A solution to a design problem in a given context. Design patterns are reusable microarchitectures that contribute to an overall system architecture. They capture the static and dynamic structures and collaborations among key participants in software designs.

**Dynamic binding**    A rule stating that the *dynamic type* of an entity determines which version of a *feature* is applied. Dynamic binding allows the choice of the actual version of a feature to be delayed until runtime. Whenever more than one version of a feature might be applicable, dynamic binding ensures that the version most directly adapted to the target object is selected. The static constraint on the entity's type ensures at least one such version.

**Dynamic type**    The *type* of the object an *entity* refers to at a given point in its lifetime. A nonexpanded entity may acquire a new dynamic type either through a creation instruction explicitly specifying this type or through any assignment instruction, including actual to formal mapping of routine parameters and assignment attempt.

**Encapsulation**    A packaging mechanism by which external aspects of an *object* are separated from its implementation. Encapsulation enables information hiding.

**Entity**    A name used in the text of an Eiffel program to handle objects. The four kinds of entities are attributes of classes, local entities of routines (including *Result* for functions), formal routine arguments, and *Current*, denoting the current object.

**Feature**    Either *attributes* or *routines* of an *object*. Features are part of the definition of classes. The routines are the only means for modifying the attributes of an object and hence its encapsulation properties. An object communicates with another through a request, which identifies either the attribute to be read or the routine to be performed on the second object. The object responds to a request by possibly changing its attributes or by returning a result.

**Feature specification**   Reflects the abstract data type view of a routine: its *signature* and *precondition*s and *postcondition*s.

**Framework**   A reusable software architecture that provides the generic structure and behavior for a family of software abstractions, along with a context that specifies their collaboration and use within a given domain.

**Garbage collection**   The automatic reclamation of unused computer storage. With many languages, programmers must explicitly reclaim heap memory at some point in the program by using a *free* or a *dispose* statement. The Eiffel garbage collector performs this function.

**Genericity**   The ability to define parameterized modules, called *generic classes*. A generic class is parameterized with formal generic parameters representing arbitrary types.

**Idiom**   A low-level pattern specific to a programming language. An idiom explains how to implement particular aspects of components or the relationships between them using the features of the given language.

**Inheritance**   A relationship between *class*es. Every inheritance relationship has parents called *ancestor*s (or superclasses) and children called *heir*s (or subclasses), and *attribute*s as well as *routine*s that are inherited. Inheritance allows for the definition and implementation of a new class by combination and specialization of existing ones. It is a mechanism for sharing commonalities (in terms of attributes and routines) between these classes, thus allowing for classification, subtyping, and reuse.

**Instance**   An instance of a *class* is an *object* belonging to this class.

**Interface**   The view an *object* offers to a set of its *clients*. Eiffel objects may present different interfaces to different clients. Indeed, you may restrict the visibility of a set of features to a nominative list of classes (and their descendants). This list may be given between brackets after a **feature** keyword. This property is sometimes called *subjectivity* because the view clients get on this kind of class depends on which client is looking (Bielak and McKim, 1993).

**Invariant**   See the entries **Class invariant** and **Loop invariant.**

**Kernel library**   The Eiffel Kernel Standard Library offers several features in such areas as array and string manipulation, object copying and cloning, input/output, object storage, and basic types. It has the same interface for every Eiffel compiler, so it allows libraries and applications to be portable across compilers.

**Loop invariant**   Characterizes what a loop is  trying to achieve, without describing how. It is a Boolean expression that must be true at the loop boundaries, just before the termination condition is evaluated. Compare with **Class invariant.**

**Loop variant**   A positive integer expression that is decreased by at least 1 at each iteration of a loop. Since by definition, it cannot go below 0, the number of iterations of a loop with a variant is bounded, and the loop eventually terminates.

**Mix-in**   A *deferred class* used to specify a common functionality or interface for a number of subclasses.

**Module**   Characterized by a well-defined *interface* and by information hiding. The interface should be small and simple for modules to be as loosely coupled as possible. The principle of modularity is the key to support modifiability, reusability, extensibility, and understandability. In Eiffel, the unit of modularity is the *class*.

**Object**   An encapsulation of a state together with a defined set of operations in that state. It embodies an abstraction characterized by an entity in the real world. Hence, it exists in time, may have a changeable state, and can be created and destroyed. Each object could be viewed as a computer (endowed with memory and a central processing unit) that can provide a set of services. The interface of an object is the set of *feature*s that can be requested by other objects; it gives the external view of the object.

**Polymorphism**   The possibility that an *entity* can assume various forms, or refer to various *object*s not necessarily having the same *type*, provided that they conform to the entity static type.

**Postcondition**   A set of *assertion*s that state the properties that a routine must guarantee at completion of any correct call. In Eiffel, a postcondition is introduced with the keyword **ensure** and appears just before the end of the routine. By providing a formal specification of what the routine should accomplish, it thus can assist in the construction of the routine and be used as a constructive proof of its correctness.

**Precondition**   A set of *assertion*s that state the conditions under which a routine may be called. In Eiffel, it is introduced with the keyword **require**. The routine caller must guarantee this condition when calling the routine; otherwise the routine work cannot be done. More formally, a precondition is a predicate that characterizes the set of initial states for which a problem can be solved. It specifies the subset of all possible states that the routine should be able to handle correctly.

**Reify**   To turn a notion into a concrete object. The Command (147) design pattern relies on the reification of the notion of a command: It makes an object out of each possible command. Reification is one of the cornerstones of the object-oriented approach.

**Routine**   Describes computations applicable to an object. A routine may be either a *function*—if it returns a result—or a *procedure*. Eiffel routines are called *methods* in Smalltalk and *member functions* in C++.

**Signature**   The name and potential list of argument and result types of a *feature*.

**Static type**   The declared *type* of an *entity*.

**Subclass**   A *class* that inherits from another class, its *ancestor*. A subclass is called a *derived class* in C++.

**Supplier**   An *object* that provides a service to a *client*.

**System assembly**   Building programs with Eiffel consists of *assembling* off-the-shelf and ad hoc software components, or *class*es. For that, you have to tell the compiler or another Eiffel environment tool, such as an interpreter, where the relevant classes are, that a particular class among them is the "root" of the Eiffel program, and that this program entry point—like the *main()* function in C—is a particular *creation routine* of the root class.

**Type**   A type characterizes a domain of values and a set of operations applicable to objects of the named type. In a typed language, *object*s of a given type may take only those values that are appropriate to the type. The only *operation*s that may be applied to an object are those defined for its type. A typing error results when one of these conditions is violated.

# Appendix B

# Design Pattern and Design by Contract Pointers

## B.1 Sources of Information

### B.1.1 Frequently Asked Questions (FAQ) (with Answers)

- **Design Patterns:** The official unofficial—or maybe it's the unofficial official—Patterns FAQ (http://g.oswego.edu/dl/pd-FAQ/pd-FAQ.html) is maintained by Doug Lea. Mail comments to dl@cs.oswego.edu.

- **Eiffel:** Franck Arnaud maintains an Eiffel FAQ. This question-and-answer list is posted monthly to the USENET news groups comp.lang.eiffel, comp.answers, and news.answers.

  Please send corrections, additions, and comments to Franck Arnaud: franck_arnaud@stratus.com.

The FAQ is abstracted and condensed from the posts of many contributors to comp.lang.eiffel and is supplemented by information from vendors. You can fetch the latest copy of the FAQ at http://www.cis.ohio-state.edu/hypertext/faq/usenet/eiffel-faq/faq.html.

### B.1.2 Mailing Lists

Several mailing lists deal with patterns and/or Eiffel.

- **patterns@cs.uiuc.edu** is for presenting and describing software patterns. They don't have to be object-oriented or design patterns, though most of them are. To subscribe, send a request containing the word *subscribe* in the *Subject* field to patterns-request@cs.uiuc.edu.

- **ipc-patterns@cs.uiuc.edu** is for presenting and creating patterns on concurrency, distribution, and IPCs (Inter Process Communications). To subscribe, send a request containing the single word *subscribe* in the *Subject* field to ipc-patterns-request@cs.uiuc.edu.

- **patterns-discussion@cs.uiuc.edu** is for discussing how to find and organize patterns or the meaning of patterns but not necessarily about particular patterns. To subscribe, send a request containing the single word *subscribe* in the *Subject* field to patterns-discussion-request@cs.uiuc.edu.

- **gang-of-4-patterns@cs.uiuc.edu** is about the design patterns in the Gang of Four's book (Gamma et al., 1995). To subscribe, send a request containing the single word *subscribe* in the *Subject* field to gang-of-4-patterns-request@cs.uiuc.edu.

- **eiffel-patterns@egroups.com** is for discussions of OO design patterns and Eiffel idioms. This mailing list is being produced by Eiffel programmers who are working together on a volunteer basis to generate a catalog of object-oriented design patterns expressed in Eiffel. To subscribe, send a request to eiffel-patterns-subscribe@egroups; or subscribe online at http://www.egroups.com/list/eiffel-patterns. This list is maintained by Stuart Hungerford (stuart.hungerford@pobox.com).

- **siemens-patterns@cs.uiuc.edu** is for reviewing and discussing the patterns described in Buschmann et al., 1996. To subscribe, send a request containing the single word *subscribe* in the *Subject* field to siemens-patterns-request@cs.uiuc.edu.

## B.1.3  World Wide Web

The Patterns Home Page, located at http://st-www.cs.uiuc.edu/users/patterns/patterns.html, is a source of information about all aspects of software patterns and pattern languages. Among the most interesting entry points located there are

**About** Patterns tutorials and introductions to patterns

**Books** that have been published about patterns

**Papers** and Bibliography, which you can download through ftp

**Conferences** about patterns

**Online patterns** and pattern languages

**Regular columns** and articles that have been published

**Presentations** on patterns

**Education** Courses on patterns

**Research projects** from around the Internet community

**Writing your own patterns** Templates, styles that can be useful

**Pattern catalogs** Tools and sample code directly relating to patterns

Douglas C. Schmidt has also an interesting page on patterns (at http:// www.cs.wustl.edu/~schmidt/patterns.html) containing

**Overview** of patterns and pattern languages

**Papers** on patterns for concurrent, parallel, and distributed systems

**Papers** on experience using patterns on commercial projects

**Online tutorials** on design patterns

**Links** to other information on patterns

The Eiffel Forum, an international user group for Eiffel users, has a Web page at http://www.eiffel-forum.org.

*Eiffel Liberty* is a Web site dedicated to exposing Eiffel and object technology (http://www.elj.com).

Yet another vendor-independent WWW page on Eiffel can be found at http:// www.cm.cf.ac.uk/CLE.

Also see Appendix D for the authors' WWW page.

## B.1.4 USENET

The following USENET newsgroups have interesting material about design patterns and Design by Contract:

- **comp.object**
- **comp.software-engineering**
- **comp.lang.eiffel**

## B.2  Software Resources

Many independent organizations, ranging from nonprofit organizations and academia to commercial companies, are making Eiffel-related products.

### B.2.1  SmallEiffel

SmallEiffel, or *The GNU Eiffel Compiler*, is a free Eiffel compiler distributed under the terms of the GNU General Public License as published by the Free Software Foundation. SmallEiffel is intended to be a complete, though small and very fast, free Eiffel compiler available for a wide range of platforms. In fact, SmallEiffel should run on any platform for which an ANSI C-POSIX compiler exists. The current distribution includes an Eiffel-to-C compiler, an Eiffel-to-Java bytecode compiler, a documentation tool, a pretty printer, and various other tools.

SmallEiffel uses an innovative strategy involving whole-system analysis, which allows compilation to be faster than the incremental compilation of traditional compilers. SmallEiffel is the result of a research project of the LORIA, a joint computer science research center in Nancy, France, involving INRIA, CNRS, University Henri Poincaré (Nancy 1), University of Nancy 2 (humanities).

SmallEiffel was developed by Dominique Colnet. This project began in 1994; since its first public release in September 1995, SmallEiffel has been used worldwide by increasing numbers of individuals and universities. You can download SmallEiffel from its WWW site at http://SmallEiffel.loria.fr/index.html.

### B.2.2  Interactive Software Engineering Inc.

This company, Eiffel's birthplace, sells the *ISE Eiffel 4 software development environment*, available on a wide range of industry platforms and providing a highly portable development environment and support for client/server and cross-platform development. This product contains

- EiffelBench, a visual workbench for object-oriented software construction, integrating an original browsing mechanism, fast recompilation with ISE's proprietary Melting Ice Technology, automatic documentation tools, visual debugging, and so on. An online Guided Tour is available for an overview of EiffelBench.

- EiffelCase, the analysis and design workbench based on the BON (Business Object Notation) method.

- Various class libraries, such as EiffelBase, the library of fundamental data structures and algorithms; EiffelLex, for lexical analysis; EiffelParse, for parsing; EiffelNet, for exchanging objects over a network; EiffelStore, the library for relational or object-oriented database access; EiffelVision, the platform-independent graphical and library; and EiffelThreads, a thread library providing the full power of multithreading.

The following are also available:

- EiffelWeb, to make it easy to process forms from the Web, avoiding the complications of CGI scripts; EiffelBuild, Eiffel's application generator and GUI builder; and DLE, to give Eiffel developers the ability to integrate new classes into their systems at runtime.

- Specific to the Wintel world: Graphical Eiffel for Windows (the full graphical ISE Eiffel 3 environment for PC users); Windows Eiffel Library (WEL), an encapsulation of Windows primitives, making it possible to have direct access to the Windows graphical API; and Eiffel Resource Bench, for using a Windows GUI builder (resource editor) to define the interface of an Eiffel application, through WEL.

For more information, contact

Interactive Software Engineering Inc.
270 Storke Road, Suite #7
Goleta, CA 93117
Phone: 805-685-1006; Fax: 805-685-6869
e-mail: info@eiffel.com
WWW://www.eiffel.com/

## B.2.3  Halstenbach ACT GmbH

Halstenbach makes the Eiffel-based development environment iss-base, a graphical object-oriented development environment with reusable modules for professional client/server applications. It supports the development cycle, from analysis, through graphical restructuring capabilities, all the way to source code. The special characteristics of Eiffel help achieve the highest possible level of flexibility in adapting to enterprise-specific operations. Business processes become easier to shape and simulate.

For more information, contact

Halstenbach ANGEWANDTE COMPUTER TECHNOLOGIE GMBH
Breidenbrucher Str. 2
D-51674 Wiehl
Germany
Phone: ++49-2261-9902-0;   Fax: ++49-2261-9902-99
Mailing address: Postfach 13 29, D-51657 Wiehl
e-mail: info@halstenbach.de
WWW://www.halstenbach.de

## B.2.4  Object Tools Inc.

Object Tools, previously known as Sig Computer GmbH, in Braunfels, Germany, produced the first commercially available Eiffel 3 compiler and now ships *Visual Eiffel*, featuring a "state of the art" compiler, workbench, and, with its newest product, DM, RAD technology for Windows.

For more information, contact

> Object Tools Inc.
> 13267 Summit Sq. Center
> Route 413 & Doublewoods Rd.
> Langhorne, PA 19047
> Phone: 215-504-0854
> e-mail: info@object-tools.com
> WWW://www.object-tools.com

# Appendix C

# Design by Contract in Other Languages

## C.1 Design by Contract in Java

### C.1.1 The iContract Tool

The novel Java tool called iContract provides developers with support for Design by Contract. Previously, the explicit specification of contracts by means of class invariants and message pre- and postconditions was available only to Eiffel developers. The iContract prototype tool, written by Reto Kramer, provides similar support for Java, offering developers the following benefits:

- Support for design testability by enhancing the system's observability (failure occurs close to fault)

- Uniform implementation of invariant, pre-, and postcondition checks among team members

- Synchronized documentation and code

- Semantic-level specification of what requirements/benefits a class/message offers

This preprocessor, which builds in checks for class invariants and pre- and postconditions that may be associated with methods in classes and interfaces, is available for free from

http://www.reliable-systems.com

Special comment tags, such as @pre and @post, are interpreted by iContract and converted into assertion check code that is inserted into the source code. The expressions are a superset of Java, compatible with a subset of the latest UML Object Constraint Language (OCL) (see Section C.2). Highlight features include quantifiers (forall, exists) to specify properties of enumerations, implications, old- and return-value references in postconditions, as well as the naming of exception classes to throw.

The iContract tool supports the propagation of invariants, pre- and postconditions via inheritance, and multiple interface implementation, as well as multiple interface extension mechanisms. The instrumentation level, such as only precondition checks, can be chosen for each file, enabling fine-grained, vertical (inheritance, implementation), and horizontal (delegation) performance control.

Due to the nonmandatory nature of the comment tags, source code that contains Design by Contract annotations remains fully compatible with Java and can be processed with standard Java compilers, enabling a risk-free adoption of the technique.

## C.1.2  A Simple Example

The following simple example[1] demonstrates the basic steps to instrument Java source code with Design by Contract enforcing checks.

The interface Person specifies methods that allow clients to set and read a person's age. The contract for both methods requires that the age must be a positive integer. iContract will instrument classes that implement this interface with the checks required to enforce the pre- and post-conditions on the clients.

Implementations of the interface Person promise that, provided the age passed to the setAge(int) method is positive, the age returned by the getAge() method is positive as well.

```
package iContract.doc.tutorial.Person;

public interface Person
{
    /**
     * @post return > 0 // age always positive
     */
    public int getAge();
```

---

1. Reproduced with permission from the iContract documentation.

```
/**
 * @pre age > 0 // age always positive
 */
public void setAge(int age);
}
```

Through the contract propagation, the class Employee (see below), which implements the interface Person, must adhere to the interface's pre- and post-conditions. In addition, the age passed to the Employee's constructor must be a positive integer.

```
package iContract.doc.tutorial.Person;

public class Employee implements Person
{
  private int age_;

  /**
   * @pre age > 0
   */
  public Employee( int age ) {
    age_ = age;
  }

  public int getAge()
  {
    return age_;
  }

  public void setAge( int age )
  {
    age_ = age;
  }
}
```

A simple example client application demonstrates the precondition check that will catch the negative age (−1) passed to the Employee's setAge(int) method:

```
package iContract.doc.tutorial.Person;

public class Main {

  /**Test driver method.
   * Create an employee and print its age.
   */
  public static void main( String argv[] )
```

```
{
  Employee employee = new Employee( 25 );
  System.out.println( "Employee's age is: " + employee.getAge() );

  employee.setAge( -1 ); // this will break!
}
}
```

The example client program prints the age of the 25-year-old employee correctly. It refuses, however, to set the age to −1 year, signaling the violation of the precondition declared in interface Person (*age* > 0).

```
> java iContract.doc.tutorial.Person.Main
Employee's age is: 25
java.lang.RuntimeException: Employee.j:22: error: precondition violated
   (iContract.doc.tutorial.Person.Employee::setAge(int)):
   (/*iContract.doc.tutorial.Person.Person::setAge(int)*/ (age > 0))
at iContract.doc.tutorial.Person.Employee.setAge(Employee.java:124)
at iContract.doc.tutorial.Person.Main.main(Main.java:14)
```

Please note that the above error message mentions both the class/method where the violation of the precondition was detected (Employee.setAge(int)) and the interface/method in which the precondition was declared (Person.setAge(int)).

# C.2  Design by Contract in UML

## C.2.1  Introduction to the OCL

In UML, a constraint can be attached to any element of a model and is syntactically represented between braces { }. The Object Constraint Language (OCL) (Warmer and Kleppe, 1999) is a formal language, easy to read and write, to describe constraints about the objects in the model. As such, OCL can be used to specify invariants on classes and types in the class model and to describe pre- and post-conditions on operations and methods. Indeed, pre- and postconditions are just constraints stereotyped ≪ *precondition* ≫ and ≪ *postcondition* ≫, which are often abbreviated as *pre:* and *post:*.

Rooted in the Syntropy method, the OCL was developed as a business modeling language within the IBM Insurance division to be easy to use for people with no strong mathematical background.

OCL is a pure expression language. Therefore, an OCL expression is guaranteed to be without side effects; it cannot change anything in the model. Thus, the state

```
┌─────────────────────────────────────────────┐
│                BankAccount                    │
│                                               │
│         { balance >= − overdraftLimit}        │
├─────────────────────────────────────────────┤
│  balance : Money                              │
│  overdraftLimit : Money                       │
├─────────────────────────────────────────────┤
│  deposit (amount : Money)                     │
│      {pre: amount > 0}                        │
│      {post: balance = balance@pre + amount}   │
│                                               │
│  withdraw(amount : Money)                     │
│      {pre: amount > 0 and                     │
│          amount <= balance + overdraftLimit}  │
│      {post: balance = balance@pre − amount}   │
│                                               │
│  setOverdraftLimit(newLimit : Money)          │
│      {pre: balance >= − newLimit}             │
└─────────────────────────────────────────────┘
```

**Figure C.1** Precise specification of a bank account in UML

of the system will never change because of an OCL expression, even though an OCL expression can be used to specify a state change, in a postcondition, for example. Values for all objects, including all links, will not change. Whenever an OCL expression is evaluated, it simply delivers a value.

## C.2.2 A Simple Example

Figure C.1 illustrates the use of the OCL to add Design by Contract information to a simple UML class modeling a bank account with an overdraft limit. The class invariant goes into the class name compartment as a constraint on the class instances:

```
{balance >= − overdraftLimit}
```

Preconditions and postconditions can be associated to a method. For example, the precondition of *withdraw* is that the withdrawn amount should be positive but less than the current balance plus the overdraft limit:

```
{pre: amount > 0 and
        amount <= balance + overdraftLimit}
```

The postcondition of *withdraw* is that the new balance is reduced by the withdrawn amount:

```
{post: balance = balance@pre - amount}
```

Note that the OCL operator *@pre* refers the value its argument had when entering the method, as with the *old* operator in Eiffel.

Not many UML CASE tools support OCL and Design by Contract yet. Look at http://www.irisa.fr/pampa/UMLAUT for a freely available example of such a UML tool, as well as more references on Design by Contract and the UML.

# Appendix D

# More Information about This Book

The authors maintain a World Wide Web server with information related to this book: http://www.irisa.fr/prive/jezequel/DesignPatterns. This WWW server should provide you with up-to-date pointers to other design pattern and Design by Contract pages. It also contains an errata list for this book, as well as the source code of all of the examples presented in this book. All of the examples have been tested with The GNU Eiffel compiler (see Appendix B.2.1).

# Bibliography

Adams, Chris. 1995. "Why can't I buy an SCM tool?" In Jacky Estublier, ed., *Software Configuration Management: Selected Papers of the ICSE SCM-4 and SCM-5 Workshops*, pp. 278–281. Springer-Verlag.

Agesen, Ole. 1995. "The Cartesian product algorithm: Simple and precise type inference of parametric polymorphism." In *Proceedings of the 9th European Conference on Object-Oriented Programming (ECOOP'95)*, pp. 2–26.

———. 1996. *Concrete Type Inference: Delivering Object-Oriented Applications*. Ph.D. diss., Stanford University. Published by Sun Microsystem Laboratories (SMLI TR-96-52).

Alexander Christopher, Sara Ishikawa, Murray Silverstein, Max Jacobson, Ingrid Fiksdahl-King, and Shlomo Angel. 1977. *A Pattern Language*. New York: Oxford University Press.

Allen, Larry, Gary Fernandez, Kenneth Kane, David Leblang, Debra Minard, and John Posner. 1995. "ClearCase MultiSite: Supporting geographically-distributed software development." In Jacky Estublier, ed., *Software Configuration Management: Selected Papers of the ICSE SCM-4 and SCM-5 Workshops*, pp. 194–214. Springer-Verlag.

Ambriola, Vincenzo and Lars Bendix. 1989. Object-oriented configuration control. In *Proceedings of the 2nd International Workshop on Software Configuration Management*, pp. 133–136. Princeton, NJ. October.

Appleton, Brad. 1997. "Patterns and software: Essential concepts and terminology, *Object Magazine Online*, May.

Bancilhon, François, C. Delobel, and Paris Kanellakis, eds. 1992. *Building an Object-Oriented Database System: The Story of O2*. San Mateo: Morgan-Kaufmann.

Belkhatir, N. and W. L. Melo. 1994. "Supporting software development processes in Adele 2." *The Computer Journal* 37 (7), pp. 621–628, May.

Bendix, Lars. 1992. "Automatic configuration management in a general object-based environment." In *Proceedings of the 4th International Conference on Software Engineering and Knowledge Engineering*, pp. 186–193. Capri, Italy. June.

Bielak, R. and J. McKim. 1993. "The many faces of a class: Views and contracts." In *Proc. TOOLS 11*, pp. 153–161. August.

Boehm, B. W. 1987. "Improving software productivity," *Computer* 20 (9), pp. 43–57, September.

Booch, Grady. 1991. *Object Oriented Design with Applications*. Benjamin Cummings.

———. 1994. *Object-Oriented Analysis and Design with Applications*, 2d ed. Reading, MA: Addison-Wesley.

Buschmann, F., R. Meunier, P. Sommerland, and M. Stal. 1996. *Pattern Oriented Software Architecture, A System of Patterns*. Wiley & Sons, British Library.

Chen, P. P. S. 1976. "The entity-relationship model: Toward a unified view of data," *ACM TODS* 1 (1), pp. 9–36, March.

Coleman, D. P., Arnold, S. Bodoff, C. Dollin, H. Gilchrist, and P. Jeremaes. 1994. *Object-Oriented Development: The Fusion Method*. Englewood Cliffs, NJ: Prentice-Hall.

Collin, Suzanne, Dominique Colnet, and Olivier Zendra. 1997. "Type inference for late binding: The SmallEiffel compiler." In *Joint Modular Languages Conference*, pp. 67–81. Springer-Verlag.

Conklin, Peter F. 1996. "Enrollment management: Managing the Alpha AXP program," *IEEE Software* 13 (4), pp. 53–64, July.

Coplien, J. O. 1995. "A generative development-process pattern language." In Coplien, J. O. and D. Schmidt, eds., *Pattern Languages of Program Design*, pp. 183–238. Reading MA: Addison-Wesley.

Coutaz, J. 1997. "PAC, an object oriented model for dialog design." In H. J. Bullinger and B. Shackel, eds., *INTERACT 87*, pp. 431–436. Grenoble: Elsevier Science Publisher.

Creel, Christopher. 1997. "Experiences of using Eiffel for embedded systems development at Hewlett-Packard color laserjet and consumables division." Business Communications, December. http://www.eiffel.com/eiffel/projects/hp/creel.html.

Dart, Susan and Joe Krasnov. 1995. "Experiences in Risk Mitigation with Configuration Management." Technical Report, 108 Pacifica, Irvine, California, Continuus Software Corporation. Delivered at 4th SEI Risk Conference, November.

Desfray, P. 1995. *Objecteering: The Fourth Dimension*. Reading, MA: Addison-Wesley.

Estublier, Jacky and Rubby Casallas. 1995."Three dimensional versioning." In Jacky Estublier, ed., *Software Configuration Management: Selected Papers of the ICSE SCM-4 and SCM-5 Workshops*, pp. 118–135. Grenoble: Springer-Verlag.

Floch, J. 1995. "Supporting evolution and maintenance by using a flexible automatic code generator." In *Proceedings of the 17th International Conference on Software Engineering*, pp. 211–219. San Francisco. April.

Gallagher, Keith B. and Lewis I. Berman. 1993. "Applying metric-based object-oriented process modeling techniques to configuration management." In *Proceedings of the 4th International Workshop on Software Configuration Management (Preprint)*, pp. 79–101. Baltimore, MD. May.

Gamma, Erich, Richard Helm, Ralph Johnson, and John Vlissides. 1995. *Design Patterns: Elements of Reusable Object-Oriented Software*. Reading, MA: Addison-Wesley.

Gentleman, W. M. 1989. "Managing configurability in multi-installation realtime programs." In *Proceedings of the Canadian Conference on Electrical and Computer Engineering*, pp. 823–827. Ottawa. November.

Goldberg, A. and D. Robson. 1983. *Smalltalk-80: The Language and its Implementation*. Reading, MA: Addison-Wesley.

Graver, J. and R. Johnson. 1990. "A Type System for Smalltalk." In *Proceedings of POPL*, pp. 139–150. San Francisco.

Guidec, F., J. M. Jézéquel, and J.-L. Pacherie. 1996. "An object oriented framework for supercomputing." *Journal of Systems and Software*, Special Issue on Software Engineering for Distributed Computing, June.

Hayes, B. 1992. "Finalization in the collector interface." In *Proc. Int. Workshop on Memory Management*. pp. 277–298. Saint-Malo, France. September.

Humphrey, Watts. 1989. *Managing the Software Process*. Reading, MA: Addison-Wesley.

Jackson, M.A. 1985. *System Development*. Englewood Cliffs, NJ: Prentice-Hall.

Jacobson, Ivar, Magnus Christerson, Patrik Jonsson, and Gunnar Overgaard. 1992. *Object-Oriented Software Engineering—A Use Case Driven Approach*. Reading, MA: Addison-Wesley/ACM Press.

Jézéquel, (J.-M.) and B. Meyer. 1997. "Design by contract: The lessons of Ariane," *Computer* 30 (1), pp. 129–13, January.

Jézéquel, J.-M. 1996a. "Engineering high performance telecom systems with Eiffel." In *TOOLS Europe'96*, pp. 67–76. Paris: Prentice-Hall.

———.1996b *Object Oriented Software Engineering with Eiffel*. Reading, MA: Addison-Wesley.

———. 1998a. "Object-oriented design of real-time telecom systems." In *IEEE International Symposium on Object-Oriented Real-Time Distributed Computing, ISORC'98*. Kyoto, Japan. April.

———. 1998b. "Reifying configuration management for object-oriented software." In *International Conference on Software Engineering, ICSE'20*. Kyoto, Japan. April.

Jones, Neil D. 1990. Partial evaluation, self-application, and types. In M. S. Paterson, ed., *17th International Colloquium on Automata, Languages, and Programming (ICALP), Warwick, England*, pp. 639–659. New York: Springer-Verlag.

Knuth, D.E. 1968. *The Art of Computer Programming*, 2nd Ed., Vol. 1. Reading, MA: Addison-Wesley.

Kramer, Reto. 1998. "iContract—The Java^tm Design by Contract^tm Tool." In *26th Conference on Technology of Object-Oriented Systems (TOOLS USA'98)*. Santa Barbara. August.

Leblang, David and Paul H. Levine. 1995. "Software configuration management: Why is it needed and what should it do?" In Jacky Estublier, ed., *Software Configuration Management: Selected Papers of the ICSE SCM-4 and SCM-5 Workshops*. pp. 53–60. Santa Barbara. Springer-Verlag.

Leblang, David B. 1994. "The CM challenge: Configuration management that works." In Walter Tichy, ed., *Configuration Management*, pp. 1–38. West Sussex, England: John Wiley.

Li, Kai. 1986. *Shared Virtual Memory on Loosely Coupled Multiprocessors*. Ph.D. diss., Yale University.

Lieberherr, Karl J. and Ian M. Holland. 1989. "Assuring good style for object-oriented programs." *IEEE Software* 6 (6), pp. 38–48, September.

Liskov, Barbara and John Guttag. 1986. *Abstraction and Specification in Program Development*. Cambridge, MA: MIT Press/McGraw-Hill.

MacKay, Stephen A. 1995. "The state-of-the-art in concurrent, distributed configuration management." In Jacky Estublier, ed., *Software Configuration Management: Selected Papers of the ICSE SCM-4 and SCM-5 Workshops*. pp. 180–193. Springer-Verlag.

McCabe, T. 1976. "A complexity measure." *IEEE Transactions on Software Engineering* 2 (4), pp. 309–320, December.

McLendon, Jean and Gerald M. Weinberg. 1996. "Beyond blaming: congruence in large systems development projects," *IEEE Software* 13 (4), pp. 33–42, July.

McNab, Andy. 1993. *Bravo Two Zero*. London: Transworld Publisher.

Meijers, Marco. 1996. "*Tool Support for Object-Oriented Design Patterns*." Master's thesis, Utrecht University.

Meyer, B. 1988. *Object-Oriented Software Construction*. Englewood Cliffs, NJ: Prentice-Hall.

———. 1992a. "Applying 'design by contract,'". *IEEE Computer (Special Issue on Inheritance & Classification)* 25 (10), pp. 40–52, October.

———. 1992b. *Eiffel: The Language*. Englewood Cliffs, NJ: Prentice-Hall.

———. 1994. *Reusable Software: The Base Object-Oriented component libraries*. Englewood Cliffs, NJ: Prentice-Hall.

———. 1997. *Object-Oriented Software Construction*, 2nd ed. Englewood Cliffs, NJ: Prentice-Hall.

Milner, R. 1978. "A theory of type polymorphism in programming." *Journal of Computer and System Sciences* 17 (3), pp. 348–375.

Mosley, Vicky, Frank Brewer, Rita Heacock, Phil Johnson, Gary LaBarre, Vince Maz and Tami Smith. 1996. "Software configuration management tools: Getting bigger, better, and bolder." *Crosstalk: The Journal of Defense Software Engineering* 9 (1), pp. 6–10, January.

Oquendo, Flávio. 1992. "Acquiring experiences with object-based and process-centered CASE enginronment architectures for configuration management systems." In G. Forte, N. H. Madhavji, and H. A. Muller, eds., *Proceedings of the 5th International Workshop on Computer-Aided Software Engineering*, pp. 14–18. Montreal, Canada. July.

Palsberg, Jens and Michael I. Schwartzbach. 1991. "Object-oriented type inference." In *Proceedings of 6th Annual ACM Conference on Object-Oriented Programming Systems, Languages and Applications (OOPSLA'91)*, pp. 146–161.

Ray, Randy J. 1995. "Experiences with a script-based software configuration management system." In Jacky Estublier, ed., *Software Configuration Management: Selected Papers of the ICSE SCM-4 and SCM-5 Workshops*, pp. 282–287. Springer-Verlag.

Render, Hal, and Roy Campbell. 1991. "An object-oriented model of software configuration management." In Peter H. Feiler, ed., *Proceedings of the 3rd International Workshop on Software Configuration Management*, pp. 127–139. Trondheim, Norway. June.

Royce, W. 1970. "Managing the development of large software systems." In *Proceedings of IEEE WESCON*, Los Angeles. August.

Rumbaugh, James, Ivar Jacobson, and Grady Booch. 1997. *Unified Modeling Language Reference Manual*. Reading, MA: Addison-Wesley.

Rumbaugh, James, Michael Blaha, William Premerlani, Frederick Eddy, and William Lorensen. 1991. *Object-Oriented Modeling and Design*. Englewood Cliffs, NJ: Prentice-Hall.

Stephan, Philippe. 1995. "Building financial software with object technology." *Object Magazine* 5 (4), July.

Suzuki, N., and M. Terada. 1984. "Creating efficient system for object-oriented languages." In *Eleventh Annual ACM Symposium on the Principles of Programming Languages*, pp. 290–296, Salt Lake City, January.

Suzuki, N. 1981. "Inferring types in Smalltalk." In *Eighth Symposium on Principles of Programming Languages*, pp. 187–199. New York, January.

Tichy, W. F. 1992. "Programming-in-the-large: Past, Present, and Future." In *Proceedings of the 14th International Conference on Software Engineering*, pp. 362–367. Melbourne, Australia. May.

Tichy, W. F., ed. 1994. *Configuration Management*. West Sussex, England: John Wiley.

Vitek, J., N. Horspool, and J. S. Uhl. 1992. "Compile-time analysis of object-oriented programs." In *International Conference on Compiler Construction*, pp. 237–250. Paslerborn, Germany: Springer Verlag.

Warmer, Joseph, and Anneke Kleppe. 1999. *The Object Constraint Language*, Precise Modeling with UML. Reading, MA: Addison-Wesley.

Wirfs-Brock, Rebecca, Brian Wilkerson, and Lauren Wiener. 1990. *Designing Object-Oriented Software*. Englewood Cliffs, NJ: Prentice-Hall.

Wiener, Richard. 1995. *Software Development using Eiffel: There Is Life other than C++*. Englewood Cliffs, NJ: Prentice-Hall.

Zendra, Olivier, Dominique Colnet, and Suzanne Collin. 1997. "Efficient dynamic dispatch without virtual function tables: The SmallEiffel compiler." In *Proceedings OOPSLA '97, ACM SIGPLAN Notices*. New York. October.

# Index

# Addison-Wesley Computer and Engineering Publishing Group

# How to Interact with Us

## 1. Visit our Web site

http://www.awl.com/cseng

When you think you've read enough, there's always more content for you at Addison-Wesley's web site. Our web site contains a directory of complete product information including:

- Chapters
- Exclusive author interviews
- Links to authors' pages
- Tables of contents
- Source code

You can also discover what tradeshows and conferences Addison-Wesley will be attending, read what others are saying about our titles, and find out where and when you can meet our authors and have them sign your book.

## 2. Subscribe to Our Email Mailing Lists

Subscribe to our electronic mailing lists and be the first to know when new books are publishing. Here's how it works: Sign up for our electronic mailing at http://www.awl.com/cseng/mailinglists.html. Just select the subject areas that interest you and you will receive notification via email when we publish a book in that area.

## 3. Contact Us via Email

cepubprof@awl.com
Ask general questions about our books.
Sign up for our electronic mailing lists.
Submit corrections for our web site.

bexpress@awl.com
Request an Addison-Wesley catalog.
Get answers to questions regarding your order or our products.

innovations@awl.com
Request a current Innovations Newsletter.

webmaster@awl.com
Send comments about our web site.

cepubeditors@awl.com
Submit a book proposal.
Send errata for an Addison-Wesley book.

cepubpublicity@awl.com
Request a review copy for a member of the media interested in reviewing new Addison-Wesley titles.

We encourage you to patronize the many fine retailers who stock Addison-Wesley titles. Visit our online directory to find stores near you or visit our online store: http://store.awl.com/ or call 800-824-7799.

**Addison Wesley Longman**
**Computer and Engineering Publishing Group**
**One Jacob Way, Reading, Massachusetts 01867 USA**
TEL 781-944-3700 • FAX 781-942-3076